About the author:

Mark Hichens is a biographer, historian and retired teacher. His publications include history books, *The Inimitable P G Wodehouse* (Book Guild), a biography and treasury of the popular writer, and collections of biographies of wives of the Kings of England, Prime Ministers' wives, and his latest, *Women of Consequence* (Book Guild, 2013).

Oscar Wilde's Last Chance – The Dreyfus Connection

Mark Hichens

Book Guild Publishing
Sussex, England

This edition published in Great Britain in 2014 by
The Book Guild Ltd
The Werks
45 Church Road
Hove, BN3 2BE

First published in 1999 by The Pentland Press Ltd

Printed and bound in Great Britain by
CPI Group (UK) Ltd, Croydon, CR0 4YY

A catalogue record for this book is available from
The British Library.

ISBN 978 1 909716 78 0

To Thetis
who instigated this book

Contents

Illustrations

Foreword

by John Blacker

THIS BOOK TELLS THE STORIES OF TWO MEN: one was convicted of a crime he had not committed; the other was convicted of something which today would not be regarded as a crime. The stories, particularly that of Dreyfus, are complex, and Mark Hichens tells them with a rare lucidity. But he also tells of the link between the two: the part which Oscar Wilde played in the Dreyfus Case, which is a little-known chapter of these sagas.

My grandfather, Carlos Blacker, played a pivotal role in the events here described. He provided Oscar Wilde with incontrovertible evidence of Dreyfus's innocence and Esterhazy's culpability of the treachery for which Dreyfus had been condemned; and he told him, in strictest confidence, of his plans to make this evidence public. But OW betrayed his trust: he divulged the plans to a hostile journalist who promptly published an account of them in the *New York Times*. As a result the plans had to be abandoned; my grandfather was vilified in the anti-Dreyfusard press and went in fear of his life. Not surprisingly, there was a bitter quarrel between him and OW. The latter described his version of the quarrel in two ugly letters, hitherto unpublished,* to his friend Robbie Ross. They are filled with mawkish self-justification, abuse of my grandfather, and make no mention of the real cause of the quarrel. That we in fact know what had really happened is due to the meticulous research of the American historian Robert Maguire, whose own detailed account of these events we are eagerly awaiting.

---

* Rupert Hart-Davis, in his editing of the Collected *Letters of Oscar Wilde*, omitted the passages in these two letters derogating my grandfather out of consideration for our family. However extracts from these letters were published by H. Montgomery Hyde in his biography of Oscar Wilde.

My grandfather died in the year before I was born. I can therefore claim no personal recollection of him; but stories of him abound in our family. One of the most vivid pictures of him was recounted by my father in some memoirs which he wrote towards the end of his life.* When my father was a small boy, the family used frequently to stay with CB's sister Carmen, who lived in Freiburg in Germany. My father and his younger brother Robin (later killed at the Battle of Loos in 1915) would be taken for walks on a hill near Freiburg called the Schlossberg. CB would often accompany them, discoursing to them on various topics and encouraging them to ask questions. On one such occasion they broached the subject of the Ten Commandments.

> My father had a quiet voice and very gentle manners. He could attune himself to children of different ages and knew exactly how to talk to them. He dealt with our questions about the Ten Commandments by telling Robin and me that these Commandments were directed to different people. Some were specially meant for children and others were more for grown-ups, but that in due course we would understand them all, and profit by them. In the meanwhile we could take it that all ten could be summed up in one comprehensive commandment, which, if acted on by everyone, would make the world a much better place than it was. What, we asked expectantly, was this commandment? My father hesitated a few seconds before answering. He then spoke the following two words: 'Be kind,' he said. After all these years I clearly remember the moment when he pronounced these words. It was a cold evening and we were standing near the seat at the top of the Schlossberg. My father was smiling with pleasure over what he was saying, and I saw his face in profile. His dark moustache was touched white with frost. He was wearing gloves and a cap. 'Be kind to one another, especially to children younger than yourselves,' he said, and, as he spoke, my father looked to us to be the kindest, wisest, and best of men.

This portrait goes a long way to explaining how he came to be so deeply involved in the Dreyfus Case. He was a man of peace and compassion; and he was also a cosmopolitan liberal who disliked bellicose chauvinism. Thus it was not simply that he was incensed by the injustice done to an innocent man; he abhorred the anti-semitism and xenophobia which

---

* *Have You Forgotten Yet? The First World War Memoirs of C.P. Blacker M.C.,* G.M., M.A., M.D., F.R.C.P., M.R.C.S., edited by John Blacker (forthcoming).

the Case excited fanning as it did the smouldering hostility between France and Germany – both countries for which he had a deep affection. Later when the hostility burst into flames in 1914, instantly engendering throughout France and England a frenzy of hatred against the Germans, 'it seemed to him,' my father wrote, 'that the world had suddenly gone mad.'

Is this the man, then, whom Oscar Wilde, in one of the two letters which he wrote to Robbie Ross, depicted as 'a Puritan, a prig, and a preacher'? OW was a complex and many-sided character. On the one hand he could be wonderfully kind and generous; but he was also fascinated by what he called 'the seduction of sin', was immensely arrogant and unwilling ever to admit that he had been at fault.

His involvement in the Dreyfus Case brought out the worst sides of his character. He was attracted by and consorted with Esterhazy largely because he knew him to be guilty of the crime for which another man had been condemned. It also reveals in him a latent anti-semitism, despite, as Mark Hichens points out, the generous help he had received from Jewish benefactors in his darkest hour. In the first letter to Ross he approvingly described the virulently anti-semitic *Libre Parole* as 'one of the first papers in France'. In the second letter he expressed the hope that 'on the day of St Hugh of Lincoln there will be a general massacre [of Jews]'.* He evidently had no compunction in betraying CB's plans to the anti-semitic journalist Rowland Strong, who, with Esterhazy, had become one of his regular drinking companions.

However, Mark Hichens also describes how, by a complex chain of events, OW's indiscretions with the information my grandfather had given him unwittingly assisted the Dreyfusards and gave their cause a crucial fillip at a time when their fortunes were at a low ebb.

So how, we may ask, is OW's role in the Dreyfus Case to be assessed? Did he in fact do more good than harm to the Dreyfusard cause? The impact which his revelations ultimately had on the course of events is difficult to assess, and it is questionable whether they made a material contribution to Dreyfus's eventual release and exoneration. Against this, OW undoubtedly torpedoed CB's carefully laid plan to publish in the British press the documents incriminating Esterhazy. The potential impact of this plan, had it materialized, is a matter of speculation which no reputable historian would like to undertake, and Mark Hichens does not attempt to do so. 'History,' an old Cambridge historian once said

---

* The allusion to St Hugh of Lincoln is explained in the footnote on p. 151.

to me, 'is the study of what was, not what might have been.' But the reader is entitled to his own conjectures, and for my part my thumb is turned down. If Oscar Wilde's disclosures had any real influence on the course of events, how much greater would have been that of the documents which my grandfather had planned to publish?

Preface

For many years now perceptions of Oscar Wilde have been indulgent. In books, plays and films he has always been portrayed as a victim rather than a villain, his virtues extolled, his faults glossed over and his treatment at the hands of the law castigated. Few today would defend his imprisonment for an offence which is no longer considered criminal or even particularly culpable. But the severity of his treatment has, perhaps, caused too great a reaction. For, as he would be the first to avow, he was no saint. He could be wonderfully kind and generous, but he could also be callous, vindictive and thoughtless. The man who would go out of his way to bring comfort to an old lady in distress or give his last penny to a beggar was also capable of neglecting his wife and family and leaving them in dire financial straits while consorting with male prostitutes and lavishing on them expensive gifts.

It is not the purpose of this book to vilify Wilde, certainly not to regress to the opinions of him prevalent a hundred years ago; but it is time for a more balanced picture, one that does not shy away from his less attractive side.

This unattractive side was strongly evident in his connection with the Dreyfus Affair. After his own experience of prison life it might seem to have been just the sort of case to have aroused his sympathy and indignation – a flagrant injustice with the victim suffering the tortures of the damned on a remote tropical island while the authorities tried to cover the matter up. This was an ideal opportunity for him to bring into play again his brilliant literary gifts. But he was not interested. When acquainted with the inside story by his friend, Carlos Blacker, he expressed only scornful indifference. 'It is always a mistake to be innocent,' he scoffed. 'To be criminal takes imagination and courage.' Even allowing that he might have been in his cups at the time these are terrible words. And his continued intimacy with the villain of the piece, Count Esterhazy, shows the extent to which he had succumbed to what he called 'the seduction of sin'.

Wilde died at the age of forty-four – diseased, impoverished, deserted by most of his friends with only the dregs of society as company. That such should have been the fate of a man of genius is a deep human tragedy.

I have had much generous help in the writing of this book. It could not have been written without the active cooperation and encouragement of the grandchildren of Carlos Blacker who had such a central role in the book's narrative. It was Thetis Blacker who urged me to write the book and gave all possible help including the brilliant design for the cover. Dr Carmen Blacker too has shown great interest and provided me with important family papers as also has Dr John Blacker who in addition has been kind enough to write the Foreword, setting out the views of the Blacker family about Carlos Blacker's friendship with Wilde and its tragic ending.

I also owe a great debt of gratitude to the American historian, Robert Maguire, who has an important collection of Wilde, Dreyfus and Blacker papers. He is a pre-eminent scholar in these fields and has published a number of articles in magazines and encyclopaedias. He is also in the course of writing a major work, and it was an act of exceptional kindness on his part to give me so much help and to give me the go-ahead to publish before he did.

Others too have taken time and trouble to give help and make suggestions. For these I would like to express gratitude to Alan Maclean, Richard Ollard and my sister, Phoebe Pearce, also to Wendy McLerie for her two excellent drawings.

Extracts from letters of Oscar Wilde are reprinted by permission of Fourth Estate Ltd from *The Letters of Oscar Wilde* by Merlin Holland and Sir Rupert Hart-Davis. Copyright letters The Estate of Oscar Wilde 1962, 1985, 2000. Merlin Holland 2000.

Mark Hichens

Dramatis Personæ

Dreyfus

Billot, General:
War Minister (1896–8); firmly opposed any reconsideration of Dreyfus Case.

Boisdeffre, General:
Chief of Staff of French Army. Strongly opposed to retrial of Dreyfus. Attempted to overawe jury in trial of Zola and to intimidate judges at second court martial of Dreyfus. Resigned after confession of Henry.

Brisson, Henri:
Prime Minister (1896). Allowed appeal of Lucie Dreyfus to proceed to Court of Criminal Appeal.

Cavaignac, Godfroy:
War Minister (1898). Believed strongly in guilt of Dreyfus and to prove it published secret documents which turned out to be forgeries. Forced confession from Henry about Faux Henry.

Cernusky, M.:
Said to be retired officer in Austrian Army of aristocratic descent. Claimed to have seen evidence of Dreyfus's espionage. Record of fraud and mental instability.

Clemencau, Georges:
Radical deputy who gave strong support to Dreyfus both in Chamber and in newspaper L'Aurore. Subsequently prime minister; came to be known as 'The Tiger'.

Conybeare, Frederick:
Oxford academic. Friend of Carlos Blacker who drew him into his plan for proving innocence of Dreyfus. When this miscarried he wrote article in English Review under pseudonym of 'Huguenot' with information supplied by Blacker. Later wrote book on Dreyfus Affair.

Cuignet, Captain:
Discovered forgery of Faux Henry.

Demange, Edgar:
Lawyer who defended Dreyfus in both courts martial.

Drumont, Edouard:
Editor of La Libre Parole. Fanatically anti-Semitic and anti-Dreyfusard. Lived to see his newspaper collapse and himself ruined.

Du Paty de Clam, Major:
Intelligence officer charged with arresting Dreyfus and extorting confession from him. Almost certain (but

unproved) that he cooperated with Henry in underhand activities including forgery and disclosing classified information to press. Killed in First World War.

Freystaetter, Captain: One of the judges at first court martial of Dreyfus. Later revealed existence of secret documents shown to judges and not to defence. Gave evidence at Rennes but restricted in what he could say.

Jaurès, Jean: Leader of Socialists in Chamber. Spoke out on behalf of Dreyfus.

Gonse, General: Assistant Chief of General Staff. Opposed retrial of Dreyfus. Obstructed prosecution of Esterhazy. Took steps to ostracize Picquart. Resigned after Henry's confession.

Henry, Major: Officer in Statistical Section. Active in compiling case against Dreyfus. Later fabricated evidence including *Faux Henry*. Committed suicide when forgery discovered.

Labori, Fernand: Lawyer. Defended Zola and with Demange defended Dreyfus in second court martial.

Lazare, Bernard: Jewish writer. At instigation of Mathieu Dreyfus wrote pamphlet setting out the injustice of Dreyfus's conviction. One-time anarchist.

Leblois, Louis: Lawyer to whom Picquart told all he knew. Passed on some information to Scheurer-Kestner. Gave evidence at Zola's trial.

Lebrun-Renault, Captain: Said to have alleged that Dreyfus confessed to him on the way to degradation ceremony. Later retracted this.

Mercier, General: Minister of War (1893–4). Took decision to prosecute Dreyfus. Remained convinced of his guilt to the end and was active in proclaiming it.

Panizzardi, Colonel: Italian military attaché in Paris. Cooperated closely with Schwartzkoppen. Friend of Carlos Blacker to whom he confided details of Esterhazy's dealings. Much abused by anti-Dreyfusards.

Pellieux, General: Conducted enquiry which whitewashed Esterhazy. Resigned from army after suicide of Henry.

Picquart, Colonel: Became head of Statistical Section in 1895. Discovered weakness and fraudulence of case against Dreyfus. Unable to persuade High Command to admit error and order retrial. Despatched to Tunisia to get out of way. Imprisoned and put on trial for disclosing secret information. Eventually acquitted. Minister of War (1906).

Quesnay de Beaurepaire: Judge. President of Civil Court who made slanderous attack on judges of Court of Criminal Appeal for pro-

	Dreyfus leanings. Later resigned in order to take part in anti-Dreyfusard campaign.
Reinach, Joseph:	Jewish Deputy. Strong and outspoken Dreyfusard. Wrote full-scale history of Dreyfus Affair.
Roget, General:	Charged by War Minister, Cavaignac, to investigate all documents relating to Dreyfus which led to discovery of *Faux Henry*.
Sandherr, Colonel:	Head of Statistical Section at time of Dreyfus's arrest. Anti-Semitic, strong believer in his guilt. Sought out all evidence against him.
Scheurer-Kestner, Auguste:	Vice-President of Senate. Made aware of Dreyfus's innocence. Urged reconsideration of the case which led to his being replaced as Vice-President.
Schwartzkoppen, Colonel:	German military attaché in Paris. Had dealings with Esterhazy. Stated publicly that he had had no dealings with Dreyfus.
Waldeck-Rousseau, René:	Lawyer. Refused brief to defend Dreyfus. Prime Minister (1899–1902). Recommended presidential pardon for Dreyfus.

Wilde

Adey, More:	Art connoisseur. Friend of Wilde; managed his financial affairs while he was in prison. Attempted to organize petition to Home Secretary for his early release.
Clarke, Sir Edward:	Barrister. Acted for Wilde against Queensberry and defended him in his two trials.
Douglas, Percy Lord Hawick:	Brother of Lord Alfred Douglas. Later 10th Marquess of Queensberry. Supplied half of bail for Wilde.
Harris, Frank:	One-time editor of *Evening News* and *Fortnightly Review*. Notorious fantasist and braggart, particularly about his sexual affairs (hetero). An admirer and staunch friend of Wilde. Took leading role in drawing up petition for his early release.
Headlam, Stuart:	Church of England parson. Supplied half of bail for Wilde, although at the time did not know him. Wilde went to his house after his release.
Healy, Christopher:	Irish journalist and poet. Secretary and companion to Rowland Strong. Informed by Wilde or Strong about details of Esterhazy-Schwartzkoppen dealings. Passed these on to Zola which resulted in 'Letter from Diplomat'. Later wrote article in English periodical showing part played by Wilde in Dreyfus Affair.

Leverson, Ada: — Wealthy Jewish friend of Wilde who provided him with accommodation between his trials. Known by Wilde as 'Sphinx'.

Queensberry, 9th Marquess: — 'Screaming scarlet Marquess'. Famous sportsman. Notorious for his outspoken views and violently eccentric behaviour. Libellous note to Wilde led to his prosecution and Wilde's downfall.

Ross, Robert: — Loyal and devoted friend of Wilde. Said to have been his first male partner. Managed his financial affairs after his release from prison. Of Canadian origins. Journalist and art critic. Wilde's literary executor.

Sherard, Robert: — Changed his name from Kennedy. Great-grandson of Wordsworth. Struggling author and journalist. Loyal friend of Wilde whom he visited in prison. Later wrote three biographies of Wilde.

Strong, Rowland: — Paris correspondent of *London Observer* and *New York Times*. Drinking companion of Wilde and Esterhazy. Informed by Wilde of some details of Dreyfus Affair, confided in him by Carlos Blacker; these he passed on to Esterhazy.

Taylor, Alfred: — Kept male *maison de rendez-vous* in College Street. Tried jointly with Wilde in first trial. Convicted. Old Marlburian.

Turner, Reggie: — Close friend of Wilde who called him 'boy snatcher of Clements Inn'. Illegitimate son of Lord Burnham, proprietor of *Daily Telegraph* in which he wrote gossip column.

Documents, Letters and Telegrams

Bordereau:

Communication from Esterhazy to Schwartzkoppen which fell into the hands of French intelligence and led to conviction of Dreyfus.

Bordereau annoté:

Copy of the *bordereau* said to have been annotated by the Kaiser with references to Dreyfus. Existence never proved.

Blanche and Speranza telegrams:

Sent by Esterhazy to Picquart in Tunisia in an attempt to incriminate him by conspiratorial messages which would be seen by the censor.

'Canaille de "D"':

An allusion in a letter from Schwartzkoppen to Panizzardi (1892) to one of his agents. Fell into hands of French intelligence officers who, two years later, believed wrongly it referred to Dreyfus.

Faux Henry:

Document forged by Henry to incriminate Dreyfus. Discovery of forgery led to suicide of Henry.

Letter from Diplomat (of Berne):

Published in *Le Siècle* (April 1898) giving, for first time, details of Schwartzkoppen's dealings with Esterhazy. Believed to have been written at instigation of Zola with information from Blacker and Panizzardi.

Petit Bleu:

Letter from Schwartzkoppen to Esterhazy which fell into the hands of French intelligence (March 1896). First indication of guilt of Esterhazy.

Weyler letter:

Addressed to Dreyfus in Devil's Island by unknown correspondent with cryptic message in invisible ink. An attempt to incriminate him.

Prelude

Chapter I

No sense have they of ills to come, Nor care beyond today.

Thomas Gray

In March 1891 Oscar Wilde was in Paris with his friends Carlos Blacker and Robert Sherard, and a visit was arranged to the foremost figure in French literature at that time, Emile Zola. With other French writers, such as André Gide and Anatole France, Wilde had formed close friendships, but it was unlikely that he would establish much rapport with Zola. The two men had little in common. Zola, the son of an Italian immigrant, had known deep poverty and had become a writer only because he had failed his *baccalauréat* which barred him from the legal profession. Intensely serious and with a burning social conscience, he regarded writing as an instrument of social justice: by means of education and medicine he believed that the human condition could be improved. In 1891 he had just completed a twenty-volume epic (Les Rougon Macquart) on the fortunes of a French family during the Second Empire. For this he had felt compelled to live at close quarters with the poorest of the poor, and the conditions he found there he described in lurid detail, so much so that some people regarded his works as pornographic. He was later described as 'the most widely read and most hated of French writers'.

Very different had been the upbringing and outlook of Oscar Wilde. The son of a well-to-do Irish doctor, he had had brilliant success first at Trinity College, Dublin and then at Magdalen College, Oxford where he had taken a double first in Greats and had then won the prestigious Newdigate Poetry Prize. In establishing himself as a writer, he held completely opposite views to those of Zola. A fervent member of the Aesthetic Movement, he believed passionately that all forms of art were sacred and totally divorced from moral, political or any other considerations. He no more believed in art as a means of social change than did Zola in 'Art for art's sake'.

In spite of the differences between them it seems that the meeting passed off amiably and courteously. Zola told of his plans for a new novel about the Franco-Prussian War of 1870–1 for which he felt it necessary to visit the battlefields and make his way through mountains of documents. Documentation, he said, was the basis of all great novels. Although this was hardly Wilde's method, he agreed warmly and said that in writing his novel, *The Picture of Dorian Gray*, he had made a careful study of long lists of jewellery. On this somewhat flippant note the meeting came to an end, and it seemed improbable that the men would meet again. As it happened, however, there was to be further contact between them, although this was not altogether harmonious. And they were both to be involved in different ways in the great 'Affair' which in a few years time was to engulf the French nation. In 1891 it seemed highly unlikely that either man would be concerned with the trial and conviction of an obscure French army officer called Alfred Dreyfus, and equally unlikely that before the end of the century both men would receive prison sentences, be subjected to violent abuse and forced to live in exile abroad.

Also at this meeting was Carlos Blacker. A gentleman of independent means with brilliant gifts, he was at that time Wilde's closest friend – a friendship based solely on harmony of minds and interests with no element of homosexuality. He was trustee of his marriage settlement and Wilde had dedicated to him one of his most successful early works, *The Happy Prince*. As a conversationalist he was second only to Wilde who used to recall how they had 'tired many a moon with talk and drunk many a sun to rest with wine and words'. Like Wilde and Zola, Blacker too was doomed to great misfortune and persecution and lived much of his life in exile abroad. And he too was to play a vital role in the great 'Affair'.

Justice Miscarried

Chapter II

The innocent always suffer. It is their métier.
(Oscar Wilde to Esterhazy)

If you are innocent you are the greatest martyr of all time.
(Du Paty de Clam to Dreyfus)

My only crime was to have been born a Jew.
(Dreyfus)

In 1891 few people had heard of Alfred Dreyfus. There was no reason
why they should. A captain of artillery of no great distinction, he led
a quiet, unpretentious life devoted to his army career and his young
family. Within four years, however, through no fault of his own, he was
suddenly to be engulfed in infamy and obloquy and, to his total bewilderment was to find himself at the centre of an unprecedented political
storm.

Dreyfus was Jewish. His ancestors had come from Eastern Europe in
the previous century and settled in the Rhineland province of Alsace,
a territory long disputed between France and Germany. Since 1648 it
had been part of France, but in the nineteenth century it still bore
German traces, and German was still the predominant language. Like
many wandering Jews the Dreyfus family had had a desperate struggle
to survive, but by dint of hard work, business acumen and some good
luck they had not only survived but prospered. The Industrial Revolution
had brought great opportunities for those with skills and enterprise, and
Alfred's father, Raphael, had been ready to grasp them. By 1891 he was
the owner of a flourishing cotton mill and was a distinguished and
prosperous citizen of the Alsatian City of Mulhouse. He was also the
father of a large family which included four sons of which Alfred was
the youngest. In the normal course of events it would have been likely
that all sons would have gone into the family business, but in 1870 the

French Emperor Napoleon III was lured into a war with Prussia, the largest and most militaristic of the German states. The result was an immediate and overwhelming French defeat. At the age of twelve Alfred had to witness a foreign invasion of his country with all the attendant horrors and humiliations – German troops strutting through Mulhouse, heavy demands for money and all sorts of goods and brutal punishments for anyone who resisted or failed to comply. And then in March 1871 came the ultimate dishonour when the French Government was forced to agree to the cession of Alsace to the newly proclaimed German Empire.

This confronted members of the Dreyfus family with a major decision. If they stayed in Alsace they would become German citizens, and the sons would be liable to conscription into the German army. But by the Treaty of Frankfort it was open to French citizens to make a choice between French and German nationality; although if they chose the former it would be necessary for them to cross the new frontier into France. In the event two of the brothers opted to remain in Alsace to take care of the family businesses while the rest moved into France where Alfred was sent to a boarding school.

The Prussian occupation of Alsace and its incorporation into the German Empire had a profound effect on the young Alfred. He had always been intensely patriotic with a deep and burning love for France. Although he paid lip service to the Jewish religion he regarded himself as first and foremost a Frenchman, and France's humiliation in 1870–1 bit deeply into him. Like many others he looked forward to a war of revenge and the regaining of the lost provinces of Alsace and Lorraine, and this must surely have been a major consideration in his decision to join the French army. In 1882 he was commissioned in the artillery and by the following year was making steady progress up the promotion ladder. Reports on him by his commanding officers had been favourable; he had a quick comprehension of all military matters and he accepted totally and gladly the customs and quirks of the French army. In 1891 he married Lucie Hadamard, the daughter of a wealthy Jewish diamond merchant which meant that his already ample private means were further augmented. Altogether his career and prospects seemed set fair, but then in 1892 came a development which was to lead to disaster: he was selected to be a staff probationer in the War Office. This entailed spending time in each of the four main departments of the War Office: those covering fortifications, artillery, troop movements and intelligence. Here again reports on Dreyfus from his superior officers were on the whole favourable, acknowledging his quick mind, wide knowledge of military matters and his skill at languages; but for the first time a note of criticism appeared – it was remarked that he was too sure of himself and apt to be pretentious. It also became evident that he was not altogether popular with his fellow officers who found him aloof and too ready to show off his superior knowledge; he also seemed to have no outside interests – in the arts or in sports – and in the mess he only ever wanted to 'talk shop' which was not thought good form. No doubt too his wealth and opulent lifestyle aroused hostility as also did the fact that he was a Jew.

Since the French Revolution with its ringing declarations about the equality and brotherhood of man anti-Semitism, as with all racism, had been officially taboo. But, of course, such things are not abolished by decree, and anti-Semitism still prevailed in some parts of France, especially where Jews were most numerous and most successful. The Dreyfus family had been subject to it in Alsace, and in Paris it was even more virulent. But although Alfred Dreyfus had encountered it in the army, it had not been a serious handicap to him in his career which in 1894

seemed promising. In addition he had no financial worries and was happily married with two young children. There appeared to be no clouds on the horizon. Disaster, when it came, came out of a clear blue sky.

On Saturday, 13 October 1894 Dreyfus was at home when a special messenger arrived, summoning him to attend an inspection of staff officers at the War Office on the following Monday. There was something slightly unusual about this, as also was the instruction to come in civilian clothes and the return of the messenger later to get a written receipt for the order. But Dreyfus was not unduly concerned and on Monday

Alfred Dreyfus in 1895

morning, promptly, he presented himself at the War Office, expecting to be taken into the presence of the Chief of Staff. Instead, however, he was shown into a room occupied by an officer of whom he was to see much in the next weeks – Major the Marquis Du Paty de Clam.

Du Paty was reputed to be a clever man (he had passed second out of the Ecole Militaire), but was also known to be unbalanced and flamboyant; with scarlet face, flowing moustache and theatrical manner (as well as a taste for transvestism), he seemed to step straight out of an act of a musical comedy. With the Major were three civilians who were later revealed as police officers. The interview began with Du Paty requiring Dreyfus to take dictation under the pretext that he had injured his finger (appropriately bandaged). Dreyfus was certainly surprised at this, especially as what he took down contained classified military information which should not have been mentioned in front of civilians; but it did not prepare him for the bombshell which followed when Du Paty suddenly and dramatically clapped him on the shoulder and declared: 'Captain Dreyfus, in the name of the law I arrest you. You are accused of high treason.' At this Dreyfus was struck dumb. Shy, inarticulate and with a thin reedy voice he could only splutter out his innocence and say that a terrible mistake had been made. It then became evident that Du Paty saw it as his role to break him down and extort a confession from him. Shouting, gesticulating, abusing, he urged him to tell all or commit suicide, for which a loaded revolver was at hand. Dreyfus, however, continued to maintain his innocence and offered full cooperation in clearing the matter up, handing over the keys of all drawers and cupboards in his house. Eventually Du Paty was compelled to realize that a confession was not going to be forthcoming and ordered Dreyfus to be taken to a military prison known as Le Cherche Midi.

The events leading up to this extraordinary situation were long drawn out and complex, and to understand them it is necessary to have a picture of the general situation in Europe at that time. After France's humiliating defeat in 1870 the country had made a good recovery and there was much talk of a war of revenge; to some this was inevitable and necessary; France's honour could only be restored by the regaining of the lost provinces and to symbolize this determination the statue representing the town of Strasbourg in the Place de la Concorde in Paris was perpetually draped in black. The German Imperial Chancellor, Prince Otto von Bismarck, was aware of this threat and took steps to guard against it: not only did he keep the German army in a state of readiness, but he also formed a Triple Alliance with Austria and Italy whereby each country would come to the help of the other in the event of war.

At first France was without allies in Europe, but following the fall of Bismarck in 1890 and the aggressive policies of Kaiser Wilhelm II, other countries in Europe took fright and France was able to make an alliance with Russia, a strange union between the most democratic of European countries and the most despotic, but both had much to fear from Germany. With Europe thus poised for war it was vitally necessary for all the powers to be as well informed as possible about the plans and armaments of the others. There was, therefore, much espionage. At the centre of this usually were the military attachés in foreign embassies. Particularly active in the early 1890s was the German military attaché in Paris, Colonel von Schwartzkoppen, who worked in close cooperation with his Italian counterpart, Colonel Panizzardi.* The French were aware of their activities and had set up a special department to deal with them which was given the cover name of the Statistical Section (SS). The SS was separate from the main body of military intelligence and was engaged mainly in the 'cloak and dagger' aspect of spying, involving such matters as the picking of locks, the bribing of servants and prostitutes, the stealing of letters, the forgery of documents and the planting of false information.

One of its agents was a domestic worker in the German embassy whose job it was to go through the waste-paper baskets and extract from them anything which looked of importance and hand it over to an agent of SS. It was possibly from this source that in late 1892 there came into the possession of the SS a letter from Schwartzkoppen to Panizzardi which said: 'Herewith twelve large-scale plans of Nice which that *canaille* (blackguard) "D" has handed to me for you.' At the time the SS could not identify "D", but later it seemed clear enough.

In July 1894 (it transpired later) a man in civilian clothes called at the German embassy and asked to see von Schwartzkoppen. The man revealed himself as Marie-Charles-Ferdinand Walsin-Esterhazy, a descen-

---

* There is some evidence that their relationship was more intimate than usually exists between military attachés. From the flowery wording of some of their correspondence in which they addressed each other as 'Alexandrine' and 'Maximilienne' and '*ma belle pitite*' and '*mon chéri*' as well as the rather ambiguous use of the French word *bourrer* (dictionary definition: 'to stuff', 'ram a charge home', 'to cram') a homosexual relationship has been surmised.

dant, albeit illegitimately, of an ancient Hungarian family, but French by birth and an officer in the French army with the rank of major. He told Schwartzkoppen that he was in desperate financial straits, confronted with the prospect either of suicide or selling military secrets which he was in a position to do as he had numerous high-ranking contacts, and had served for a time in the Statistical Section. He was aware that such conduct would be regarded with the utmost contempt by Schwartzkoppen, and defended himself on the ground that he was not a true Frenchman and would have preferred to serve in the German army; and, moreover, he had come to feel the greatest contempt for the French army and in particular for its senior officers. Schwartzkoppen was, indeed, disgusted by such behaviour on the part of an aristocrat and an officer, and his first instinct was to have nothing to do with him; but when he realized the scope of the information he had to offer, he felt he must communicate with his superiors in Berlin who told him to maintain contact. And so for the next two years money was passed to Esterhazy for military information, alleged later to have been some 162 communications in all at the rate of 80,000 francs a year. Usually these transactions passed off smoothly, but there was one which was to have momentous consequences.

On 1 September 1894, about a month after he had first made contact, Esterhazy left at the German embassy a document or *bordereau* as it subsequently came to be known. This *bordereau*, which was unsigned and undated, contained no secret information itself but listed a number of items which the writer claimed to be able to provide. Somehow, it later transpired, it had been found by the French domestic worker in the German embassy who was in the pay of the SS and who, having first torn it up, then delivered it to French intelligence. The reason for tearing it up was that a document stolen from the German embassy was equivalent to abstracting it from German territory which might lead to a diplomatic incident; by tearing it up it was made to appear that Schwartzkoppen had read the document, torn it up and then thrown it into the waste-paper basket from where it might have fallen into the hands of someone outside the embassy, and thus outside German territory. The items listed in the *bordereau* mainly concerned artillery – how guns behaved, how they were disposed and a note on covering troops, as well as a secret Firing Manual of the Field Artillery. In addition it also offered information on an impending expedition to Madagascar, and ended by saying that the writer was just off on manoeuvres. Such a document was naturally of great concern to the SS. It had been known there for some time that information was being leaked to the Germans, and this was the first opportunity to track down its source. In doing so the intelligence officers were struck by one point – the variety of the information on offer which would not have been available to many staff officers. As has been seen the French War Office was divided into four sections, and although these were not watertight, it would be unusual for one man to have access to all the subjects mentioned. That it was an officer on the staff they had little doubt, and then it occurred to them that the most likely candidate was one of the probationers (*stagiari*) who was going the rounds of the different departments as part of his training. And looking down the list of these one name stood out prominently – that of Alfred Dreyfus: he was an artillery officer, he had the reputation of being a loner, he came from Alsace with its German connections and he spoke German fluently; in addition he was a Jew which to some people meant that his loyalty to France was suspect. There were, however, cogent reasons why it should not have been Dreyfus: there was total lack of motive – Dreyfus was known to be amply well off, and when the *bordereau* came to be examined carefully it was seen that it was unlikely to have been written by an artillery officer; there were technical mistakes and the title of the artillery manual was misquoted; in addition Dreyfus had no connection whatever with the Madagascar expedition and he was not just off on manoeuvres (although the *bordereau* being undated, this was not conclusive). Certain general points about the *bordereau* also became apparent: the information offered was not of vital importance and not all of it was secret, in particular the artillery manual; there was too a feeling of unreality about it; it seemed unlikely to have been written by a professional spy who would almost certainly have made some mention of payment.

Of course the crucial matter was that of the handwriting. Did this match up with that of Dreyfus? Here there was uncertainty and dis- agreement. There was, indubitably, some similarity. Army intelligence officers, who had no great expertise, were divided on the issue: some said definitely that it was not, others that it could be or might be a case of self-forgery – Dreyfus disguising his own handwriting. Later the top graphologist from the Bank of France was called in and, after some hesitation, stated definitely that the handwriting was not that of Drey- fus. However, he was not regarded as infallible and the case against Dreyfus was not dropped. Too many people in the army needed a conviction to save their reputations, in particular the head of the SS, Colonel Sandherr. Sandherr was from Alsace and a strong anti-Semite and seems to have convinced himself that Dreyfus was guilty and was covering his tracks with devilish cunning. He therefore instituted an investigation to find out all that was unfavourable to him. Some officers came forward to say that he was aloof and inquisitive, often enquiring into matters that did not concern him. The Paris police were asked to investigate his private life which they did with some thoroughness; they were not able to come up with much, but such as it was was exaggerated and distorted: he had made some unauthorized visits to his family in Alsace where he might have been in touch with German agents; he had visited racecourses, so he might be a compulsive gambler anxious to make good his losses; a casual acquaintance with an Austrian lady was transformed into an expensive and dangerous liaison with a sinister foreigner.

Immediately after his first interview Du Paty had gone straight to Dreyfus's house where with his usual bluster he had tried to extort a confession from his wife, but without success; and Lucie had then cooperated fully in his search of the house and removal of a quantity of papers, none of which subsequently were found to be in any way incriminating, and it was notable that there was no sign of the type of paper on which the *bordereau* had been written. When she heard what had happened to her husband Lucie's first instinct had been to send for Alfred's elder brother, Mathieu, who of all men was the closest to him, but this was forbidden by Du Paty. 'One word from you,' he said, 'a single word and he will be ruined. The only way to save him is through silence.'

After being taken to the Cherche Midi military prison Dreyfus was left in solitary confinement for three days when at times his reserve broke down and he raged frenziedly round his cell, banging his head against the wall and shouting that he was innocent and that his only crime was to have been born a Jew. At the end of that time Du Paty reappeared, hoping that by then he would have been sufficiently 'softened up' for a confession to be forced from him. To this end he wanted to burst in on Dreyfus at the dead of night with a bright light which he would flash in his eyes, but this was prohibited by the prison governor. But what was Dreyfus to confess to? He still had not been told the details of the charges against him. It was not until the eleventh day that he was at last shown a copy of the *bordereau*; and of this he denied all knowledge, pointing out that it was not in his handwriting and contained items of which he could have no knowledge. Meanwhile his mental and nervous state continued to deteriorate and his thoughts turned increasingly to suicide, but from this he was dissuaded by the prison governor, Major Ferdinand Forzinetti, who had become convinced of his innocence and did all he could to support him, urging that he must at all costs keep going as suicide would be taken as proof of guilt and his family would never live down the disgrace.

By the end of October it was evident that the case against Dreyfus was a weak one, and the decision had to be taken as to whether to abandon it or proceed with it and bring Dreyfus to a court martial. The decision on this rested with the Minister for War, a retired general of no great distinction whose political career at that time was at a low ebb. Auguste Mercier, like many military men, was not an adept politician and he was being hard pressed in the Chamber of Deputies for his maladministration of the army; it was also rumoured that he had lost the confidence of the Prime Minister who might be about to dispense with his services. To save his political career he badly needed a success and this might be provided by the uncovering of a spy in the War Office. But he also realized how insubstantial was the case against Dreyfus, and if he were to be put on trial and acquitted, it would mean further loss of face. There were several people at the time who urged him to take no action and hush the matter up. General Saussier, Military Governor of Paris and a highly popular figure with a splendid record on the battlefield (and in the boudoir),* urged him not to proceed against Dreyfus but 'to despatch him to the colonial frontiers and see he doesn't come back'. The Foreign Minister too was apprehensive, fearing that the affair would put more strain on France's relations with Germany, especially if it became known that French intelligence was keeping an agent among the domestic staff of the German embassy.

But then there was another development: the matter was leaked to the press. This, it was later discovered, was the work of a Major Henry of the SS, no doubt with the agreement of Colonel Sandherr, whose object was to stir up the anti-Semitic press and so bring pressure to bear on Mercier to continue with the case against Dreyfus. In this they were successful. The newspaper chosen, *La Libre Parole*, was viciously anti-Semitic and its editor, Edouard Drumont, was obsessed with secret Jewish syndicates and the idea that traditional French values were being undermined by Jewish big business. It was not a subject on which he could think rationally, and when he heard that a Jewish officer was being held

---

* At the time he was living in a ménage à trois with a Jewish officer and his wife.

on a charge of treason it was grist to his mill. He assumed at once, without any evidence, that he must be guilty and that a sinister Jewish conspiracy was bent on covering the matter up. He even intimated that Mercier might be part of this plot. Other organs of the press joined in this manic campaign, and Dreyfus and his family were reviled and accused of every imaginable crime. Not all the press, it should be noted, debased itself in this way; there were honourable exceptions who proclaimed that Dreyfus, like anyone else, 'had the right to be innocent', and that 'the arrest of a French officer on the charge of high treason without serious proof would be a crime as abominable as treason itself.' But these were lone voices and the general atmosphere in the last months of 1894 was frenzied and highly charged.

Auguste Mercier was no coward; he had shown at other times that he was prepared to take an unpopular stand and confront the press; but on this occasion he must have been aware of the abuse and scandalous imputations that would be levelled against him if he allowed the case against Dreyfus to be dropped. He may also have been convinced, however wrongly, that Dreyfus was guilty. The officers of the SS would have seen to it that all documents pointing to his guilt would have been shown to him while others indicating his innocence would have been withheld. And so his final decision, taken, it should be noted, with the backing of nearly all his cabinet colleagues, was that the prosecution of Dreyfus should go forward and he should be brought before a court martial.

Just before this decision was taken Lucie Dreyfus had at last been allowed by Du Paty to make contact with Mathieu Dreyfus who set out at once for Paris where for the next four years he was to devote himself unsparingly to his brother's cause. In this he was to be endlessly frustrated, violently abused and in constant personal danger; his only advantage was that he had ample financial resources. His first task was to obtain the services of the best possible lawyer which was not easy as some shied away from such an unpopular brief; but in the end he was able to engage one of the highest standing, Edgar Demange, who made it a condition that he must be convinced of Dreyfus's innocence. And so, after three weeks in solitary confinement, Dreyfus was at last allowed to see a lawyer, and after only a brief interview it was clear to Demange that he was being wrongly accused and the case against him was totally inadequate. It seemed to rest solely on the *bordereau* about which there were many peculiarities; and still no plausible motive could be found. In a civil court of law the case would soon have been demolished, but it would be a different matter in a court martial. Here the judge and jury would be seven middle-ranking officers with little or no experience of legal affairs. It would be wrong to suppose that they might be suborned, but they must certainly have been aware that it would be embarrassing to the high command if Dreyfus were to be acquitted.

Three weeks before the court martial was due to open Mercier took the unusual and highly improper step of giving an interview to a newspaper in which he is alleged to have said that 'there were crying proofs against Dreyfus and the only question was whether he had been paid'. At the time he denied having given the interview, but years later he admitted it. The reports of this interview, along with allegations in the press that it was to Germany that Dreyfus had been passing information, caused great bewilderment in the German and Italian embassies. Schwartzkoppen and Panizzardi knew that they had had no contact with Dreyfus and could only assume that he must have been in direct contact with Berlin or, maybe, a military attaché in another country. The German ambassador in Paris, Graf von Münster, was an aristocrat of the old school who disapproved strongly of espionage, and when Schwartzkoppen told him that he had had no dealings with Dreyfus (keeping from him his contact with Esterhazy), he published a statement in a French newspaper making the position clear. This was followed a few days later by similar statements from the Italian and Austrian embassies. But these made little impression, the general attitude to them being 'they would say that, wouldn't they'.

As the day of the trial approached Demange made great efforts to see to it that it was held in public, but the first action of the court when it convened was to hold the trial in camera 'in the interests of national security'. It was, of course, highly undesirable that it should be made public how the *bordereau* had been filched from the German embassy, and it was also undesirable that it should be seen by the public how weak was the case against Dreyfus.

The trial, when it took place, was heavily one-sided; the evidence unfavourable to Dreyfus was highlighted and exaggerated while that favourable was passed over lightly or omitted. Even so at one stage the case seemed to be in danger of collapsing, and it was then that Major Henry of the SS committed flagrant perjury. He had already given evidence once, but then asked to be recalled as he had something further to say. He then told how before the discovery of the *bordereau* the SS had been warned by 'a man of honour' that there was a traitor in the War Office whom he later identified. 'And there he is!' shouted

Henry, pointing at Dreyfus. This was a complete fabrication and unacceptable as evidence unless his informant was named and brought to court to testify under oath and be cross-examined. This was immediately pointed out by Demange, but Henry refused to give a name, saying 'There are secrets in an officer's head that even his képi should not know.' In a civil court such a statement would have been disallowed, but in a court martial the army officers, impressed by the need for secrecy in certain circumstances, merely told Henry to swear on oath that Dreyfus was the man named, which he had no qualms in doing. And this was not all that was illegal in the trial. Realizing that more evidence than the *bordereau* must be found to secure Dreyfus's conviction, Sandherr and Henry, abetted by Mercier, had been searching in the records of the SS for documents that could be used to incriminate him. They had not been able to come up with much, but there were intercepted letters between Schwartzkoppen and Panizzardi about espionage activities, as well as the one referring to '*ce canaille de D*'. The proper procedure would have been for these to be produced in court and shown to the defence counsel, but he, they realized, would then have little difficulty in casting doubts on them. And so it was decided that they should be withheld from Dreyfus and Demange and shown to the judges privately after they had withdrawn to consider their verdict. This was certainly illegal and, if it had been discovered, would have rendered the trial invalid. But the judges were told that it had to be done this way as the information was so sensitive that if it were to be revealed in court, even a court in camera, it might cause a European war. This seems to have been accepted by the judges,* who were convinced by the documents (subsequently known as the Secret File), and they brought in a unanimous verdict of guilty. Until recently such a verdict would have resulted in a sentence of death, but this was no longer available, and Dreyfus was given instead the heaviest sentence possible – that of deportation for life to a fortified place, to forfeiture of his rank and to degradation, a grisly ceremony in which he would be publicly humiliated. He might have had a modified sentence if he had made a confession, but this, despite great pressure, he refused to do. He was allowed to appeal, but within just over a week this had been rejected.

And so on 3 January 1895 Dreyfus was handcuffed and in full military

---

* Years later one of the judges was to break ranks and reveal what had happened.

uniform brought into a court-
yard where detachments of
troops from all the regiments
serving in Paris were assembled.
The sentence of the court was
read out whereupon Dreyfus, as
loudly as his weak voice would
allow, proclaimed his innocence. Then, while bells rang
and drums rolled, a warrant officer stepped forward and
solemnly stripped his uniform of
all badges, gold braid, buttons,
even the red stripes from his
trousers. He then took his sword
and snapped it across his knee.
Dreyfus was marched round the
parade ground while the assembled troops looked on in silence
as he again tried to declare his
innocence and while the crowd
that had gathered outside yelled
death cries and anti-Jewish
abuse.

Dreyfus is degraded

From then on Dreyfus was treated with the greatest harshness and
cruelty. Four weeks later he was transferred from the Santé prison in
Paris to one in La Rochelle on the west coast. To avoid crowds the
journey was made at great speed in the middle of the night; half-dressed
but in handcuffs and leg-irons, he was hustled out of his cell and then
into a tiny compartment in an ice-cold train with no food or water for
the four-hour journey. At La Rochelle word had spread of his arrival
and he was awaited by a mob, screaming and spitting and ready to lynch
him.* Only just preserved, he was then packed off to the Ile de Ré from
where a ship would take him to the bleakest, most inhospitable part of
the French Empire, the Iles de Salut off the coast of French Guiana.
Until then he was kept in conditions which a visitor described as

---

* Next day in *La Libre Parole* there appeared the insane suggestion that the
  crowd was in Jewish pay, and that their object was to rescue Dreyfus and
  waft him to safety.

'absolutely barbarous, monstrous and revolting'. He was allowed some heavily censored mail from his family, as well as a few brief, closely supervised visits from Lucie. In these it was permitted to talk only of private family matters; no mention could be made of his trial or of future plans for clearing his name. But Lucie was able to let him know that she and Mathieu would never weaken in their efforts to achieve this, and at the same time she urged him vehemently that for the sake of his family he must never entertain thoughts of suicide.

Finally on 22 February 1895 he was taken on board ship, and put in a wire mesh cage, exposed to the bitter winter winds, for the voyage to a destination which had not yet been revealed to him. Eighteen days later the ship reached the Iles de Salut on one of which, known as Devil's Island, it was intended that he should remain for the rest of his life.

Three weeks after Dreyfus reached the Iles de Salut Oscar Wilde was arrested and charged with homosexual offences for which he was subsequently imprisoned for two years. At the time it seemed inconceivable that there could ever be any connection between Wilde in Reading gaol and Dreyfus on Devil's Island. Apart from being on different continents the two men had nothing in common. There seemed to be no reason why their fates should ever cross.

Justice Misplaced

Oscar Wilde — a favourite subject for cartoonists

Chapter III

Somehow or other I will be famous. If not famous, notorious.
(Oscar Wilde)

*A man who can dominate a London dinner table can dominate the
world.*
(*Ibid*)

And every one will say
As you walk your mystic way,
If this young man expresses himself in terms too deep for me,
Why, what a very singularly deep young man this deep young man
must be.
(W.S. Gilbert – *Patience*)

At the time of his visit to Zola in 1891 Wilde had not reached the
zenith of his career; the four great comedies for which he was to become
famous had not been written, and his literary reputation rested on some
scholarly and provocative essays and a number of short stories including
some delightful ones for children (although he always maintained that
these were written 'not for a child but for childlike people from eighteen
to eighty'); there was, too, a volume of poetry which had had a mixed
reception including charges of plagiarism (because of which a presenta-
tion copy to the Oxford Union was rejected – an unprecedented rebuff).

Although these works had brought some acclaim, they had not
brought great financial reward, and it had been necessary for Wilde to
undertake a certain amount of journalism including a stint as editor of
a woman's monthly magazine. Such fame as he had achieved derived
not so much from his literary works as from his wit, his enthralling
conversation and a flamboyant lifestyle. It was the latter which first
attracted public attention notably when, in an attempt to gain publicity
for his poetry, he had for a time disported what purported to be aesthetic

costume – velvet coat, knee breeches, loose shirt and flowing tie. This outfit, combined with a pose of drooping languor and absorption with corruption and decay, had caused outrage among the more conventional. In particular it had caught the eye of the sharp-witted and acerbic satirist, W.S. Gilbert, then at the height of his fame for his operettas written in conjunction with Arthur Sullivan. In one of their most beguiling works, *Patience*, Wilde and the Aesthetic Movement were ridiculed caustically. In fact Wilde's flirtation with medieval costume was short-lived and less ostentatious than generally supposed. It is doubtful if he ever 'walked down Piccadilly with a poppy or a lily in

Wilde lectures the Americans on Dante Gabriel Rosetti (cartoon by Max Beerbohm)

his medieval hand', but he might have done. As he himself remarked: 'To have done it was nothing, but to make people think one had done it was a triumph.' In the event the highly popular operetta brought him much notoriety (to which he had no objection) as well as an arduous and surprisingly successful lecture tour of America, organized by D'Oyly Carte, the Gilbert and Sullivan producer, as a publicity stunt for *Patience*. In the course of this, as well as lecturing socialites, students and Gilbert and Sullivan enthusiasts on a wide variety of subjects, he also addressed more rugged audiences – on one occasion going down a silver mine and talking to the awe-struck miners on the art of Benvenuto Cellini.

In 1890, eight years after his American tour, Wilde published his first (and only) novel, *The Picture of Dorian Gray*, which caused a considerable furore. The story, not altogether original, was of a beautiful young man who sold his soul to the Devil in exchange for the gift of everlasting youth and beauty, and how, while he lived a life of the wildest debauchery, instigated by his evil genius, Lord Henry Wotton, his portrait became decayed and depraved and he remained as young and beautiful as ever; and how in the end Nemesis (goddess of retribution and vengeance) closed in on him. This torrid, erotic story, with strong homosexual undertones, fascinated some and scandalized others. It was, indeed, a critical step in Wilde's rise to fame and then to ruin. Like Dorian Gray he too was leading a life of dangerous depravity and he too was on the way to an encounter with Nemesis.

The year 1891 was to be a fateful one for Wilde – on the face of it a year of great achievement and success. Under a mask of extreme boredom he saw the publication of two volumes of short stories, a collection of essays, a controversial political tract (*The Soul of Man under Socialism*) and two plays – *Salome* based on a biblical theme and *Lady Windermere's Fan*, the first of his modern comedies. But it was also the year in which he first met Lord Alfred Douglas.

At first his main hopes were for *Salome*, the story of the seductive dancer who on the instigation of her mother, Herodias, beguiled King Herod into having the head of John the Baptist brought to her on a charger. His hopes for this were enhanced when Sarah Bernhardt, the greatest living actress, agreed to take the title role, and there was much curiosity as to how, aged thirty-seven, she would perform the Dance of the Seven Veils (in answer to enquiries she only smiled enigmatically and said: 'Wait and see'). A magnificent production was envisaged, but, unfortunately, no heed was taken of British censorship laws, one of which, dating from Puritan times, forbade the portrayal of Biblical characters on the stage, and so the production had to be abandoned. The operation of this archaic law made Wilde furious and he talked about emigrating and taking out French citizenship. That he did not eventually do so may have been in part due to the consideration that if he had, he might have become liable to military service – a prospect regarded with some hilarity by elements of the British press. But the main reason was the great success of his other play, *Lady Windermere's Fan*. This had been dashed off at great speed while on holiday in the Lake District – from where he had taken the names for the leading characters. At first he had not attached great importance to it, describing it as 'One of those drawing room plays with pink lampshades'. On the surface it did not seem to be more than a vehicle for Wilde's choicest epigrams, and as such it was instantly popular. To those who looked at it more closely, however, there were elements of a more disturbing nature. It is unlikely that Wilde intended the play to have a moral; he would certainly have denied it strongly. Nevertheless, a moral did emerge and, as always with Wilde, a paradoxical one – that the greatest harm is often done by conventional, unthinking 'good' people, and that good is more likely to be done by people who have fallen from grace and have no pretensions to virtue. One of the characters in the play is made to say: 'I am afraid that good people do a great deal of harm in this world. It takes a thoroughly good woman to do a thoroughly stupid thing.' And again: 'What are called good women may have terrible things in them, mad moods of recklessness, assertion, jealousy, sin. Bad women, as they are termed, may have in them sorrow, repentance, pity, sacrifice.'

Remarkable too in the play is a passage in which Lady Windermere is warned of the fate that would befall her if she broke the laws by which society was governed: 'You don't know what it is to fall into the pit, to be despised, mocked, abandoned, sneered at – to be an outcast, to find the door shut against one, to have to creep in the hideous byways, afraid every moment lest the mask should be stripped from one's face, and all the while to hear the laughter, the horrible laughter of the world, a thing more tragic than all the tears the world has ever shed.' Four years later, almost word for word, this was the fate which was to overtake Wilde himself.

The great popularity of *Lady Windermere's Fan* made it inevitable that Wilde would be under pressure from theatre managements to write another play of the same sort, and this he did in the following year. Once again it was written at speed while on holiday, first near Cromer in Norfolk (hence such names in the cast as Hunstanton, Brancaster and Illingworth) and later at Babbacombe in Devon. *A Woman of No Importance* was in many ways similar to *Lady Windermere's Fan*, containing as it did a multitude of epigrams, brilliant people (most of them fashioned in Wilde's own image), a demure Puritan lady whose rigid goodness brings her into deep waters, as well as a dramatic secret to be revealed at the appropriate moment. But the play has weaknesses. Of Wilde's four main comedies it is, perhaps, the least distinguished, being laden with such Victorian banalities as a wicked lord, a virtuous woman he has wronged and 'the son of her shame'. And the plot was stereotyped; Wilde himself derided it, saying he had taken parts of it from *The Family Herald*, but 'Plots,' he said, 'are tedious. Anyone can invent them. Life is full of them. Indeed one has to elbow one's way through them as they crowd across one's path.' Another weakness, more in evidence than in *Lady Windermere's Fan* was the inadequacy of the emotional scenes: these have been described as 'conventional and adolescent', and reflect Wilde's own emotional immaturity. All his life he glorified youth and dreaded it slipping away. In *A Woman of No Importance* he reveals these feelings which are expressed by his alter ego, Lord Illingworth, eloquently but, as always, with flippancy: 'Remember that you've got on your side the most wonderful thing in the world – youth! There is nothing like youth. The middle-aged are mortgaged to life. Youth has a kingdom waiting for it. Everyone is born a king, and most people die in exile, like most kings. To win back my youth, there is nothing I wouldn't do – except take exercise, get up early or be a useful member of the community.' This imbalance between a highly developed mind and an undeveloped emotionalism may have produced brilliance but also abnormality.

In spite of its flaws the play was another great popular success. The wit and the dialogue ensured that. The Prince of Wales (later Edward VII) came on the second night, and when Wilde told him that he was thinking of making some cuts, he implored him not to cut a line, a royal command he was happy, if mistaken, to obey.

Two great theatrical successes in two years meant that Wilde had achieved his ambition of becoming the best-known and most talked about writer in London. Not only was the *beau monde* flocking to see his plays, but he was in ever greater demand by the aristocracy for their dinner parties where he would fascinate the assembled company with his talk. In the present age, when conversation as an art is a rarity, it is difficult to imagine a party of twenty or thirty dinner guests, including some of the highest in the land, sitting sometimes for hours, spellbound by a flow of talk, but that this was the case with Wilde has been testified by several of his hearers. Wilfred Blunt, who had heard all the great men of the day and was himself no mean exponent of the conversational art, has recorded: 'He was without doubt the most brilliant talker I have ever come across, the most ready, the most witty, the most audacious. Nobody could pretend to outshine him or even to shine at all in his company.' And Lord Alfred Douglas (perhaps not a disinterested witness) recalled how 'without any apparent effort he exerted an enchantment which transmuted the ordinary things of life, investing them with a strangeness and glamour.' Although his talk might seem spontaneous and effortless, Wilde had been at great pains to perfect it: with him it was an art, and like all arts had to be cultivated. For this, certainly, he had wonderful gifts – a beautiful voice ('the texture of brown velvet and played like a cello'), boundless imagination, a vivid dramatic sense (with all the tricks of a skilled actor), and a prodigious memory which enabled him to recall instantly everything he had heard or read. But he was acutely sensitive to the moods and disposition of his hearers – as to whether they wanted to be amused or impressed, and which subjects would hold their attention. And he was always careful not to be overbearing or arrogant. This was noted by Arthur Conan Doyle (the creator of Sherlock Holmes), who has written: 'He towered above us all and yet had the art of seeming to be interested in all that we could say.' And Laurence Housman, dramatist and novelist: 'He was not only the best talker, but also the most courteous and most charming.'

The general tone of Wilde's talk, as with his writing, was essentially flippant. 'Life is far too important a thing,' he said, 'ever to talk seriously about it.' His aim was always to surprise, to shock and, above all, to entertain. But he felt himself bound by certain rules; he never used obscene or blasphemous language or referred to anything that was in any way risqué or improper; in this he always respected his listeners' susceptibilities. It was also *de rigueur* with him never to contradict or to be drawn into an argument. 'It is only the intellectually lost who ever argue,' he once said, and Lady Bracknell in *The Importance of Being Earnest* is made to declare: 'I dislike arguments. They are always vulgar and often convincing.' He was, however, always ready to shock his hearers by standing accepted values and cherished beliefs on their heads and by flaunting outrageous views. 'Duty,' he proclaimed, 'is what one expects from others, not what one does oneself.' Or: 'Morality is simply the attitude we adopt towards people whom we personally dislike.' Or again: 'Don't be led astray into the paths of virtue.' By some people such aphorisms were taken with a pinch of salt. It was assumed, particularly by the aristocracy, that he did not really mean what he was saying and he was putting on an act. The reaction of many was probably similar to that of Lady Hunstanton in *A Woman of No Importance* who says after Lord Illingworth has been talking in the mode of Oscar Wilde: 'Now I am quite out of my depth. I usually am when Lord Illingworth says anything ... I have a dim idea, dear Lord Illingworth, that you are always on the side of sinners, and I know I always try to be on the side of the saints, but that is as far as I can get.' Or again the Duchess of Berwick to Lord Darlington in *Lady Windermere's Fan*: 'Do, as a concession to my poor wits, Lord Darlington, just explain to me what you really mean.' To which Lord Darlington replies: 'I think I had better not, Duchess. Nowadays to be intelligible is to be found out.'

Sometimes he held rapt the most unlikely audiences. On one occasion he walked into a room full of hard-boiled country gentlemen who turned their backs on him to show their disapproval of his arty ways and effeminate looks. But Wilde, not the least put out, started to talk and, one by one, they found themselves compelled to listen to him. With so many falling so readily under his spell it was always likely that Wilde himself would be affected by his talk. Disraeli once said of Gladstone that he was 'inebriated with the exuberance of his own verbosity', and the same might apply to Wilde. He once admitted as much to Conan Doyle: 'Between me and life there is a mist of words always. I throw probability out of the window for the sake of a phrase, and the chance of an epigram makes me desert truth.' In *An Ideal Husband* this is put more succinctly when the Earl of Caversham, who has just been subjected to a flow of Oscariana from his son, Lord Goring, looks at him dazedly and says: 'Do you always really understand what you say, sir?' And Lord Goring replies: 'Yes, father, if I listen attentively.'

Of course not everyone found Wilde's wordplay amusing. There were always the respectable and the humourless ('the dullard and the doctrinaire', as he called them) who found him trivial and flippant and even dangerous. But there were, too, people of some discernment, including a number of fellow writers – Henry James, George Meredith, W.E. Henley and even George Bernard Shaw – who were among his detractors. As long as he was riding high with a succession of popular plays, and his private life was not exposed to view, little heed was taken of their murmurings, but if he should be in trouble their cries would grow louder.

Before this happened he wrote two more plays, generally regarded as his best. In *An Ideal Husband*, written in a holiday home in Goring, the ingredients are much the same as in his first two comedies – a witty and world-weary milord, a fallen woman, a Puritan lady, and a guilty secret. But there are differences: Lord Goring, unlike Lord Illingworth in *A Woman of No Importance* proves to be a noble character, the fallen woman is evil, and the Puritan lady less severe and unreasoning. Generally the play is more warm hearted and less of a vehicle for epigrams, although these are still plentiful. Once again the play was a great box office success. It opened in January 1895 just over a year before Wilde's downfall. And once again, as in *Lady Windermere's Fan*, he seems to have had a premonition of this when Sir Robert Chiltern, an eminent and moralistic politician, is warned of the fate in store for him if ever his secret is found out: 'Think of their loathsome joy, of the wild delight they would have in dragging you down, of the mud and mire they would plunge you in. Think of the hypocrite with his greasy smile penning his leading article and arranging the foulness of the public placards.' And later reference is made to those men who have worse secrets in their own lives which is the reason they are so pleased to find out other people's secrets which will distract public attention from their own. Fifteen months later Wilde was to have bitter experiences of them.

After three successful plays Wilde was a rich man: his income for 1894 was of the order of £8,000 (worth nearly £400,000 today), but he never had any money sense and it was all squandered – some on himself, too little on his family and too much on worthless company. By the end of the year he was once again in financial straits and living from hand to mouth. For many months he had been inactive, apparently unable to summon the necessary energy and willpower to write anything. But then, suddenly and very quickly, he produced his greatest masterpiece. Bizarre as it may seem *The Importance of Being Earnest*, one of the greatest comedies of the English theatre, was written in three weeks in a seaside boarding house (The Haven, 5 Esplanade, Worthing) where Wilde had reluctantly joined his family for a holiday.

Wilde later described the play as being 'exquisitely trivial, a delicate bubble of fancy', but with a philosophy which was that one should treat all the trivial things of life very seriously and all the serious things of life with sincere and studied triviality. It differed in a number of ways from the previous comedies: there was no hidebound Puritan lady, no fallen woman, no agonizing situations, and nothing that could be taken at all seriously.* As one reviewer put it: 'The author has found himself at last as an artist in sheer nonsense ... There is no discordant note of seriousness.' Gentle mockery, of course, it did contain, as usual, of those things most highly regarded by the respectable – birth, baptism, love, marriage, illegitimacy and death, but so lightheartedly and farcically that only the most humourless could take offence. The play was received with rapture by West End audiences and the critics were much more forthcoming in their praise; but there was a dissenting voice, that of Bernard Shaw who said that it was all froth and no pith. 'Unless a comedy touches me as well as amuses me, it leaves me with a sense of having wasted my evening.'

The Importance of Being Earnest came just in time. Only four days after the opening night events were set in motion which were to lead to Wilde's ruin. Three months later he was in gaol. At the peak of his powers his literary career came to an end.

---

* One thing it did contain, like the other comedies, was an orphan brought up by foster parents, leading to speculation as to whether this was connected with the two or more illegitimate children of Wilde's father.

Chapter IV

The fatal concept of the allure of sin.
Oscar Wilde)

Tired of being on the heights, I deliberately went to the depths in the search for new sensations.

(Ibid.)

It was like feasting with panthers. The dirtier and more debased the better.

(Ibid.)

I lulled myself into long spell of senseless and sensual ease.
(Ibid.)

It seems that Oscar Wilde was not at first primarily homosexual; his early love affairs, of which there were several, were with women, notably with a colonel's daughter whom he courted for two years. When he did marry, at the age of twenty-eight, it was to Constance Lloyd, an attractive and gifted lady with a modest fortune. It seems that at the time the two were deeply in love. To a friend he met on his honeymoon Wilde expatiated on the joys of married life, particularly the physical ones, and this was borne out by the birth in quick succession of two sons.

This state of affairs, however, was not to last, and after two years the marriage began to fall apart. No doubt Wilde's emotional immaturity had much to do with this, but it was due in the main to the ever more apparent incompatibility between him and Constance. It would need a remarkable woman to make a successful marriage to Oscar Wilde. Constance was no simpleton; she spoke fluent French and Italian, was an accomplished pianist and had a discerning appreciation of art, although her views on the subject – that there is no perfect art without perfect morality – were the opposite to those of her husband. But she did have basically a conventional mind and a limited sense of humour; and much as she admired Oscar's wit and brilliance, she was sometimes overwhelmed by them. In some ways she resembled the virtuous women in his plays, taking an active interest in philanthropic projects including missionary work, and she must have been dismayed by some of his more cynical comments. 'Philanthropy,' he once declared, 'seems to me to have become simply the refuge of people who wish to annoy their fellow creatures.' As for missionaries, 'they are the divinely provided food for destitute and underfed cannibals. Whenever they are on the brink of starvation, Heaven in its infinite mercy sends them a nice plump missionary.' Like others she may have thought that he did not really mean what he said and was only talking for show, but more and more his clever talk jarred on her, especially when she had heard it often before; while Oscar, for his part, became increasingly irritated by her disapproval and what he regarded as her naive and unnecessary inter-ruptions. By 1886, then, they were beginning to lead separate lives with Oscar spending longer times away from home, but still drawn back by his love for his sons and the need for a home base. By then the physical side of the marriage had come to an end, and one reason for this may have been the recurrence of syphilis which Wilde is believed to have contracted while at Oxford (allegedly from a notorious whore known in Magdalen as 'Old Jess'). The evidence for this is not conclusive but is borne out by the blackness of his teeth which could have been caused by mercury, used at that time for the cure of syphilis, also by his final illness which could have been derived from the disease.

It must be certain that the failure of Wilde's marriage was a factor in his growing obsession with homosexuality. This had always been latent and was evident at Oxford notably in his ardent Hellenism. Afterwards too it had occasionally come to the surface, and years later he recalled a bizarre incident when he was out shopping with his wife and was waiting for her outside the department store of Swan and Edgar in Piccadilly when a highly coloured youth passed by and gave him a look which 'clutched at my heart like ice'. There were, it seems, strains in his character which made homosexuality attractive – the thrill of doing something outrageous, of shocking the conventional and respect-able, the fascination of sin and the perversities and dangers attached to it.

It seems that it was in 1886, when he was thirty, that Wilde became an active homosexual. In that year he made the acquaintance of Robert

Ross who years later let it be known that he was Wilde's first partner. Ross was to play a major role in the Wilde drama. Of Canadian origins he had no great literary or artistic talents nor a particularly striking personality, but he did have charm and good looks as well as an instinctive ability to ingratiate himself with whatever company he might be in, and this varied from the highest in the land to the lowest. His relationship with Wilde was to have its ups and downs, but in the days of disaster no one supported him more loyally and devotedly.

In the years that followed Wilde became more and more involved in London's homosexual underworld which at that time was extensive, in spite of draconian penalties. Until 1861 sodomy was punishable by death; in that year the penalty was reduced to penal servitude of between ten years and life; but lesser homosexual practices were not then illegal. In 1885, however, Parliament passed an act to protect women and young girls from being victimized and to suppress female brothels, and on to this was tacked at the last moment an amendment which made gross indecency between adult males a misdemeanour punishable by two years hard labour. This was initiated by a radical Member of Parliament, Henry Labouchere, old Etonian, nephew of a lord, who saw his main role in Parliament as being the exposure of fraud and scandal in high places. He was editor of a weekly paper, *Truth*, a nineteenth-century version of *Private Eye*, like which he was much involved in suits for libel. It was under his amendment that ten years later Wilde was to be convicted.

After the passing of the Act prosecutions for homosexual offences became more frequent and, for the most part, attracted little attention, but in 1889 there was a notorious case involving men in high places which gave rise to great interest and scandal. It began when police investigating the theft of money at the Central Telegraph Office became aware that certain messenger boys were earning money on the side by providing sexual services at a male brothel in Cleveland Street.* It then emerged that among their clientele were some very eminent personages including Lord Arthur Somerset, the son of a duke, a major in the Blues and an equerry to the Prince of Wales; and the Earl of Euston, also the

---

* Messenger boys were a favourite target of homosexuals who sent frequent telegrams to each other of no importance, their object being to provide a visit from a telegraph boy – a clear example of the medium being the message, thus anticipating in rather a different sense a dictum of a twentieth-century theoretician.

son of a duke and a virile military figure with a considerable reputation for heterosexual prowess.* The police were ready to press charges at once, but the government ministers involved (at that time of a Conservative administration under Lord Salisbury) put a brake on proceedings and did all they could to hush the matter up. The reason for this was not to protect the two noblemen (in the event Lord Arthur Somerset had to go into exile abroad and Lord Euston brought a successful libel action against a newspaper editor) but because the Prime Minister had become aware that an even more eminent name was implicated, that of Prince Albert Victor, eldest son of the Prince of Wales and second in line of succession to the throne – a gentle, ineffective character about whom a number of legends were invented including the ludicrous one that he was Jack the Ripper. He was to die of pneumonia in 1892, but if it ever became known that he had been a visitor to a homosexual brothel, it might have been a death blow to the monarchy, and to prevent this Lord Salisbury, one of Britain's more honourable prime ministers, was prepared to go to any lengths. In doing so he was strongly attacked and rigorously quizzed, but for the time being Prince Albert was shielded.

The Cleveland Street scandal should have warned Wilde of the hazards of descent into the homosexual underworld, but instead of exercising discretion he became ever more reckless, associating with the dregs of society and wining and dining them at expensive restaurants and staying with them at leading hotels. This recklessness was to become all the more flagrant when Lord Alfred Douglas appeared on the scene.

Lord Alfred was the third son of the Marquess of Queensberry. Nature had bestowed on him attractive gifts including charm, great good looks and a talent for writing poetry; but others had been withheld, notably discretion, self-control and integrity; and lack of these was to make much of his life a torment. His childhood had been turbulent, caught in the middle of a bitter quarrel between his father who neglected and despised him, and his mother who pampered him; it was from her that he got the pet name 'Bosie' (originally 'Boysie') which stuck to him for the rest of his life.

---

* Lord Euston's marital affairs had been unusually complicated. At the age of twenty-three he married a music hall star, Katie Smith who, it later transpired, was already married but to a man who was also already married. Divorces at that time were not easily obtained, but in the circumstances it was considered that Lord Euston did have sufficient grounds.

Like other boys of his class Bosie had been sent off to boarding school at an early age, first to a preparatory school and then to Winchester where his father thought he would be less mollycoddled than at Eton. But in the early 1880s Winchester was not the august, enlightened seat of learning it is sometimes imagined to be. Conditions were better than at the beginning of the century when they were often anarchic: riots were not uncommon, and on one occasion the military with fixed bayonets had to be called in to restore order. But the school was still something of a roughhouse: bullying was rife, discipline veered from the lax to the brutal and malpractices were prevalent.

Later in life Douglas was to describe it as 'a sink of iniquity', and claimed that he arrived there 'a sensitive, dreamy child, passionately pure and devoted in my heart to every noble ideal', and that he left 'a finished young blackguard, ripe for any kind of wickedness'. He also said that, apart from the first eighteen months which were a nightmare, he had enjoyed himself thoroughly and still had a great affection for his old school.* From Winchester he went on to Oxford where, again on his own admission, he led a far from blameless life, and in spite of his considerable talents failed to take a degree. At twenty-one he had become an attractive, sensual, wayward, entirely selfish young man.

Douglas and Wilde met for the first time in 1891 when Douglas was an Oxford undergraduate and Wilde was having his first successes as a playwright. Predictably they made a great impression on each other. Douglas was dazzled by Wilde's wit and worldliness, while Wilde was greatly attracted by a young man who, as well as being exceptionally good-looking, was also a poet and a lord. The meeting led to a friendship which within a year had become a love affair. Douglas wrote later that he regarded Wilde then as the most wonderful man he had ever met and that he really adored him. Wilde, for his part, was totally infatuated, writing Douglas ecstatic love letters, lavishing him with expensive gifts and delighting in gratifying his every whim. Before they met both men

---

* Douglas was perhaps fortunate in the House to which he was sent – that founded not long before by Trant Bramston, a benign and enlightened man who tried to create a gentler, more civilized atmosphere. The reputation of 'Trant's' as a cultivated, mildly eccentric House prevailed over the years in the course of which it harboured such diverse characters as Oswald Mosley, Hugh Gaitskell, Rupert D'Oyly Carte (as well as, on a very different level, the present author).

Oscar and Bosie in 1893

were active homosexuals but it seems that between themselves physical relations were limited. For although Wilde was strongly attracted by Douglas, the taste of the latter was for younger men. Years later, soon after he had been converted to Roman Catholicism, Douglas wrote in his autobiography that between him and Wilde there had been 'familiarities of the kind which not infrequently take place among boys at English public schools; but of the sin which takes its name from one of the Cities of the Plain there never was the slightest question, and I give this on my solemn word before God, as I hope to be saved.' At the time, it has to be said, Douglas had become 'a stranger to truth', but on this point he is to be believed.

The fatal consequences of their friendship soon became evident. Both had a taste for low life which became more and more addictive. Douglas introduced Wilde to one Alfred Taylor, an old Marlburian (pupil of Marlborough public school) who ran an exotic male brothel in Little Smith Street in Westminster. Through him he was put in touch with various grooms, potboys, bookmakers' touts and messenger boys who were ready to supplement their incomes by prostitution. How a man of genius and the greatest erudition could become besotted by the likes of these and persuade himself that their views on art and life were of greater interest than those of educated people is, indeed, a mystery. Later, when he was in prison, he attempted an explanation in the long letter he wrote to Douglas which came to be called *De Profundis*:

> People thought it dreadful of me to have entertained at dinner the evil things of life, and to have found pleasure in their company. But they, from the point of view through which I, as an artist in life, approached them, were delightfully suggestive and stimulating. It was like feasting with panthers. The danger was half the excitement. I used to feel as the snake charmer must feel when he lures the cobra to stir from the painted cloth or reed-basket that holds it, and makes it spread its hood at his bidding, and sway to and fro in the air as a plant sways restfully in a stream. They were to me the brightest of gilded snakes. Their poison was part of their perfection.

The dangers of his obsession must soon have become evident to him, as he became the target of blackmailers. Some of his more passionate letters to Douglas fell into the hands of miscreants who demanded large sums for their return. They were treated airily by Wilde who told one of them that he was fascinated by the 'wonderfully wicked life' he was leading. Some of the letters he regained, but others, or copies of them, remained with the blackmailers and were later to be used against him when he came into court.

It is a sad paradox that the years in which Wilde's genius was at its peak should also have been the years of his greatest depravity. Success and self-indulgence brought out the worst in him. Physically he became gross and unhealthy and at the same time more arrogant and exhibitionist and more blind to the consequences of what he said or did. There was an embarrassing exhibition of this arrogance on the first night of *Lady Windermere's Fan* when at the end of the play there was a call for the author and he came on stage smoking a cigarette, looking deadly bored and in tones of the utmost condescension addressed the audience:

> Ladies and gentlemen, it's not perhaps very proper to smoke in front of you, but it is not very proper to disturb me when I am smoking. I have enjoyed this evening immensely. The actors have given us a charming rendering of a delightful play, and your appreciation has been most intelligent. I congratulate you on the great success of your performance, which persuades me that you think almost as highly of the play as I do myself.

Later that evening his wife went home while he went out to dine with a group of fawning young men. When taken to task for the way he had behaved he was far from penitent, declaring; 'Humility is for the hypocrite, modesty for the incompetent. Assertion is at once the duty and privilege of the artist.'

To some people such arrogance was no more than a pose put on to amuse his audience who were either entertained by it or dismissed it as of no importance. But there were others who found it deeply offensive and thought it no mere pose but part of his nature. Since the appearance of *The Picture of Dorian Gray* with its sinister and erotic undertones the number of Wilde's detractors had been growing and their ranks were swollen later in the same year when he published a socialist tract, *The Soul of Man Under Socialism*. His flirtation with Socialism was brief and unconvincing and was the result of hearing a talk on the subject by Bernard Shaw. But political theory was not his strong suit and there was little likelihood of his taking up the subject seriously and joining the Fabian Society (an association of British Socialists founded in 1884 to promote the cause of democratic socialism) where he and the likes of Beatrice and Sidney Webb would have made strange bedfellows. But although hostility to him might be mounting and some friends and acquaintances were distancing themselves from him, people were still flocking to his plays, and the highest in the land were still seeking after him to entertain their dinner parties. And unless there was a public scandal this would continue.

Wilde had always had a premonition that his life would end in disaster and at times seemed to be wanting this. It was, he felt, his fate and it would be unavailing to try to avoid it. And so he turned a deaf ear to all warnings and made no amends; there was never any question of his becoming a reformed character. In view of such an attitude it was inevitable that Nemesis would move in on him. But the instrument used by Nemesis to bring him down was bizarre – a half-crazed nobleman full of hatred for his fellow men and in particular for his own family.

Chapter V

Why has destruction such a fascination? Why is it that one runs to one's ruin?

(Oscar Wilde)

Why when one stands on a pinnacle must one then throw oneself down?

(Ibid.)

Blindly I staggered as an ox in the shambles.

(Ibid.)

He once played dice with his father for my life and lost.

(Ibid.)

At first sight John Sholto Douglas, 9th Marquess of Queensberry would seem to be no more than a brute and a madman. His flaming temper, physical violence, crazy public utterances and vicious treatment of his wife and family would leave one in little doubt. But this was not the complete picture; he did have some fine qualities, and his life, though a tragic one, was not without its achievements.

Although of a wealthy aristocratic family, he had not been brought up in the lap of luxury, and when still a boy had been sent to endure the rigours of life in the Royal Navy in which he served for seven years. Thereafter his great passion in life had been for hard, masculine sports. As a boxer he became amateur lightweight champion, and then used his high rank and no mean attainments to bring order into the sport, instituting the Queensberry Rules which have been accepted throughout the world ever since. As a horseman too he was outstanding, riding fearlessly not only to hounds but also in steeplechases including the Grand National. In sporting circles, in the company of jockeys, prize-fighters and gamekeepers where he was treated with considerable awe,

The 9th Marquess of Queensbury

he was in his element. The great tensions that beset him were eased and he became comparatively reasonable and contented. But outside these circles it was a different story. His behaviour knew no bounds. Self-restraint, prudence, any consideration for others were all alien to his nature. Any kind of opposition sent him into a frenzy, and he was always ready for the direct confrontation and recourse to violence. Among his many phobias was a raging antipathy to all forms of religion, particularly Christianity, and, being the man he was, he could not keep this under reasonable control, but had to be constantly blazoning it abroad regardless of the pain and embarrassment it might cause. The oath of loyalty to Queen Victoria, which it was necessary for him to take before being admitted into the House of Lords, he described as 'Christian tomfoolery', and when this resulted in his being barred, he felt deeply aggrieved.*

As a family man Queensberry was a monster. Twice married and twice divorced (once for adultery and once for non-consummation) he treated his wives outrageously, particularly the first one, a gentle, saintly character who endured him for twenty years and only divorced him when he proposed to move a mistress into the family home and set up a *ménage à trois*. In his children he showed no interest and had little contact with them. It was, of course, a great tragedy for a man such as he that two of his four sons should be homosexual. His eldest son, Viscount Drumlanrig, was private secretary to the Foreign Secretary, Lord Rosebery, and when the suspicion arose that there might be a too intimate relationship between them, Queensberry went berserk and followed Rosebery out to Germany where he threatened to belay him with a horsewhip. Soon afterwards Drumlanrig died in mysterious circumstances; it was held to have been a shooting accident, but it was thought by some to have been suicide brought on by the possibility of revelations of a homosexual scandal. His second son, Lord Douglas of Hawick, was a noble, generous character but infuriated his father by marrying the daughter of a clergyman. At the time Queensberry was being driven into even greater dementia by the humiliating circumstances of his second divorce,† and then came the realization that his

---

* Bearing a Scottish title it was necessary for him to be elected to the House of Lords by his fellow Scottish peers which his forbears always had been as of right; but his unorthodox views put him out of the running.

† Actually an annulment in which allegations were made of frigidity and impotence as well as 'malformation of the parts of generation'.

third son had formed a close and possibly improper relationship with Oscar Wilde. In the circumstances it was, perhaps, too much to expect a man such as he to behave rationally.

Like his brothers Bosie had been a great disappointment to his father who found him soft, spoiled and lacking in manly qualities, and during his childhood there had been practically no communication between them apart from occasional words of reproof and abuse. Later, particularly when he left Oxford without taking a degree, his father's criticism became more outspoken, but he was not at first unduly hectoring and intolerant and continued to pay him an allowance. By 1893, however, when Alfred was twenty-three and showing no signs of taking up a useful or profitable occupation, but to the contrary was leading an idle and profligate life in the company of an older man of great brilliance but suspect reputation, he could bear it no longer; and he wrote to him telling him bluntly that Wilde was not a fit companion for him and his association with him must cease forthwith. No doubt he expected that Bosie would instantly comply with his wishes, but Bosie had inherited much of his father's obstinacy and temper, and had no intention of being dictated to by him as to who should be his friends. He had never liked his father and lately had come to hate him because of his treatment of his mother, and was quite ready to defy him and to insult him.

With all these family troubles that were besetting him at this time Queensberry became more and more deranged and his behaviour more and more unpredictable. There was an extraordinary incident, early in 1894, when he came across Wilde and Douglas dining together at the Café Royal. For a time he sat and glowered at them, but then was persuaded to come and join them, when, miraculously, he fell under the spell of Wilde's charm and conversation and sat listening rapt for over an hour. 'He is a wonderful man,' he told Alfred when they parted. 'I don't wonder you are so fond of him.' Soon afterwards, however, the spell was broken, and his next letter was more unbalanced and choleric than ever. He first stated that if it was Alfred's intention 'to loaf and loll about and do nothing' he utterly declined to supply him with sufficient funds for this purpose. He went on to say that he would cut off all money supplies at once unless he ceased his 'intimacy with that man Wilde'. He did not accuse them of homosexual activity but 'to pose as a thing is as bad as to be it'. He then let loose a torrent of abuse:

With my own eyes I saw you both in the most loathsome and disgusting relationship as expressed by your manner and expression. Never in my experience have I ever seen such a sight as that in your horrible features. No wonder people are talking as they are. Also I now hear on good authority, but this may be false, that his wife is petitioning to divorce him for sodomy and other crimes. Is this true, or do you know of it? If I thought the actual thing was true, and it became public property, I should be quite justified in shooting him at sight. These English Christian cowards and men, as they call themselves, want waking up.

Bosie's response to this outburst was impish and reckless. He sent an open telegram to his father beginning: 'What a funny little man you are!' As intended this sent Queensberry into further paroxysms of rage. His return letter began: 'You impertinent young jackanapes', and threatened him with the thrashing he deserved if he ever wrote to him like that again. He added that if he ever caught him with Wilde again he would 'make a public scandal in a way you little dream of'. In reply Bosie was once again provocative and insolent, and the marquess, now almost out of his mind, called on Wilde in his home in Tite Street, Chelsea, abused him and threatened him with violence. What happened next is not certain but, according to Wilde, he stood his ground and outfaced the 'screaming, scarlet marquess' who was obliged to make a humiliating exit. Bosie then added fuel to the fire by writing another letter, taunting his father: 'Ever since your exhibition at O.W.s house, I have made a point of appearing with him at many public restaurants ... and I shall continue to go to any of these places whenever I choose and with whom I choose. I am of age and my own master. You have disowned me at least a dozen times, and have meanly deprived me of money. You have therefore no right over me, either legal or moral. If O.W. was to prosecute you in the Central Criminal Court for libel, you would get seven years penal servitude for your outrageous libels. Much as I detest you, I am anxious to avoid this for the sake of the family; but if you try to assault me, I shall defend myself with a loaded revolver, which I always carry; and if I shoot you or he shoots you, we shall be completely justified, as we shall be acting in self-defence against a dangerous and violent rough, and I think if you were dead not many people would miss you.'

In this letter, Bosie's purpose, although he disclaimed it, became clear – to provoke his father into some rash, unlawful act or some blatant libel which would take him to court and perhaps to prison. Wilde in the meantime was becoming increasingly uneasy at being caught in the crossfire between father and son. He had been horrified at Bosie's telegram to his father. 'It was,' he said, 'a telegram of which the commonest street boy would have been ashamed.' His instinct was to calm things down rather than stir them up, but Bosie, headstrong and vindictive, had the bit between his teeth and was out of control. Wilde, his willpower sapped, could only look on helplessly and let events take their course.

Inevitably they went from bad to worse. In September 1894, two months after the Tite Street episode, a novel, *The Green Carnation* was published. The green carnation, of which the colour was artificially induced, was said to be a blend of art and nature, and was the insignia of homosexuals, and Wilde was seldom without one. The novel, by Robert Hichens, was a portrayal of the relationship between a highly sophisticated middle-aged man and a young aristocrat, easily recognized as Wilde and Douglas, and told how the life of the latter had become engulfed in that of the former. The book caused a furore: gossip about Wilde and Douglas, already prevalent, redoubled, as also did the fury of Queensberry. He now became obsessed with the idea of bringing disgrace to Wilde; this, he hoped, would end his relationship with his son and at the same time, of equal importance, cause his son great distress.

In the months that followed Bosie behaved more and more selfishly and neurotically, making ever greater demands on Wilde and throwing fits of temper to see they were satisfied. He was always insisting on being taken to expensive restaurants and running up large hotel bills not only for himself but also for companions of his choice. And in January 1895, just as *The Importance of Being Earnest* was going into rehearsal, he made Wilde go with him on a sex-based trip to Algiers. As always Wilde was threatening to leave him, but as always Bosie made a scene and Wilde relented.

Meanwhile manic ideas were seething in Queensberry's mind. He determined to attend the first night of *The Importance of Being Earnest*, provided with a 'phallic bouquet', consisting of turnips and carrots, which he would fling at Wilde when he appeared on stage at the end of the play, and then burst into a tirade against him. But his plan became known and he was barred from the theatre, every entrance being guarded and he could do no more than prowl around menacingly outside and leave the bouquet for Wilde at the stage door. The failure of this ploy further demented him so that he resorted to even more desperate measures, and on the following day delivered to Wilde's club, the

Albemarle, his visiting card on which was scrawled, misspelt and hardly legible: 'For Oscar Wilde posing as somdomite'. The porter at the club, somewhat baffled but suspecting it to be improper, put it into an envelope which he handed to Wilde when he next came to the club ten days later.

That the words were actionable was certain. But would Wilde take out a criminal prosecution? The wise counsel was that he should tear up the card and forget about it. Nobody had seen it except the porter, who did not fully understand it, and it would not have reflected on Wilde if he had taken no action. But he was becoming exasperated by Queensberry's lunatic ways and wanted to bring the persecution to an end. And Douglas, of course, urged him on vehemently: he longed to see his father in the dock and himself appearing as a witness and exposing the sham of a noble, pathetic old man struggling to save his son from corruption – an old man who, nevertheless, had himself led a flagrantly immoral life (with one divorce and one annulment) and whose interest in his son until then had been minimal. Still Wilde hesitated and at one point tried to get out of taking action by pleading inadequate funds; but Bosie then persuaded his mother and elder brother* to guarantee the costs. It was very unfortunate at this juncture that Wilde could not obtain the services of the solicitor who had advised him wisely before, Sir George Lewis, who would have urged him to tear up Queensberry's card and forget about it; but he had already been engaged to act for Lord Queensberry, and so it was necessary to find someone else, and the substitute, C.O. Humphreys, proved a bad choice. Perhaps scenting a sensational case, he advised Wilde to prosecute, and finally Wilde agreed, so on 1 March 1895 went to Marlborough Street Police Station where he took out a criminal prosecution for libel against Lord Queensberry.

And so the die was cast. Queensberry was arrested and then released on bail. To avoid conviction and a possible prison sentence it was necessary for him to put in a plea of justification and prove to the jury that the words he had written were true and publication of them was in the public interest. In the card he had left at the Albemarle Club he had been canny enough not to accuse Wilde of being a sodomite, only that Wilde's writings and lifestyle gave credence to such an act.

---

* Percy, Lord Douglas of Hawick, now heir to the marquisate. He had quarreled violently with his father, so much so that they had come to blows in Bond Street and had been arrested and bound over to keep the peace.

At first the evidence for this was thin, consisting of no more than Wilde's published works and some of his exotic letters to Bosie which Queensberry had managed to obtain from the blackmailers. Queensberry's new solicitor, Charles Russell (Sir George Lewis having withdrawn on the grounds that he had a social relationship with Wilde), realized that more would be needed, and so he employed a private detective to investigate Wilde's private life. At first this was unavailing, but then help came from an unexpected quarter. A second-rank actor, Charles Brookfield, who had profited much from his acquaintance with Wilde and at the time had a minor part in *An Ideal Husband*, had conceived a great hatred for him and gave the investigator information that led him to Alfred Taylor's establishment in Little College Street. Here he made contact with some of the male prostitutes who testified that they had been solicited by Wilde and had committed indecent acts with him. Help was also forthcoming from female prostitutes who were indignant that males were doing them out of business.

At the same time Russell was trying to engage the services of one of the most formidable barristers of that time, Sir Edward Carson. Like Wilde Carson came from Ireland and they had been at university together where they had had a slight acquaintance. Partly for this reason and partly because of the sparsity of evidence at first Carson was reluctant to become involved, but when the shocking evidence of Wilde's association with male prostitutes came to light, he felt that in the interests of justice he must accept the brief.

The first stage in proceedings was a formality: Queensberry was summoned to appear before a magistrate on 9 March to answer the charge of libel. He then pleaded justification and was committed to trial at the Old Bailey. In the three weeks before this took place Wilde's solicitor managed to engage Sir Edward Clarke, a QC of great eminence, who had been Solicitor-General for six years. He too was unwilling to become involved in the case and only did so after he had obtained from Wilde a solemn assurance that he was innocent of all charges that were being brought against him, which Wilde had no compunction in giving as at that time the only charges of which he was aware were the immorality of his writings and his letters to Douglas.

So confident was Wilde of success at first that he chose this moment to go on a trip with Bosie to Monte Carlo. Soon after he came back, however, he was confronted with the Plea of Justification which Queensberry's solicitors had drawn up and which he was entitled to see. This was a great shock as it contained a number of new charges about

Wilde's association with young men, and put a new aspect on the case. Several people then came forward to urge Wilde to abandon the case and get out of the country while he could; these included Bernard Shaw and another writer of note at that time, Frank Harris, who were convinced that in the existing climate of opinion he was bound to lose. But Wilde was not to be moved; he still had a strong sense of doom – that he was fated to disaster and that his life would be incomplete without it. He even likened his fate to that of Jesus – at one moment great triumph with the crowds shouting hosannas and laying palms before him, and soon afterwards disgrace and everyone clamouring for his death. In more rational moments he realized that this was fantasy, but in moments of crisis his intellect was always liable to be overwhelmed by his sense of drama; and if he did ever falter there was Douglas to taunt him with cowardice and urge him to persevere. Later, when he was in prison, he wrote how mistaken he had been: 'I admit I lost my head. I was bewildered, incapable of judgment.'

The case of Oscar Wilde versus the Marquess of Queensberry opened at the Old Bailey on 3 April 1895. As might be expected a suit between a world-famous dramatist and a notorious and highly eccentric sportsman who was also a lord attracted great attention, and the court was full to overflowing, although there were no ladies present. The trial had a strong Irish flavour: as well as the two main antagonists, Wilde and Carson, the judge, Mr Justice Henn Collins, was an Irishman, as also was Carson's junior counsel, Charles Gill.

The trial opened with a statement from Wilde's counsel, Sir Edward Clarke, who described Wilde's eminence as a dramatist and poet and insisted that from such a man exotic and extravagant language was to be expected, even in his private letters, and although this might seem strange to those 'whose correspondence was mainly commercial', it should not be looked on as denoting immorality. To some people, particularly Douglas, Clarke's opening speech was too mild and bland. He made no effort to denigrate the character of Queensberry or to show that his supposed concern for his son's moral welfare was not credible in view of his past neglect and ill-treatment. To make this point as forcibly as possible Douglas was very eager to be called as a witness and was bitterly angry with Clarke for not agreeing; but it is doubtful if this would have been permitted by the judge. Of Clarke's opening speech Carson was later quoted as saying that 'both matter and manner were superb'. Clarke also kept silent about the charges in Queensberry's Plea of Justification concerning Wilde's association with young men. He then called Wilde into the witness box and asked him a number of innocuous questions designed to present him as a gifted, kindly, unconventional man. It was then the turn of Carson to cross-examine him, and battle began.

Carson started by pointing out that Wilde had just been untruthful about his age, stating that he was two years younger than he actually was – a small point but a telling one as it served to emphasize the difference in ages between himself and Douglas. He then brought up the subject of Wilde's published works, in particular *The Picture of Dorian Gray*, picking out certain passages and asking whether these were not immoral and indicative of an unnatural relationship between two men; but Wilde had little difficulty in fending off these charges, saying that the language was that of an artist and that only a philistine could find anything immoral in it. It was the same when Carson produced copies of some of Wilde's letters to Douglas (obtained at a price from the blackmailers) with their references to 'those red rose-leaf lips of yours' and 'your slim gilt soul walks between passion and poetry'. 'Is not this an exceptional letter?' Carson asked. To which Wilde replied amidst laughter: 'It is unique I should say.' And again after reading another letter: 'Is that an ordinary letter?' Giving Wilde a splendid opportunity which he did not miss: 'Everything I write is extraordinary. I do not pose as being ordinary.'

So far Wilde was winning on points. Carson had not succeeded in discomposing him and he himself was being made to look tasteless and inept. But he was not worried. He knew how deadly was the evidence he still had in store – concerning Wilde's relations with young men of a very different type to himself. When this subject was brought up Wilde was not at first disconcerted; he continued to answer easily and humorously and was ever ready with a sharp and witty retort.* A lesser man than Carson might have been nettled by this but he kept his calm; he was confident that in time Wilde would overstep the mark and come up with a serious indiscretion. In the meantime he kept on remorselessly asking him about his association with 'homeless and shiftless boys'. 'Were not grooms and valets strange companions for an artist?' 'Did he dine

---

* Perhaps the most notable instance of this was when Carson, probing the subject of the champagne dinners he had given some of the youths, asked him whether he himself drank much champagne, to which he replied that it was a favourite drink of his although strongly against his doctor's orders. 'Never mind your doctor's orders,' said Carson. 'I never do,' replied Wilde.

with them for purpose of having an intellectual treat?' 'Was it really in the best interests of a paper boy from Worthing to be dressed up as a gentleman and be given a cigarette case and a silver-mounted walking stick?'

On the second day of the trial Wilde seemed to be more subdued, as Carson continued to press him about his connection with Alfred Taylor and the young men he had met at his establishment in Little College Street. 'Had you given them expensive gifts?' 'Had you taken them out to dinner?' 'What could you possibly have in common with rough, uneducated types such as these?' For a time Wilde kept his end up, maintaining that he got great pleasure from the company of those who were 'young, bright, happy, careless and free' and that he had 'a passion to civilise the community'. But Carson was closing in, and at the appropriate moment delivered his trump card when he announced that one of the young men, Charles Parker, an unemployed valet, would be appearing in court to give testimony. This took everyone by surprise as it was assumed that this could not be done, as no immunity could be granted to such witnesses, and they must necessarily incriminate themselves.*

This was one of the turning points in the trial and another occurred soon afterwards when Wilde at last made a seriously damaging remark. Carson had asked him about a youth called Grainger. 'Did you kiss him?' he asked. 'Oh, dear no,' Wilde replied. 'He was a peculiarly plain boy.' Carson knew then that he had him on the ropes and moved in for the kill. 'Was that the reason you had never kissed him? Why had you mentioned his ugliness?' And Wilde was left floundering, muttering that he had been stung by insolent questions into being unduly flippant.

Soon afterwards Carson proceeded to his opening speech in defence of Lord Queensberry and repeated that he was proposing to put into the witness box some of the young men who had been associated with Wilde. By then Sir Edward Clarke had become seriously worried: it was becoming apparent to him that Wilde had been less than candid when he had assured him that there was no truth in any of the allegations in Queensberry's Plea of Justification. He saw that if the trial took its course and the young men gave evidence, not only would Queensberry be acquitted but the judge would order the arrest of Wilde in open court. To avoid this he urged Wilde to withdraw his prosecution and

---

* Immunity can only be given to Crown witnesses and in this case, of Wilde versus Queensberry, the Crown was not involved.

accept a verdict that he had posed as a homosexual which was not a criminal offence. This might lead to charges being brought against him, but Clarke hoped that he would take the opportunity to leave the country. To this advice Wilde felt compelled to agree, and next day, while Carson was still in full fling, Clarke interrupted him to announce the withdrawal of the prosecution and acceptance of a verdict of not guilty in so far as the offending words referred to posing as a sodomite. This was accepted by Carson on behalf of Queensberry and by the judge, and the jury was directed to bring in the appropriate verdict which they duly did to loud applause from the public gallery.

This took place in the morning of 5 April and from then on events moved swiftly. Immediately after leaving the court Wilde dashed off a letter to the *Evening News* saying that it would have been impossible for him to have proved his case without Lord Alfred Douglas giving evidence against his father in the witness box; this he was willing to do but Wilde would not allow it and so had decided to retire from the case. At the same time Queensberry's solicitors at once sent round full details of the evidence that had been given, along with the statements made by the young men who had not been called, to the Director of Public Prosecutions. He immediately made contact with the Home Secretary, Herbert Asquith, the future Liberal Prime Minister, whom Wilde had known socially; he made contact with the law officers of the Crown and it was agreed that application should be made straight away for a warrant for Wilde's arrest.

When this was made to the Bow Street magistrate he delayed for an hour and a half before granting it. Whether this was done deliberately to allow Wilde time to leave the country is not certain, but it is certain that this was an option open to Wilde and he did not take it. Nearly all his friends urged him to go, but once again he seems to have been unable to make a decision or take any action. All he could do was to wait on events in the Cadogan Hotel where Douglas had taken rooms. These were not long in coming. At 6.30 that evening two detectives arrived and took him into custody. In a somewhat inebriated condition, as he had been fortifying himself for some time with hock and seltzer, he was then taken to Scotland Yard where he was formally charged with committing acts of gross indecency with various male persons. He was then taken to Bow Street police station where he was locked up in a cell for the night. Next day he was removed to Holloway prison where he was remain for a month, as applications for bail were refused, the Bow Street magistrate remarking that this was not possible as he did not think there was a worse crime than that with which the prisoner was being charged.*

During this inter-trial period many of Wilde's friends, including even Robert Ross, felt it prudent to absent themselves abroad out of reach of the law. The one exception was Douglas who visited Wilde every day in Holloway and tried hard, albeit unavailingly, to obtain bail for him. Someone else not to desert Wilde at this time was Sir Edward Clarke who, as soon as he knew that he was to be prosecuted, offered to act for him again free of charge, an offer that was gratefully accepted. At the same time the press in particular and the public in general gave themselves up to an orgy of self-righteousness and moral indignation. Typical of this tone was an article in the *National Observer*:

> There is not a man or woman in the English-speaking world possessed of the treasure of a wholesome mind who is not under a deep debt of gratitude to the Marquess of Queensberry for destroying the High Priest of the Decadents. The obscene imposter, whose prominence has been a social outrage ever since he transferred from Trinity Dublin to Oxford his vices, his follies and his vanities, has been exposed, and that thoroughly at last.

Some of Wilde's fellow writers led the pack. The poet, W.E. Henley, wrote at the time:

> Yes: Oscar at bay was on the whole a pleasing sight ... Holloway and Bow Street have taken his hair out of curl in more senses than one. And I am pretty sure that he is having a damn bad time ... I hear that he is ill, and am very glad to hear it.

Perhaps the most ridiculous and hypocritical instance of this hysteria was the blotting out of Wilde's name on the billboards advertising *The Importance of Being Earnest*, the management seeming to feel that if this were done, patrons could see the play with a clear conscience. The prevalent attitude at that time was summed up by Frank Harris, one of the few writers to stick by Wilde:

> His arrest was the signal for an orgy of Philistine rancour such as even

---

* Surely a strongly prejudiced view from an officer of the law, as Wilde's alleged crime was no more than a misdemeanour carrying a maximum penalty of two years in prison. There were many crimes for which there were much heavier penalties.

London had never known before. The Puritan middle class, which had always regarded Wilde with dislike as an artist and an intellectual scoffer, a mere parasite of the aristocracy, now gave free scope to their disgust and contempt, and everyone tried to outdo his neighbour in expressions of loathing and abhorrence.

And so the nightmare sequence of events continued to unfold. On 19 April Wilde was committed to trial along with Alfred Taylor who, alone of his accomplices, had refused to give evidence against him in return for a free pardon, a noble act certainly, but it did Wilde no good to be aligned with a man of his reputation. On 24 April, two days before the beginning of the trial, a further dreadful disaster overtook Wilde. He was heavily in debt, notably to Queensberry for the costs of his failed libel action. These had been guaranteed by Queensberry's family but they were unable to honour their obligations, and so Wilde was put into bankruptcy and the bailiffs entered his house in Tite Street where they held a hastily rigged sale of all his possessions. In this the prices obtained were derisory – valuable pictures, first editions, Wilde's own manuscripts and other treasured objects going at give-away prices, although Ross and other friends were able to save some items by buying them in and later restoring them to Wilde.

Chapter VI

There are moments when life takes you like a tiger by the throat.
(Oscar Wilde)

We know no spectacle so ridiculous as the British public in one of its periodical fits of morality.
(Lord Macaulay)

. . . compound for the sins they are inclined to by damning those they have no mind to.
(Samuel Butler)

When on 26 April 1895 Wilde came into the dock in the Old Bailey, he was showing signs of his ordeal of the last three weeks. Apart from the rigours of prison life and the disasters that had overtaken him, he had been subjected to the most virulent abuse from all quarters. He looked thinner and more downcast; his hair had been cut, and the jauntiness of the previous trial had disappeared. He faced at first a total of twenty-five charges of gross indecency, conspiracy to commit indecent acts and sodomy. In the course of the trial six of the charges were withdrawn including all those on the last two counts, which was as well as the penalty for sodomy at that time could be life imprisonment. To all the remaining charges he pleaded not guilty which he felt he had a right to do even though, on his own admission later, he was on some of them, in fact, guilty.

The justification for this was maintained not only by himself but also by Bernard Shaw: 'Guilty or not guilty is a question not of fact but of morals: the prisoner who pleads not guilty is not alleging that he did this or did not do that; he is affirming that what he did does not involve any guilt on his part.' Whether or not this is so is, perhaps, open to question, but it is certain that such a course of action would necessarily involve repeated perjury.

However strong might seem to be the evidence against him, under British Law Wilde was innocent until proved guilty and was entitled to a fair and impartial trial; but this in the circumstances he was unlikely to get. In the previous weeks the press had mounted a vicious campaign against him and had seemed to assume his guilt. He was also handicapped by the refusal of bail which meant that he had not been free to organize his defence fully. A more serious disadvantage was that he was being tried jointly with Alfred Taylor against whom there was much more damning evidence, and this would inevitably reflect on him. But there were too some points in his favour: he was being represented free of charge by one of the ablest and most respected members of the bar, and the judge before whom he was appearing, Mr Justice Charles, was a man of great integrity and fairness. Also he was not again to be confronted by Sir Edward Carson; in this trial the prosecution was led by Charles Gill, a less formidable adversary.

The case for the prosecution was certainly strong. All the witnesses unearthed by Queensberry and his solicitor could in this case (as the Crown was prosecuting) be offered a free pardon if they gave evidence, and as the alternative was the possibility of being prosecuted themselves, they were naturally ready to do so. The first three days of the trial were to be taken up by the evidence of this grisly mob, with one exception men of the lowest character – prostitutes, blackmailers and extortioners – who were led to describe how they had been introduced to Wilde (sometimes by Taylor), how he had wined and dined them at fashionable restaurants, stayed with them at well-known hotels, made them expensive gifts, and then had sex with them. There were other witnesses too: Taylor's landlady at Little College Street described the heavily curtained, incense-filled rooms with women's clothes lying around although no women ever called there. And there were a number of hotel employees, mainly chambermaids, but including, rather strangely, a 'professor of massage' who gave lubricious evidence as to what they had seen in Wilde's rooms and the state of his sheets.

In opening the case for the defence Sir Edward Clarke first deplored the disgraceful conduct of the press in abusing Wilde and prejudging the trial. He then attacked Gill for attempting, as Carson had done before, to incriminate Wilde by his literary works. Wilde was, he said, an artist, and, like many artists his work might contain matters that some people found offensive, but he was not to be condemned by his books, for these might be misunderstood when hidden meanings were unjustly read into them and a prurient construction placed on them.

And if it was wrong to judge Wilde by his own works, how much more so was it to judge him by the works of others. And yet in the Queensberry trial it had been attempted to blame him for articles appearing in an undergraduate magazine with a strong homosexual flavour which were not written by him and some of which he had condemned. He then called Wilde into the witness box and went through with him the main events of his life and his rise to fame, presenting him always as a brilliant but eccentric artist who had been grossly abused and misunderstood, but who was basically a kind and honourable man. Wilde was then cross-examined by Gill. Compared to his confrontation with Carson this was a low-key affair. Gill was less aggressive and Wilde was more subdued, showing less inclination to be clever and to score points off his inter-rogator. In spite of the fact that the judge in the previous trial had said they were of no real significance, Gill did bring up again the matter of the articles in the undergraduate magazine and questioned him in particular about the meaning of one line of poetry: 'I am the love that dare not speak its name.' Until then Wilde had seemed reticent, almost apathetic, but now suddenly he roused himself and spoke as only he could:

> The love that dare not speak its name in this century is such a great affection of an elder for a younger man as there was between David and Jonathan, such as Plato made the very basis of his philosophy, and such as you find in the sonnets of Michelangelo and Shakespeare. It is that deep, spiritual affection that is as pure as it is perfect. It dictates and pervades great works of art like those of Shakespeare and Michelangelo, and those two letters of mine, such as they are. It is in this century misunderstood, so much misunderstood that it may be described as the 'Love that dare not speak its name', and on account of it I am placed where I am now. It is beautiful, it is fine, it is the noblest form of affection. There is nothing unnatural about it. It is intellectual, and it repeatedly exists between an elder and a younger man, where the elder has intellect and the younger man has all the joy, hope, and glamour of life before him. That it should be so, the world does not understand. The world mocks at it and sometimes puts one in the pillory for it.

Everyone in court was clearly moved by these words and there was loud applause. It was Wilde's finest moment, although it was not difficult for the prosecution to point out later that the love such as he had described could hardly be felt for the sordid and disreputable creatures who had just given evidence. As regards these Wilde did not deny that he had associated with them, taken them out to dinner and given them presents, but totally denied any improper behaviour. Gill then questioned him further about his relationship with them, and once again he seemed subdued and disinclined to show off, but there were occasional flashes of wit as when Gill brought up his visits to Little College Street and asked if this was not 'a rather rough neighbourhood' to which Wilde replied that he did not know about this; all he knew was that it was near the Houses of Parliament. And when Gill was questioning him about his exaltation of youth and asked him if he therefore preferred puppies to dogs and kittens to cats. 'I think so,' Wilde replied. 'I should enjoy, for instance, the society of a beardless briefless barrister quite as much as the most accomplished QC.'

Clarke's final speech for the defence was, by general consent, a masterpiece. He first stressed in strongest terms that Wilde and Taylor should have been tried separately and that evidence against Taylor, particularly from the youths who frequented his rooms, should not be considered as evidence against Wilde. He then attacked Gill for alluding to Wilde's letters to Douglas. These were irrelevant. Wilde was a poet and wrote letters 'in a tone which to others may seem high-flown, inflated, exaggerated and absurd'. He had said that the affection described in them was 'pure and true, absolutely unconnected with, alien to, irreconcilable with the filthy practices which the band of blackmailers you have heard has been narrating'. Clark ended with a strong, emotional appeal to the jury to put aside all feelings of shock and disgust in reaching their verdict. He knew how difficult this was but implored them to make the effort and be guided only by the evidence of those witnesses who were worthy of belief. If they did this he trusted that 'the result of your deliberations will be to gratify those thousands of hopes which are hanging upon your decision, and will clear this fearful imputation from one of our most renowned and accomplished men of letters today and, in clearing him will clear society from a stain.' Wilde was in tears by the end of this speech.

In Gill's final speech he told the jury that in the Queensberry trial Wilde had been compelled to accept that he had been posing as a sodomite, and his sudden withdrawal of the prosecution had led to his being in the dock today. In deciding whether or not Wilde had done more than just pose, he urged them to consider in particular the evidence of the one witness, Edmund Shelley, who was neither a prostitute nor a blackmailer and had shown himself to be 'an absolutely respectable and trustworthy witness'. As for the other witnesses they should not be

ignored as 'they can have no conceivable object in bringing the accusations against the accused, unless the charges they have made are true
in substance and in fact. He ended by telling the jury that they had a
duty to society, however sorry they might feel themselves at the moral
downfall of an eminent man, to protect society from such scandals by
removing from its heart a sore which cannot fail in time to corrupt and
taint it all. The judge in his summing up was scrupulously fair. He told
the jury that on any point on which they might have doubt, it was
their duty to give the benefit of it to the accused. Also they should not
be influenced by any of Wilde's published writings, much as they might
disapprove of them, nor by his letters to Lord Alfred Douglas which
were not necessarily incriminating and he did not agree with Sir Edward
Carson who had said in the previous trial that they were 'of a horrible
and indecent character'. He also pointed out that it was to Wilde's
credit that he had not been afraid to bring an action against Lord
Queensberry, that when this failed, he had made no attempt to leave
the country, and in the present trial had been ready to come into the
witness box. He warned the jury that they must treat with caution the
evidence of the prosecution witnesses, but it was for them to decide on
which side the balance of credibility lay. He concluded by saying that
the case was of great importance to the community at large as well as
to the accused. If they believed the evidence that had been presented
it was their duty to the public to say so, but it was also of vast importance
that people should not be convicted of acts which they had not committed. The jury then withdrew and deliberated for nearly four hours
after which the leader had to inform the judge that they could not agree
on a verdict and there was no likelihood of this happening.* And so
the judge had no option but to order a retrial. The agony was to be
prolonged.

On the day after the trial ended Wilde's solicitor applied to a judge
in chambers for bail which was granted, the money for this being supplied
partly by Lord Douglas of Hawick (Bosie's elder brother and Lord
Queensberry's heir) and partly by a clergyman, the Rev. Stuart Headlam
who was unknown to Wilde but who admired his works and felt that
he had not had a fair trial. Wilde was then to have three weeks of
freedom before the prison walls finally closed in on him, but this was
to bring him little relief. In his frenzied hatred Queensberry had hired

---

* Later one of the jury was said to have let it be known that they were split
11–1 in favour of a conviction.

a gang of thugs who hounded his footsteps and saw to it that he was turned away from every hotel. Finally, in a state of near collapse, he was forced to take refuge with his mother and elder brother, Willie, in Chelsea.

Oscar Wilde's mother was a large, eccentric lady with a strong taste for the dramatic. Known as 'Speranza' (Italian for hope) she loved to wear theatrical costume (flowing robes, towering headdress, clusters of heavy jewellery) and to declaim on people's wrongs, especially those of the Irish. She also wrote inflammatory poetry. 'I express the soul of a great nation,' she declared. 'Nothing less would content me, who am the acknowledged voice in poetry of all the people of Ireland.' Bosie once described her as a 'parlour Fenian' (Irish terrorist). She made no great personal sacrifice for the Irish cause and had been ready to accept a pension from the English 'oppressor'. She had had a troubled life. Her husband, Sir William Wilde, was a Dublin surgeon of international reputation but a loose-living and unfaithful husband, begetting three illegitimate offspring and becoming involved in a lawsuit regarding a woman patient in which he was fortunate to be acquitted. When he died he left his wife in straitened circumstances, and she decided to come and live in London to be near her two sons. She was devoted to Oscar and gloried in his literary fame, and he loved her dearly and had perhaps exaggerated ideas about her abilities, describing her as a mixture of Elizabeth Barrett Browning and Madam Roland.* Her elder son, Willie, was less of a joy to her. His career as a journalist had been unsuccessful and he thought to solve his problems by marrying a wealthy widow from New York, declaring that what New York needed was a leisured class and he meant to introduce one. However, the widow soon got rid of him saying that he was of no use to her either by day or night. He then returned to England where he lived with his mother in Oakley Street, Chelsea.

Willie had never been on good terms with his younger brother and had been jealous of his success. And so when disgrace came to him, he was not as distressed as he might have been; and when Oscar arrived at Oakley Street late at night, 'collapsing across the threshold like a

---

* Elizabeth Barrett Browning, the wife of Robert Browning, was an intellectual and perhaps the leading poetess of the time. Madam Roland was an impassioned and beautiful leader of the French Revolution. But she fell foul of Robespierre and other extremists and was guillotined, declaring before she died: 'Oh, Liberty, what crimes are committed in thy name!'

wounded stag', he allowed himself a certain amount of moral severity. It was, he said, Oscar's duty as an Irish gentleman to face the consequences of his misdeeds bravely and to have no thoughts of taking refuge abroad. His mother also took this line powerfully, and told him that she could forgive him anything except running away. What with Willie's righteousness and his mother's histrionics, life at Oakley Street became claustrophobic, and Oscar accepted gratefully the offer of a Jewish friend of his, Ada Leverson, of a room in her house where he could live quietly and simply until his next trial.*

During this time a number of his friends called to give him support and nearly all of them urged him to jump bail and get out of the country while he could. Foremost among these was Lord Douglas of Hawick who said he would willingly forfeit the money he had put up for bail if Wilde was likely to be convicted. Bosie too sent word that he should join him in France at once, and Constance Wilde added her voice. Her life in the last weeks had been desperately miserable: apart from the disgrace of her husband, she was being cold-shouldered by friends, gaped at by passers by and racked with anxiety about what to do with her two young sons. But to all pleas that he should go Wilde turned a deaf ear. For once he made a decision and stood by it. 'I cannot see myself,' he said 'slinking about the Continent, a fugitive from justice.' And besides he could not be persuaded that he did not have a good chance of being acquitted.

When in Wilde's second appearance in court the jury had been unable to agree on a verdict, there were those who thought that there was no need for another trial and that Wilde had already suffered enough. This was the view said to have been taken even by Sir Edward Carson who was not sympathetic to Wilde and had done as much as anyone to bring about his downfall. But the Solicitor-General, Sir Frank Lockwood, was adamant that the prosecution must proceed. No doubt he remembered the agitation that had arisen when a previous government had tried to hush up the Cleveland Street scandal (see p. 34–5). And there was another reason. In the second trial there had been a number of allusions to people in high places, including the Prime Minister, Lord Rosebery, and so the government would have been particularly vulnerable if there had been any signs of a cover-up.

And so the trial went ahead. For Wilde the outlook this time was

---

* Apart from a daily visit from his hairdresser to wave his hair and a daily delivery of a green carnation for his buttonhole.

less favourable than before. The Solicitor-General decided that he would lead the prosecution himself, and, as well as being more aggressive than Gill and carrying more weight, he would as a law officer of the Crown have the right to say the last word to the jury, a notable advantage. This was a right that law officers of the Crown did not always exercise, and Sir William Clarke said that when he was Solicitor-General he had never done so, but Sir Frank Lockwood insisted on it. There was also a new judge. Mr Justice Charles had been a model of fairness and impartiality, but in his place there was now Mr Justice Wills who conducted the case with correctness but was basically more hostile to Wilde and showed himself at the end to be a judge of great severity, passing on him the maximum penalty.* One advantage for Wilde this time was that he would not be tried jointly with Alfred Taylor, although this was offset by Taylor being tried immediately before him, and the details of his trial, along with his almost certain conviction, would be given great publicity which could not but prejudice Wilde's chances.

In presenting the case for the prosecution the Solicitor-General made no mention of Wilde's literary works; in the previous trials attempts to incriminate him by these had failed, and so he proceeded at once to the calling of witnesses. These were the same as before and he started with Edward Shelley who was the only one on whom any reliability could be placed. But Sir Edward Clarke was able to show in his cross-examination that he was of unstable mind, and the judge agreed with him and ordered the charge relating to Shelley to be withdrawn. This was a considerable success and Clarke was also able to throw great doubt on the evidence given by the domestic staff of the Savoy Hotel, their eyesight, hearing and memory all being called into question. In opening for the defence Sir Edward Clarke drew attention to the fact that the charges against Wilde were gradually being whittled down – from twenty-five to eight. He said that in spite of having been weakened by his ordeal, Wilde would, for the third time, be going into the witness box and submitting to cross-examination. Surely not the action of a guilty man! He then took Wilde over the same ground that had been covered twice before – the main events of his success as a writer – always representing him as a brilliant, unconventional, flamboyant artist

---

* It is believed although it cannot be certain, that if Wilde had been found guilty in the previous trial, Mr Justice Charles would have given him a less harsh penalty. And so the lone juror who held out in his favour unwittingly did him a disservice.

whose language and lifestyle might be unorthodox and at times bizarre. The Solicitor-General in his cross-examination could only repeat the same questions as before; he was more probing than Gill in the previous trial, but his general tone was moderate. Sir Edward Clarke in his final speech said that this trial seemed to be operating as an act of indemnity for all the blackmailers of London who, in return for testifying on behalf of the Crown, had gained freedom from arrest for all their past crimes and indecencies. The case against Wilde now rested basically on the evidence of two men of the lowest character which could not be accepted without corroboration. This had not been produced and so he hoped the jury would see fit to save from absolute ruin a distinguished man of letters whose genius and gifts to our literature had not yet reached maturity. The Solicitor-General in his final speech inveighed mightily on the crimes of which Wilde was accused and how vital it was for the welfare of society that these should be stamped out utterly.

The judge in his summing up was not unfair but was less evenhanded than Mr Justice Charles. He reminded the jury that when Wilde withdrew his prosecution of Queensberry he had had to concede that the words 'posing as a sodomite' were justified. He said that Queensberry was right to be offended by the tone of Wilde's letters to his son, particularly the one that addressed him as 'my own boy' and referred to his 'rose-leaf lips and slim gilt soul'; and he was entitled to do all he could to rescue his son from an association which he regarded as evil. It was for the jury to decide whether or not the letter was an indication of unclean sentiments and appetites. Speaking for himself it was a letter of which it was difficult for him to speak with calmness, as addressed from one man to another. At one point in his summing up the judge was interrupted by the foreman of the jury who asked a question, which might have occurred to many people, as to why it was, in view of his close involvement in the case and his intimacy not only with Wilde but also with some of the prosecution witnesses, that Lord Alfred Douglas had not been arrested and charged. As has been seen Douglas had been eager to give evidence on Wilde's behalf but had been prevented from this both by Clarke and Wilde himself and had been persuaded to go abroad while the trial was on so that he could not be involved in it. But it seems that the prosecution, like the defence, had no wish to call him as a witness; it is possible that Queensberry had been able to arrange this. In reply to the foreman the judge was courteous but firm that this trial was not concerned with any misdeeds of Douglas, only with those of the prisoner in the dock. In concluding the judge told the jury that it was essential, in view of the disreputable character of the prosecution witnesses that their evidence should be corroborated, and it was up to them the jury, to decide whether this had been done. The basic question they must answer was whether there was evidence of guilt or only suspicion.

The jury then withdrew for two hours, and on their return the foreman said they were in agreement and on the seven charges with which Wilde

The downfall of Oscar Wilde from The Illustrated Police News *of 4 May*

was still charged their verdict was guilty. On this the judge felt no further need to be judicious or impartial, he could speak his mind frankly and in passing sentence made no attempt to temper justice with mercy. He told Wilde:

> The crime of which you have been convicted is so bad that one has to put stern restraint upon oneself from describing, in language which I would rather not use, the sentiments which must rise to the breast of every man of honour who has heard the details of these two terrible trials. That the jury have arrived at a correct verdict in this case, I cannot persuade myself to entertain the shadow of a doubt ... People who can do these things must be dead to all sense of shame, and one cannot hope to produce any effect on them. It is the worst case I have ever tried ... That you, Wilde, have been the centre of extensive corruption of the most hideous kind among young men, it is equally impossible to doubt.
>
> I shall, under such circumstances, be expected to pass the severest sentence that the law allows. In my judgment it is totally inadequate for such a case as this. The sentence of the Court is that each of you* be imprisoned and kept to hard labour for two years.

The impact of these terrible words left Wilde swaying and gasping and trying to speak, but at a gesture from the judge he was hustled away by the warders. Present in court was a young actor, Seymour Hicks who later wrote: 'I have seen many awful happenings at the Old Bailey, but to me no death sentence has ever seemed so terrible as the one which Mr Justice Wills delivered when his duty called upon him to destroy and take from the world the man who had given it so much.'

In the street outside a noisy and bawdy scene was being enacted. A crowd was cheering and jeering, and a group of female prostitutes had gathered to celebrate the removal of what they regarded as a threat to their livelihood, and were dancing and kicking up their skirts and shouting obscenities.

Later that day, on a different level, but just as horrible, Lord Queensberry and the two actors who had aided him in his case, Charles Brookfield and Charles Hawtrey, dined together to celebrate their triumph.

---

* For sentencing Wilde had been joined in the dock by Taylor.

Chapter VII

The vilest deeds like prison weeds bloom well in prison air:
It is only what is good in man that wastes and withers there.
We turn the crank, or tear the rope,
Each in his separate hell.

(Ballad of Reading Gaol)

The dreadful dress that makes sorrow grotesque to look at, the
silence, the solitude, the shame.

(De Profundis)

In 1895 Britain's prison system was harsh and brutal. Old ideas still persisted that the way to prevent crime was to make life in prison as unpleasant as possible. The emphasis was all on deterrence; little was done positively to reform and rehabilitate prisoners. The dehumanizing process started on arrival when a prisoner was made to hand over all possessions, strip off his clothes take a bath in dirty water and dry himself on a towel that had also been much used. He then put on the prison uniform of coarse cloth covered with arrows and was conducted to a solitary cell containing small table, tin chamber pot and plank bed with no mattress. There he was left for the night. For a man of Wilde's background such a life was a living hell. Later he described it as 'a fiendish nightmare, more horrible than anything I had ever dreamed of. After spending a night, shivering and sleepless, he was roused in the early morning to clean out his cell and was given a breakfast so nasty that he could not bring himself to eat it. For prisoners on hard labour work of some sort had to be found, and as useful work was seldom available, it might be something totally useless like the treadmill or the crank.* In view of

---

* The treadmill was a large cylinder kept moving by people treading on steps which gave way under them. The crank was a handle which had to be turned endlessly. Neither served any useful purpose.

his physical condition Wilde was put on light labour which usually meant sewing mailbags or unravelling old ropes (known as picking oakum) which, as well as being deadly dull, broke his fingernails and took the skin off his fingers. In time hunger forced him to eat the prison food, but this gave him diahorrea which made the air in his cell unbearably foul.

At first the only books he was allowed were the Bible, the Prayer Book and Hymn Book; and his only visitors, apart from warders, were (on rare occasions) the prison governor and the chaplain – more absurd than any stage parson – who suggested to him that his present predicament was due to the fact that he had not held family prayers at home. Later another chaplain, when told by Wilde that he missed not being able to see the clouds out of his narrow cell window, replied that he should concern himself not with the clouds but rather with his Heavenly Father who was above the clouds. For one hour a day he was allowed out of his cell for exercise with other prisoners in total silence.

For the first three months of his sentence he was allowed no visitors from outside and only one letter in and one out (both closely censored). In effect he was in solitary confinement for twenty-three hours a day apart from occasional interruptions such as a cell inspection when the least shortcoming would be punished by a spell in a darkened cell on bread and water.

The first break in this terrible routine came with a visit from a Liberal member of parliament, R.B. Haldane, later the holder of several high political offices including that of Lord Chancellor. At the time he was a member of the Home Office Committee looking into prison administration. He had known Wilde socially and liked him and was deeply distressed by the thought of what he must be suffering. He wanted to do anything he could to help him, but at first he was met with a blank wall. Wilde would not speak to him. But he persisted with kindly words and good advice and held out the hope of providing him with more books and even writing materials. At this Wilde broke down and burst into tears; it was the first kindness he had received since his imprisonment and more deeply affecting than any brutality.

Some six weeks after beginning his sentence Wilde was moved from Pentonville to Wandsworth, possibly at the instigation of Haldane who thought the regime there would be less oppressive, but in this he was mistaken. It proved to be just as harsh if not more so – rigid routine, petty and foolish rules, unimaginative treatment, and further agonies from what Wilde called his three great torturers – hunger, insomnia and disease. Haldane was able, however, to obtain for him some of the books he wanted. After a few weeks the time came when he was allowed to receive his first visitors from outside and his first letter. His first visitor was Robert Sherard* who found him depressed and on the verge of tears; his hair was unkempt and his face so thin that he hardly recognised him. For the one letter he was allowed he chose that from his brother-in-law Otho Holland with news of his family rather than one from Bosie. Holland told him that Constance was under great pressure from her legal advisors to sue for divorce, and if Wilde wanted to avoid this he should write to her at once, pleading for a reconciliation. This he then did in such passionate terms that Constance not only called off divorce proceedings but also applied for permission to come and visit him. As he had already had one visitor he was not strictly allowed to have another for three months, but for once the prison governor was flexible. A special visit was arranged; but this was to prove deeply painful; they saw each other through iron bars and were separated by a passage in which there was a warder listening to everything they said. 'It was, indeed, awful,' wrote Constance, 'more so than I had any conception it could be. I could not see him and I could not touch him. I scarcely spoke.'

Further disasters crowded in on Wilde. Queensberry had not let up on his vendetta and, implacable as ever, sued for his costs in the libel action Wilde had brought against him and filed a petition in the Bankruptcy Court, asking for a receiving order. As has been seen these costs had been guaranteed by Queensberry's family, but they had not been forthcoming. And so on 26 August 1894 Wilde was declared bankrupt which necessitated a humiliating visit to London for it to be formally registered. This caused Wilde great bitterness; it seemed to him the culmination of Queensberry's triumph: 'The fact the he was able not merely to put me into prison for two years but to take me out for an afternoon and make me a public bankrupt was an extra refinement of pleasure that I had not expected. It was the crowning point of my humiliation and of his complete and perfect victory.' And later he wrote in despair: 'The Law has taken from me not merely all that I have, my books, my furniture, pictures, my copyright in my published works, my copyright in my plays, everything in fact from The Happy Prince and Lady Windermere's Fan down to the stair carpets and door-scraper of my house, but also all that I am ever going to have.'

---

* One of Wilde's most faithful adherents. At the time of his trial he challenged Queensberry to a duel on French soil but this was not taken up.

Soon after this Wilde suffered a serious accident when he had a fainting fit in the prison chapel and had a fall which did permanent damage to one of his ears and affected his hearing. At the time he was near to a physical and mental breakdown and was taken to the prison infirmary where he remained for several weeks, being well treated and nursed back to health. He was also examined by a mental specialist who reported that he found no evidence of madness in him.

While he was still in the infirmary Wilde was transferred to Reading Gaol, it being felt (perhaps again by Haldane) that in a comparatively small country gaol there would be a more relaxed atmosphere, and light duties in the way of gardening, bookbinding and library work would be available to him. At first, however, the move was dogged with misfortune. On the journey to Reading he had a traumatic experience at Clapham Junction where, handcuffed and in prison uniform, he had a wait of half an hour during which he was jeered and spat at by a gathering crowd. The incident made a deep impression on him and he referred to it constantly afterwards as one of the most painful and unpleasant of his imprisonment. And when he arrived at Reading he did not find at first the mild, enlightened regime he had expected. The governor, Colonel Isaacson, proved to be a petty-minded martinet who announced his intention of 'knocking the nonsense out of Wilde', which he set about doing by persecuting him with a series of punishments for minor infringements of discipline. Later Wilde was to say of him that he could not sit down to breakfast until he had punished someone and that he had 'the eye of a ferret, the body of an ape and the soul of a rat'.

Soon after Wilde's transfer to Reading efforts were made by some of his friends to obtain for him remission of sentence. It was argued, with some reason, that he had suffered enough, that his health was on the verge of a breakdown and this would be an incalculable loss to English literature. But shamefully the plea fell on deaf ears: of the eminent figures in art and literature who were approached to sign the petition nearly all (including Bernard Shaw, George Meredith, Henry James, Zola, Holman Hunt and Burne-Jones) found some reason for withholding their support; and the Home Secretary, Herbert Asquith, had no hesitation in rejecting it. Soft feelings towards Oscar Wilde at that time, it was felt, would be politically damaging.

At the same time as this great disappointment Wilde received yet another heartbreaking blow when his mother died suddenly. Of all women she was the one for whom he had the greatest love and on whose behalf he felt the greatest shame. 'Her death was so terrible to me,' he wrote, 'that I, once a lord of language, had no words in which to express my anguish and shame.' So that the news should be broken to him gently Constance made the long journey from Italy, where she had taken refuge with her sons, 'to break the tidings of so irreparable, so irredeemable a loss'. The meeting between husband and wife was to be a long and gentle one; they came to an agreement on financial matters and it seemed that a reconciliation might be possible. But sadly the meeting was to be their last; soon afterwards, largely because of the ineptness of their advisers, differences arose mainly about money and they were to remain apart.

For the rest of his sentence Wilde was visited every three months by faithful friends. In May 1896 Sherard and Ross found him much thinner; his eyes were 'terribly vacant' and he cried the whole time; his ear was still giving him pain, but he did not like to mention it to the prison doctor who was unsympathetic and always accusing him of malingering. Wilde later wrote of him that he was 'brutal in manner, coarse in temperament and utterly indifferent to the health and comfort of prisoners'. Wilde's greatest fear was that he was going insane and shortly after this visit he made another impassioned appeal to the Home Secretary for his release. In this he admitted the terrible offences of which he had rightly been found guilty, acknowledged the 'perverse passions' to which he was liable, but hoped that these might be considered a disease for cure rather than a crime for punishment. 'Though prison may not seek to make men better,' he pleaded, 'yet it does not desire to drive them mad.' But once again the petition was rejected. There had to be no question of giving him preferential treatment.

However, a wind of change was blowing in governing circles at the time. A new attitude towards prisons and prisoners was gaining ground; the latter were no longer being regarded always as hopeless and worthless members of society for whom 'hard labour, hard fare and hard bed' were the only remedy. This new perspective reached Reading gaol with the appointment of a new governor. At the end of July Colonel Isaacson, 'the mulberry coloured dictator', was replaced by Major Nelson, a man of a very different hue. Wilde was later to describe how under his governance the atmosphere of the prison changed completely; the rules remained the same but their application was altered; sympathy and kindness were occasionally shown and, as always, Wilde was deeply affected by such treatment. Major Nelson became to him 'one of the most Christlike people he had ever met'.

For the last ten months of his imprisonment, then, Wilde's life became more bearable; he was found more congenial work, he was no longer being continually punished for trivial offences, he was allowed more books to read and, most important of all, he was provided with writing materials and given more freedom as to what he might write. In making this concession Major Nelson was bending prison rules; perhaps he hoped Wilde would produce something comparable to *Pilgrim's Progress* (written by John Bunyan in Bedford gaol), or perhaps he just thought that writing would save him from insanity.

What Wilde actually did produce was a massive letter (some 30,000 words) addressed to Douglas which was later given the name (actually by Ross) of *De Profundis* ('out of the depths'). In this he discoursed on a number of subjects including the deadening effect of prison life, the changes that had come about in his character and thinking and his new attitude to religion. He also sought to explain (not, he emphasized, to defend) his past conduct. But most of the letter was taken up with a bitter and relentless outpouring against Douglas.

Since his imprisonment relations between the two men had cooled, but such a paroxysm of hate and contempt was unexpected and out of character. After Wilde's action against Queensberry had broken down and he was on remand in Holloway prison, it seemed that he and Douglas were still devoted to each other. Douglas visited him every day and Wilde's letters to him were as ardent and effusive as ever. 'I think of you as a golden-haired boy with Christ's own heart in yours,' he declared in one of them, and again: 'What wisdom is to the philosopher, what God is to his saints, you are to me.' It seems that down to the time of his conviction these feelings were undimmed. For three months afterwards no communication between them was possible, but when the time came for Wilde to receive one letter and he chose one from his brother-in-law, Otho Holland, rather than one from Douglas, the latter was evidently piqued by this, and there were other matters too which caused dissension.

When Sherard came on his first visit he told Wilde that Douglas was proposing to write an article for a French magazine about their friendship; this was affectionate and strongly supportive but was to include quotations from the letters Wilde had written to him while he was in Holloway. This outraged Wilde who considered these letters sacrosanct and certainly not to be published in a magazine. He told Sherard to do everything in his power to prevent such a thing happening. which in the event he was able to do; but it caused Douglas some offence and the matter continued to rankle with Wilde. There was another incident too which upset him, perhaps disproportionately, when Douglas sent him a cryptic message by means of a solicitor's clerk who was visiting him in prison in connection with his bankruptcy. Wilde was surprised and temporarily mystified when the clerk suddenly whispered that Prince Fleur de Lys wished to be remembered to him. Then he recalled that he had once given this name to Douglas, and he was very scornful that he should have used it again in present circumstances. 'You were in your own eye,' he wrote in *De Profundis*, 'still the graceful prince of a trivial comedy, not the sombre figure of a tragic show.' It seemed that Douglas could do nothing right at that time, and Wilde again became furiously indignant when he heard that Douglas was about to publish a volume of poetry with a dedication to him. He told Ross to tell Douglas that such an idea was 'revolting and grotesque' and he would never agree to it. In carrying out this instruction it is possible that Ross, who had no love for Douglas, may have exceeded his brief and told him that Wilde had turned against him and wanted nothing more to do with him, which may account for the fact that from then on Douglas remained silent and absent – no offer of help about the bankruptcy proceedings, although his family was responsible for them, not even a word of sympathy on the death of his mother. And all the time Wilde's anger was mounting. On his next visit Ross was told to get back from Douglas all the letters he had written to him and all the presents he had given him; but here Douglas was defiant, saying that his possession of them prevented him from ending his life and that he kissed them and prayed over them morning and evening. Finally the great change in Wilde's feelings was set out in searing terms in *De Profundis*. Here he launched into the attack in the first paragraph:

'After long and fruitless waiting I have determined to write to you myself, as much for your sake as for mine, as I would not like to think that I had passed through two long years of imprisonment without ever having received a single line from you, any news or message even, except such as gave me pain.' He then went on to spell out in detail how everything had changed. When he was in Holloway, awaiting trial he had written: 'Nothing but Alfred Douglas's daily visits quicken me into life.' In Reading he wrote: 'By your actions and by your silence, by what you have done and what you have left undone you have made every day of my long imprisonment still more difficult for me to live through.' Their friendship, once described as 'beautiful and noble' had now become 'ill-fated and lamentable', and their life together one of 'froth and folly'.

Remorselessly he drove home the point that far from inspiring him to great works he had prevented them. 'As long as you were by my side,' he declared, 'my life was entirely sterile and uncreative.' And, brutally, he made clear that intellectually he was unworthy of him: 'with no powers of intellectual concentration your interests were merely in your meals and moods ... and a life of reckless profusion'. As to the letters, which had once been such a joy to him, they were like 'froth and foam on the lips of an epileptic'.

In detail he went over the events of their life together, dwelling always on the unhappy ones rather than those that had brought joy. This was done consciously: 'Had our life together been as the world fancied it to be, one simply of pleasure, profligacy and laughter, I would not be able to recall a single passage in it. It is because it was full of moments and days tragic, bitter, sinister in their warnings, dull or dreadful in their monotonous scenes and unseemly violence, that I can see or hear each separate incident in its detail.' In particular he listed all the money he had spent on Douglas – the expensive gifts, the hotel bills, the trips abroad, the restaurant meals. 'I spent hours entertaining you and going about with you ... You demanded without grace and received without thanks.' And then came the dreadful charge that it was he who had put him in prison. It was at his insistence that he took action against his father, and by trying to put him in prison had ended up there himself. 'Blindly I staggered as an ox into the shambles.' And it was not because of any evil or cruelty that he had been brought down, but rather by his generosity and kindness. From *King Lear*, he alluded to the lines:

> The gods are just, and of our pleasant vices
> Make instruments to plague use

'The gods are strange,' he wrote. 'It is not of our vices only they make instruments to scourge us. They bring us to ruin through what in us is good, gentle, humane, loving. But for my pity and affection for you and yours, I would not now be weeping in this terrible place.'

But after this terrible tirade he knew that he must forgive Douglas. 'The first thing I have got to do is to free myself from any possible bitterness of feeling against you ... I didn't write this letter to put bitterness into your heart but to pluck it out of mine.' This, then, was the main purpose of the letter – to vent the venom of his spleen, to soothe the agonies of his years in prison, to steady his mind. His friendship with Douglas had been a turbulent one, but it was not the misery and frustration he portrayed. And it must be that he was unjust to Douglas: it was not the case that he was always seeking to end their relationship while Douglas persisted in maintaining it; and it is certainly untrue that he did not write a single line while Douglas was with him; all his greatest works were written during the years of their friendship.

As became evident later, Wilde's outburst against Douglas did not represent his true feelings; it was the product of an unbalanced mind, apt to go from one extreme to another or, as a friend described it, 'the passing delirium of gaol moral fever'. Deep down, below the rhetoric and the obloquy, he knew that his love for Douglas remained intact. At the end of *De Profundis* there is evidence that he did not regard the letter as a final parting: 'At the end of a month, when the June roses are all in their wanton opulence, I will, if I feel able, arrange through Robbie to meet you in some quiet foreign town ... I hope that our meeting will be what a meeting between you and me should be, after everything that has occurred. In old days there was always a wide chasm between us, the chasm of achieved Art and acquired culture: there is a still wider chasm between us now, the chasm of Sorrow: but to Humility there is nothing that is impossible, and to Love all things are easy.' Perhaps, as has been suggested by Richard Ellman, *De Profundis* was in reality a love letter.

As each sheet of *De Profundis* was finished it had to be handed in to the prison authorities; owing to its length and the nature of its content the completed version was not allowed to be sent outside, but on his release it was restored to Wilde who handed it over to Ross with instructions to have copies made and one to be sent to Douglas. It is not certain if this was done; Ross said that it was, but this was denied by Douglas who claimed that he did not see the parts relating to himself until twelve years after Wilde's death when he and Ross were involved in a lawsuit. As may be imagined he was bitterly hurt and outraged. Never one for moderation he described it as 'a dreadful piece of cold-blooded malignant malice, hypocrisy and lying, and almost every word it contains is a lie or distortion of the truth ... The whole letter is the raving of a lunatic, a man driven mad by impotent rage and malice and malevolent desire to injure at all costs the friend he professed to love.' He was particularly vitriolic on the subject of money and Wilde's 'appalling bad taste' in referring to it, so different from 'the generous, hospitable, open-handed man he had once been'. He claimed that he too had made financial sacrifices and after Wilde's release had given him sums of money in excess of anything he had ever had from him.

This matter is examined in more detail in a later chapter where it will be seen that the whole truth is not easily discovered.

The tirade against Douglas was the least edifying part of *De Profundis*. Some people were deeply shocked by it. Bernard Shaw called it 'most amazingly undignified', and even Ross thought he had gone too far, and when, after Wilde's death, he presented the manuscript to the British Museum, he stipulated that it should not be made public for fifty years (until 1960).

The remainder of *De Profundis* contains some autobiography and philosophical reflexions. It suffers somewhat from the conditions under which it was written – in a prison cell, in an unbalanced frame of mind and with the necessity of handing in all written sheets at the end of the day and not getting them back until the day of his release, thus making rereading and revision impossible. In consequence the work is at times discursive and repetitious. It is, nevertheless, of great interest and quite different to anything else Wilde wrote. Gone was the flippant playwright and the arrogant show-off, as also the brilliant essayist looking always for paradox and perversity. It was the nearest he came to being completely serious.

Because of the restrictions on the books allowed him in prison, Wilde was to find himself reading the Bible more often and with greater attention than he had done before. His views on religion were unorthodox and personal: 'The faith that others give to what is unseen I give to what one can touch and look at. My Gods dwell in temples made with hands.' He made clear that in prison religion was of no help to him, but reading the Bible did make a great impression. He was delighted by the stories in the Old Testament, and had ideas of dramatizing some of them after his release. But what struck him most forcibly was the personality of Christ whom he regarded not so much in a religious light as the Son of God but as 'the greatest of artists', 'a supreme poet and precursor of the Romantic Movement', and 'the most complete individualist in history'. In essence an idealized version of himself. He marvelled too at Christ's love for ignorant people and his indifference to the respectable and pretentious, and above all at his care for sinners who seemed to be nearer to God than the righteous. He delighted too in the idea of a young Galilean peasant imagining he could take on himself the sins of the world. Through Christ, as well as his own experiences, he became convinced that sorrow was the only truth and the supreme emotion of which man was capable and that only through sorrow and suffering were the secrets of life revealed. It followed, then, that he should not try to forget the horrors of prison life; to do so would be to stunt his growth. 'The plank bed, loathsome food, hard rope shredded into oakum until one's finger tips grow dull with pain, the menial offices with which each day begins and finishes, the harsh orders that routine seems to necessitate, the dreadful dress that makes sorrow grotesque to look at, the silence, the solitude, the shame – each and all of these things I have to transform into a spiritual experience. I have got to make everything that has happened to me good for me.'

At the same time he was convinced that prison could never reform a man's morals; it might make him a deeper man but not a better one. His attitude to the crimes of which he himself had been convicted was ambivalent. At times he seemed to be penitent: 'I let myself be lured by spells of senseless and sensual ease. I became the spendthrift of my own genius. Tired of being at the heights I deliberately went to the depths in the search for new sensations.' But at other times he had apparently, no regrets: 'Along with genius goes often a curious perversity of passion and desire ... What paradox was to me in the sphere of thought, perversity became to me in the sphere of passion ... I don't regret for a single moment having lived for pleasure. I did it to the full, as one should do everything that one does to the full. I went down the primrose path to the sound of flutes. I lived on honeycomb.'

Although in the last months of his imprisonment the treatment meted out to Wilde was milder and more humane, he still had to endure some deeply painful experiences. One day he became aware of wild yells of pain coming from the lower regions of the prison which later proved to have been caused by the flogging of a mentally defective prisoner for so-called 'malingering'. And at the end of his sentence he was appalled to see some very young children being locked up; they had been caught poaching and did not have the money to pay the fine. Wilde could well imagine the cold, the hunger, the terror they would suffer in a dark, solitary cell, and begged to be allowed to pay their fines for them. But the most terrible experience of all was when the death sentence was carried out on a prisoner, a soldier who had cut the throat of his unfaithful wife. Later this was to prompt from Wilde his greatest work of poetry, *The Ballad of Reading Gaol*.

In personal matters too he had troubles. His relations with Constance went into a decline. It has been seen that when she visited him in prison at the time of his mother's death there was harmony between them: he agreed that she should appoint a guardian to help her in the bringing up of the children; in financial matters it was agreed that she would make him an annual allowance of £200 and in return he would give up the life interest which he held in her marriage settlement; and she insisted, and he agreed, that this would be an informal agreement not binding by law. All might have been well if this had been allowed to stand but unfortunately there was interference from Constance's legal advisors and from Wilde's friends.

Wilde's financial affairs were in the hands of Robert Ross, but in late 1896 he had to retire from the scene because of a major operation and handed over the management to his close friend, More Adey.* Adey's devotion to Wilde was to be selfless and steadfast, but his judgement was unsound, and he became obsessed by the matter of Wilde's life interest in the marriage settlement; it seemed to him essential that Wilde should hold on to this, otherwise he would be completely dependent on Constance and, if she predeceased him, on her lawyers, with no legal rights of his own. Wilde being in bankruptcy, the life interest was regarded by the Official Receiver as a saleable property which he proposed to put up for auction where it was expected to fetch no more than £25. This Constance proposed to buy and Wilde assured her he would not make any difficulties nor bid against her. Adey, however, took it upon himself to do so with a sum of money he had collected from Wilde sympathizers, and in this he persisted although Wilde had made his wishes perfectly clear. That such a course was mistaken and fraught with danger was pointed out to Adey, forcefully and emotionally, by one of Wilde's chief benefactors, Adela Schuster, a Jewish lady of considerable means who had already given generous financial assistance and was prepared to do so again, but not towards the purchase of the life interest. She pleaded with Adey that more important than anything was a good relationship between Wilde and Constance, far more so than any financial consideration. She pointed out that such an action would infuriate Constance who would suspect that Wilde was double-dealing and that this might lead to a divorce in which case the life interest would automatically come to an end. In addition it would surely be preferable that the sum raised be devoted to Wilde's immediate needs after his release from prison. But, obstinately, Adey was not to be deflected. He had a great dislike of Constance (warmly reciprocated) as well as a strong distrust of her legal advisors. And so when the life interest came up for sale he obtained it for £75 (plus £25 costs). When this became known the consequences were as Adela Schuster had

---

* A minor literary figure and joint director with Ross of an art gallery.

predicted: Constance, who felt very strongly on the subject, was furious, felt that Wilde had deceived her and had thoughts of divorce. Wilde himself, in the last stages of his imprisonment and in an emotional state writing De Profundis, was appalled when he received 'a violent and insulting letter' from Constance's lawyer. 'It fell on me like a thunderbolt,' he wrote. In the end an agreement was negotiated with Constance's lawyers whereby Wilde surrendered his life interest and Constance undertook to pay him an annual allowance of £150 – less than before because it had been borne in on Constance that her husband's financial resources were greater than she thought. At the same time it was borne in on Wilde that his financial affairs had been thoroughly mismanaged, and in a letter to Ross he let himself go on the subject:

'In point of fact, Robbie, you had better realise that of all the incompetent people on the face of God's earth in any matter requiring wisdom, common sense, straightforwardness, ordinary intelligence, More Adey is undoubtedly the chief … in matters of business he is the most solemn donkey that every stepped … If you have ever thought him sensible, give up the idea. He is incapable, as I have written to him, of managing the domestic affairs of a tom-tit in a hedge for a single afternoon.'

It is pleasant to be able to record some relief from gloom in the last months of Wilde's imprisonment. It gave him great pleasure to hear that his play Salome was to be put on in Paris. 'It is something,' he wrote, 'that at a time of disgrace and shame I should still be regarded as an artist.' And at the same time his life was lightened in other ways when he was put in the charge of a new warder. Thomas Martin developed an affection and admiration for Wilde and was ready to bend and even openly disobey prison rules to make his life easier, smuggling into him extra food, newspapers and other comforts. Inevitably, perhaps, such a gentle and humane man did not survive in the prison service, and he was subsequently dismissed (presumably by the 'Christlike' Major Nelson) when he was caught giving biscuits to child prisoners.

As the day of Wilde's release approached careful arrangements were made to see that it passed as smoothly and painlessly as possible. During his imprisonment he had been well served by a faithful few: Robert Ross, Robert Sherard, More Adey and Frank Harris had all been tireless and courageous in their efforts on his behalf – getting him the books he wanted, drawing up petitions for his release, trying to sort out his tangled finances and visiting him and writing to him whenever it was allowed. There was too the Rev. Stuart Headlam, an avant garde

Anglican clergyman involved in Christian Socialism, who had not met Wilde until the time of his trial, but then stood bail for him and drove him to and from court every day, and on his release put his house at his disposal, thereby bringing on himself great obloquy and danger. And there were two women, both Jewish, who stood by him throughout: Ada Leverson who had taken him into her house at his darkest moment, and Adela Schuster who had provided a gift of £1,000 (worth £50,000 today) when it was desperately needed. The bravery and loyalty of these friends gleam brightly in the Oscar Wilde tragedy.

Chapter VIII

The profound, eternal, torturous silence.
(Alfred Dreyfus)

I only ask one thing, to be able to go to my grave, knowing my children's name has been cleared of this terrible stain.
(Ibid)

I put Dreyfus in prison and all France cannot get him out.
(Esterhazy to Oscar Wilde)

On the day that Oscar Wilde was released from Reading gaol (19 May 1897) Alfred Dreyfus had been on Devil's Island for over two years and a further two years still lay ahead of him. Brutal and inhuman as had been the treatment of Wilde it was as nothing compared to that meted out to Dreyfus. Deprived of the death penalty France's rulers were determined to make the rest of Dreyfus's life as near to a living hell as possible. Devil's Island was a barren, rocky strip of land which had once been used as a leper colony. Here he was kept alone – no other prisoners on the island – in a makeshift tin hut in conditions of the utmost squalor and wretchedness. Infested with vermin – ants, mosquitoes and sometimes crabs and snakes – and the tropical sun beating down, at times bringing the temperature into the 120s, life was a perpetual torment. Food was disgusting and often uneatable and he was allowed one bucket of warm, dirty water a day for drinking, washing and cooking which he had to do himself. And at all times he was under close surveillance by guards who had orders never to speak to him and to report him for punishment if he ever addressed a word to them. If he wished to make a communication of any sort it had to be in writing and then, as often as not, it would be ignored. Perhaps the most terrible part of his punishment was what he called 'the profound, eternal, torturous silence'. Sleep was his only refuge but in such conditions this was often impossible, and when it did come he was usually woken by the clanking of the changing of the guards and sometimes by nightmares. To survive such conditions for four and a half years was a miracle of endurance, especially as he was denied access to a hospital when malaria afflicted him and he was only ever given the most rudimentary medical attention.

While making life unendurable for him the authorities were at the same time much concerned about the possibility of suicide. And so, as well as keeping a permanent watch on him, they denied him the use of anything with which he might harm himself – china, glass, knives, razor blades. They were even more obsessed about the possibility of an escape; they seemed haunted by the fear that an international Jewish syndicate was planning a rescue attempt, and to guard against this they went to ludicrous lengths. Periodically his clothing and mattress were torn apart to see if they contained secret messages, and a cannon was maintained at the ready to open fire on any unidentified vessel coming within three miles of the island.* Even a flock of harmless wild goats was removed lest Dreyfus, like Ulysses escaping from the cave of Polyphemus, should attache himself to the underbelly of one of them and strike out into the shark-infested ocean.

It was inevitable that in such conditions Dreyfus's mind should turn to suicide. 'I would like,' he wrote, 'to close my eyes and no longer see, no longer think, no longer suffer.' And again: 'Human strength has its limits and my anguish overwhelms me ... Almost superhuman force is needed in order to resist.' But always, when such thoughts came upon him, he was restrained by one consideration, that suicide would be taken as an admission of guilt and that his children would have to bear the disgrace of a dishonoured and traitorous father. 'If only I were alone in the world,' he wrote, 'I would have been in the grave long ago ... I only ask one thing, to be able to go to my grave, knowing my children's name has been cleared of this terrible stain.' And so to survive became his great preoccupation, and in this he would surely not have been successful without the devoted support of his wife and brother. Theirs is, indeed, a heroic story. For nearly five years, in spite of hate campaigns,

---

* Not as far-fetched as it might seem. When war threatened between England and France over the Fashoda incident (see p. 125) Admiral Fisher, in command of the British fleet in the West Indies, is said to have been planning a descent on Devil's Island to rescue Dreyfus. Just as well this did not happen as Dreyfus would have been shot instantly.

constant harassment and perpetual obstruction, Lucie and Mathieu dedicated their lives entirely to the establishment of Alfred's innocence and at the same time giving him all possible support so that he could endure his dreadful ordeal. They were under no illusions as to how great were his sufferings. 'Every passing hour,' wrote Mathieu, 'is a century of suffering for Alfred Dreyfus, and another step towards death.'

Lucie had originally applied for permission to join her husband, as she was legally entitled to do, but this was refused, and she then saw it as her mission to do all she could from afar to maintain Alfred's morale and keep at bay all thoughts of suicide. She was quick to notice any feelings of despair in his letters and to reply at once with advice as to how these might be overcome. She told him how important it was at all times to keep his mind occupied and to find as many things as possible that interested him. In particular she urged him to write to her fully and often, not only because such unburdening of griefs would be a relief to him but also because his letters were the only thing she cherished in life. She was also able to send out to him help of a different kind – parcels of food (although many of these were pilfered), as well as books and writing materials which were a great comfort. Before his imprisonment Dreyfus had not been a reader, but now he became absorbed by some of the great classics – the philosophical works of Voltaire and Montaigne, the novels of Tolstoy and Dostoevsky and, above all, the works of Shakespeare. In order to read these in the original he set about learning English* and became fascinated by the great tragedies – *King Lear*, *Hamlet* and *Othello* whose agonies made them his 'immortal friends'. One passage from Othello made a deep impression on him:

> Good name in man and woman, dear my lord,
> Is the immediate jewel of their souls;
> Who steals my purse steals trash: 'tis something, nothing;
> 'Twas mine, 'tis his, and has been a slave to thousands;
> But he that filches from me my good name
> Robs me of that which not enriches him,
> And makes me poor indeed.

One source from which Dreyfus obtained no comfort was religion. He had long been a lapsed member of the Jewish faith, and Christianity

---

* This he did with the help of phrase books which caused great suspicion among his guards who thought that they were part of a secret code.

had little appeal to him. Religion he regarded as the 'domain of dreams' and wrote that 'being numbed by the passivity of religion is the fate of the weak.' What did give him strength were the principles which had been imbued into him during his military training – duty, honour, discipline, self-sacrifice. His belief in these never faltered. At no time did he lose his love for France or feel any disloyalty towards the army which had treated him so unjustly. He believed sincerely that the punishment meted out to him 'befitted the scoundrel he was taken to be'. He would, though, not have been human if he did not at times have bouts of fury about 'the wretch who had committed the infamous crimes' of which he had been convicted. No fate was too harsh for him: 'I would like to see him suffer all the tortures I have had to endure. Without pity I would rip at his heart and his entrails.' But he did not allow such thoughts to obsess him and somehow, during four and a half years, he maintained his faith that one day justice would be done to him.

Justice Revised

Chapter IX

No hand was held out to us; every door was obstinately closed. On the street people who knew us fled from us. We were the plague-stricken.

(Mathieu Dreyfus)

Fanaticism begins at the point where evidence stops short.

(Thierry Maulnier)

Even before Alfred left France Lucie and Mathieu had become aware of what a hard and frustrating struggle lay ahead of them. It seemed that every door was closed to them. Alfred had been convicted by a unanimous verdict of his fellow officers and nearly everyone was of the opinion that justice had been done. As the trial had been held in camera the public did not know how inadequate was the evidence against him or how the trial had been rigged. The general inclination was to trust the politicians and generals when they declared their complete conviction that Dreyfus was guilty, and not to enquire too deeply into the matter.

Mathieu's first task then was to awake in people a feeling that a great injustice had been done, that an innocent man was suffering the tortures of the damned for a crime he had not committed and that the honour of the French army and of the Third Republic was at stake until this wrong had been put right. But for all too long his pleas fell on deaf ears.

In breaking down public indifference Mathieu realized that he must proceed discreetly; it would be easy to do more harm than good. To work up a public outcry in Parliament and the press would, almost certainly, be counterproductive: the army would become stubborn and resentful, and the anti-Jewish lobby would be stirred up to fresh bouts of frenzy. It was essential at all times not to question the army's integrity nor to show any disloyalty or lack of patriotism. Rather he must rely on persuasion and diplomacy and bend all his efforts to finding new evidence which would lead to the true culprit and so to the clearance of Alfred. But this could not be done without some help from the government and the army and this was not forthcoming. He hoped that some support might come from the German and Italian embassies where the truth of the matter must surely be known. But the ambassadors had already issued denials of any dealings with Dreyfus which had been disregarded. That they would reveal the name of the true spy was expecting too much. However, in his determination to 'knock on every door' Mathieu decided to pursue this line and for the purpose engaged the services of an English private detective. In years ahead this source proved fruitful, but not at first.

The first gleam of light was to come from an unexpected and unorthodox channel. A friend of Mathieu, a Dr Gibert, urged him to make contact with a clairvoyant in whom he had great faith. Mathieu, who had been much beset by cranks and charlatans offering help at a price, was at first sceptical, but Dr Gibert was a man of some standing as well as being physician and friend to the French President, Félix Faure. And so Mathieu agreed to see the clairvoyant, a heavily built Norman peasant woman known as Léonie. In the ensuing trances Léonie told Mathieu much that he knew already but also made vehement and repeated references to 'secret documents' which had been shown to the judges at the Dreyfus trial. Mathieu would probably not have given much attention to these but soon afterwards Gibert was told by President Faure that there had actually been secret documents at the trial which had been shown to the judges and to no one else. This was an extraordinary admission in view of the illegality of such a procedure, and even stranger was it that Gibert was given permission to pass this information on to Mathieu. Mathieu, however, was also told that it was strictly unofficial and that Faure would deny it if questioned about it in public; also that Faure personally was convinced that Dreyfus was guilty. At the same time Maître Demange, who had defended Dreyfus at his trial, also heard rumours of a 'secret file' which had not been shown to him as it should have been. These reports gave Mathieu hope, but with the President remaining silent and the army refusing to comment 'in the interests of national security', it seemed that once again a dead end had been reached.

By this time Dreyfus had been on Devil's Island for nearly eighteen months and was nearly at the end of his tether. Lucie and Mathieu could tell from his letters that he was becoming desperate. In one of them he wrote of 'situations which no human being can bear indefinitely'. According to Mathieu this was the bleakest and most hopeless period of their long struggle. It seemed they were making no progress and the Dreyfus Case was sinking into oblivion. In these circumstance Mathieu became convinced that something of some sort must be done at once to bring the name of Dreyfus to public attention. And so he agreed to a somewhat bizarre plan of his English detective that it should be arranged for an article to appear in an English newspaper to the effect that Dreyfus had escaped from captivity. It was expected that the article would be reproduced immediately in the French press and be denied by the authorities, but it would, nevertheless, bring the name of Dreyfus to public attention. In this, as will be seen, it was eventually successful, but in the first instance it backfired badly when the Minister for the Colonies, fearful of the anti-Jewish press, ordered the military commander in Cayenne to redouble his efforts to prevent an escape attempt. In consequence the unfortunate prisoner was shackled to his bed in irons at night and was confined to his hut for twenty-four hours a day while a seven-foot-high palisade was constructed round his hut which excluded all view of the ocean, until then 'one of his supreme comforts'. This was almost too much for him to bear and he wrote home in desperation: 'I cannot take it any longer, everything is giving way in

Dreyfus's prison compound on Devil's Island

me.' But by dint of great willpower and stoicism he did survive, and if he had but known it, significant developments relative to his fate were beginning to take place in France.

These developments were also unknown to Mathieu as they were occurring behind the scenes in the Statistical Section. Here in July 1895, some six months after Dreyfus's conviction, a new chief had been appointed in succession to the anti-Semite Colonel Sandherr – Georges Picquart, a man of courage and integrity. On his appointment to the post he had been told by his superiors to find evidence which would prove conclusively that Dreyfus was guilty, and so lay the matter to rest. This task he set about with a will, as at that time he himself had no doubts on the subject; but facts then came to light which made him change his mind. In the first place it became evident that information was still being leaked to Germany; and in March 1896 there was discovered a document which came to be known as the *Petit Bleu* (after the colour of the paper on which it was written). Like the *bordereau* this emanated from the German embassy and it too had been torn into pieces to disguise the fact that it had been stolen. When put together the note contained little of importance apart from the fact that it was addressed to Major Esterhazy and showed that he was in correspondence with someone in the German embassy and was providing him with information. To Picquart it was then certain that the army had another traitor on its hands, but what was not immediately clear was whether both Esterhazy and Dreyfus were traitors or only Esterhazy. The crucial question was whether Esterhazy's handwriting was the same as that on the *bordereau*. For some reason it took Picquart time to obtain a specimen of Esterhazy's handwriting, but when he did he had no doubt that it matched exactly.

At the same time Picquart was becoming convinced that Dreyfus was innocent. Reports had come to him from a double agent in Berlin that no one in German intelligence had had any dealings with him. Also he had had the opportunity of going through the secret file on Dreyfus kept in the SS, and had found there nothing of any substance. By August 1896 his doubts had become a certainty and he passed on what he had discovered to the chief of staff of the French army, General Boisdeffre, a distinguished soldier who had recently played an important part in France's historic treaty with Russia (see p. 11). At the news that another traitor had been discovered in the army he was dismayed; he had no wish to go through again all the ferment stirred up by the Dreyfus Case, and his immediate reaction was to cover the matter up. 'Let Esterhazy be forced to retire from the army and no more be said about the matter' summed up his attitude. He then handed the matter over to his deputy, General Gonse.

General Gonse was not a strong man nor an honourable one. He was greatly agitated by what Picquart had to tell him and at first could only urge him over and over again to act with the greatest prudence. But later it became evident that he was intent on covering up for Esterhazy and preventing a retrial of Dreyfus. At one stage, according to Picquart, he asked him:

'Why do you make such a point of Dreyfus leaving Devil's Island?'

'But, General, he is innocent,' replied Picquart.

'That is unimportant,' said Gonse. 'That is not a consideration which should be brought into the reckoning.'

To Picquart, however, such thoughts were shameful and totally un-acceptable.

'I will not carry this secret to my grave,' he said, and he refused to be silenced.

Gonse's motives in taking the line he did can only be surmised. One factor was likely to have been that he knew of the illegality in the Dreyfus trial – the showing of secret documents to the judges – and realized that a retrial might bring this to light and so bring shame and possibly legal action on senior army officers. But there may have been other considerations as well. If Dreyfus were found to be innocent it would be deeply humiliating to those officers, including the highest in the land, who had staked their honour that he was guilty. Gonse then sought to avoid the prosecution of Esterhazy, as the more guilt that was attached to him, the weaker would become the case against Dreyfus. It is true that at first the case against Esterhazy was not strong, resting solely on the *Petit Bleu*, and would not have stood up in a court of law; but further investigations would have brought more to light, and these Gonse tried to obstruct, even forbidding Picquart at one stage to employ a graphologist to identify Esterhazy's handwriting on the *bordereau*. One further matter, although speculation, might have weighed with Gonse. Esterhazy was an aristocrat of a sort and as such mixed socially with senior officers, and it could have been that these had sometimes been indiscreet and let slip information which Esterhazy had then passed on to German intelligence. This meant that he was in a position, if he were so minded, to compromise them and even to level blackmail. There is no proof of this, but there is circumstantial evidence, and in later years Esterhazy, in his cups, used to boast that the French high command would never dare to bring him to trial.

At the time when Picquart was discovering the guilt of Esterhazy and the weakness of the case against Dreyfus, there were signs that others in the War Office, beside Gonse, were becoming alarmed and were resorting to fraudulent and underhand devices. Soon after Picquart's interview with Gonse the censors intercepted a letter to Dreyfus on Devil's Island from a character calling himself Weyler; this said nothing of great significance but on examination there was discovered a cryptic message in invisible ink. The letter was later shown to have been bogus and had been concocted presumably with the intention of providing further evidence of Dreyfus's criminality. Coming as it did almost at the same time (4 September) as the letter in the *Daily Chronicle* about Dreyfus's alleged escape, it caused something of a stir and a Deputy (André Castellin) gave notice that he would be putting a question on the matter in the Chamber of Deputies to the Minister of War. Soon afterwards (10 September) an extraordinary article appeared in the newspaper *L'Eclair*, stating positively that Dreyfus had not been convicted on the *bordereau* alone and alleging that he had made some sort of confession. The article was unattributed but it seemed that it must have come from someone with inside information, and this was confirmed four days later when another article appeared from the same source which was more explicit. This gave details of the *bordereau* and stated for a fact that secret documents had been shown to the judges at Dreyfus's trial, and in addition quoted the letter from Schwartzkoppen to Panizzardi referring to 'ce canaille de D.', (see p. 11) but falsifying it so that the 'D' was transformed into 'Dreyfus'. Clearly such an article could only have come from someone in the SS, and there can be little doubt that it was from Major Henry who, it was becoming evident, was determined at all costs to maintain the conviction of Dreyfus. But to have revealed what he did was an act of gross folly as it exposed the illegality of Dreyfus's trial. This was not lost on Mathieu Dreyfus who, when the statement was not denied by the government, prompted Lucie to appeal to the Chamber of Deputies for a retrial of her husband. And further revelations were to be made. The detractors of Dreyfus, so it seemed, felt they had still not done enough to blacken his name, and so four weeks later (10 November) there was published in *Le Matin* a facsimile of the *bordereau*. Accompanying it in somewhat florid terms was an explanation for its publication:

> Dreyfus is indeed guilty of the greatest of all crimes. And in order to stop all pity for him, by leaving it no time to be born, no possibility

thereof, it is our duty to produce the material and undeniable proof of his misdeed ...

In order to achieve this work, both patriotic and health-giving, we publish the facsimile of the famous bordereau, written with Dreyfus's own hand. To anyone who has been able to compare the admitted writing of Dreyfus with that of the document which we here reproduce, it will be clear that it was his hand which traced these lines.

But it was not at all clear. If it had been *Le Matin* would surely have printed beside the facsimile a sample of Dreyfus's 'admitted' writing, but this it did not do. Who was responsible for publishing the facsimile is not known for certain, but the style of the explanation indicates Du Paty who was working in collusion with Henry at that time.* But whoever it was made a gross blunder which backfired completely – one of which Mathieu was to take full advantage.

In the autumn of 1896, as has been seen, Mathieu decided that there should be a change of strategy in his campaign. Until then he had been keeping a 'low profile', and had tried to keep the Dreyfus Case out of the limelight. But this had achieved nothing and he now felt the time had come to bring it out into the open. He was well aware what would be the consequences of this: the greater the publicity, the more violent and hysterical would become the opposition. He and other members of the Dreyfus family had already experienced much danger and abuse. Ever since Alfred's conviction (and before) they had been beset by hate mail and death threats, had been followed and harried by undercover agents and had often been obliged to assume false names and make frequent changes of lodgings. Insults from strangers were hard enough to bear, but friends too were keeping their distance, and they were aware of hostility even from other Jews, angry with them for stirring up anti-Semitic feelings. As Mathieu wrote at the time: 'No hand was held out to us; every door was obstinately closed. On the street people who knew us fled from us. We were the plague-stricken.'

Mathieu knew, then, what he was bringing on himself, but there was no holding him back. In November 1896 he cooperated with a young Jew, Bernard Lazare, in printing an impassioned pamphlet setting out the injustice of Dreyfus's conviction – the inadequate evidence, absence

---

* There is also a theory, unconfirmed, that the facsimile was provided to *Le Matin* by one of the handwriting experts who had managed to keep a copy and was seeking to make money out of it.

of motive, the untrue story of a confession and the use in the trial of secret documents not shown to the defence counsel. Three thousand copies were printed and circulated to Deputies and other eminent figures, but for the most part they fell on deaf ears. Brilliant and articulate as Lazare might be, he had the reputation of a wild extremist with anarchist sympathies,* and was therefore treated with some scepticism.

At first, as might be expected, Mathieu's more open campaign met with setbacks. On 18 November the Dreyfus Affair was brought up for the first time in the Chamber of Deputies in response to the 'interpellation' of André Castellin. This drew from the War Minister, Billot, a retired general turned politician, a stonewalling statement to the effect that Dreyfus had been lawfully convicted by a unanimous decision of a court martial, his appeal had been rejected also by a unanimous decision and that the matter was settled (*chose jugeé*) and could not be retracted. He also added that he personally had no doubts about Dreyfus's guilt. This was the position behind which the government was to shelter for as long as it could, and for the time being it was a strong one. Billot's statement was received with general approval, no one seeking to question him about the truth of the recent articles in *L'Eclair* and *Le Matin*. And soon afterwards Lucie's appeal for a retrial was rejected by a large majority.

---

* Anarchists were a terrorist group whose basic belief was the abolition of all forms of government. Their faith was in 'the unquenchable spirit of destruction and annihilation which is the perpetual revival of new life'.

Chapter X

*There is no disgrace in making good an error. But it would be an
irreparable disgrace to support an iniquitous act even though it had
not been deliberately perpetrated.*

(Pécaut)

*That is unimportant. That is not a consideration which should be
brought into the reckoning.*
(General Gonse to Colonel Picquart on the
innocence of Dreyfus)

The Dreyfus Case was not always to be treated in the Chamber of
Deputies with the complacency and consensus that was accorded to it
at first. In time it was to give rise to the most uproarious scenes with
members screaming insults at each other, coming to blows and demand-
ing satisfaction in duels. It was noticeable, however, that these clashes,
when they came, did not necessarily follow party lines. The Dreyfus
Affair cut across political parties just as it cut across families and
long-standing friendships.

Parties in the Chamber at that time were many and diverse. On the
extreme right were the Monarchists and Bonapartists who looked back
with longing on France's past glories under kings and emperors and
dreamed of reviving them. They regarded with scorn the Third Republic,
and, as they saw them, the weak and lacklustre governments it produced
and looked for a heroic, charismatic figure who would overthrow the
Republic, unite and inspire all Frenchmen and lead them to victory
over Germany and recover the lost provinces.* With their intense

---

* With these hopes in mind a number of right wing deputies had recently
  (1889) given their support to the attempted coup d'état of General
  Boulanger, a soldier of no great distinction who, for some reason, had
  attracted popularity and support. But it soon became evident that he was

devotion to the French army there was little likelihood of sympathy for Dreyfus from this quarter; to the contrary they tended to regard him as a tiresome Jewish troublemaker. This group was, however, dwindling and becoming increasingly insignificant. More important on the political Right were the supporters of the Roman Catholic Church, then locked in controversy with successive governments over the rights and status of the Church, and they were unwilling to be diverted from these delicate negotiations by the alleged wrongs of a Jewish army officer. The parties from which most support might have been expected were those on the Left – the Radicals and Socialists who regarded themselves as guardians of the French Revolution, the upholders of liberty and the rights of man, and who tended to look with suspicion on the army, fearful that it might become too powerful and pose a threat to the Republic and democracy. But their support too was not always dependable; in their hearts many left-wingers were strong patriots and did not want to see the army humiliated. Some Radicals, like Georges Clemenceau, gave strong support, but generally on the Left help was sporadic.

In the early years of the Third Republic there was little likelihood that any parties of the extreme Right or Left would ever form a government as they were always heavily outnumbered by the Republican Party of the Centre. Since 1871 it was from this group that all governments had been formed, but here too there was disunity, and administrations were forever changing: between 1881 and 1894 there had been no less than fifteen, all similar but with a new prime minister and with the rest of the pack shuffled. For the most part they consisted of safe, moderate men seeking, as one of them put it, to avoid both reaction and revolution, and to give France a period of peace and prosperity so that the newly established Republic could settle down and come to be regarded as France's natural form of government. They also sought to avoid all adventures abroad and scandal and turmoil at home, but this was not possible. The Boulanger Affair had caused great excitement, and there had been a number of major financial scandals (notably that of Panama), but the greatest uproar of all was yet to come.

When the Minister for War made his statement in the Chamber of Deputies it had shown that most people in the country, who gave the matter any thought, believed Dreyfus to have been fairly judged and found guilty. Eminent politicians and senior army officers had affirmed

---

(cont.) no heroic leader and the movement fizzled out. Subsequently he committed suicide in exile in Belgium on the grave of his mistress.

his guilt many times, and there was, as yet, no strong reason to disbelieve them. However, following the discoveries of Picquart, the articles in *L'Eclair* and the pamphlet of Bernard Lazare doubts were beginning to appear. Picquart continued to urge his superiors to come clean and admit that a mistake had been made – that Dreyfus was innocent and Esterhazy was guilty. He was sure that this was not only the most honourable course but also the most prudent. If they gave way now gracefully there would be some embarrassment but nowhere so much as there would be if the full facts became known later and they were compelled to yield under duress. But there were others who took a contrary view – that all that was necessary was for everyone concerned to keep silent and to suppress any evidence which might be compromising. This was the view of General Gonse, but it was to become apparent that there were others in the War Office, actually within the SS, who were prepared to go further and not only to suppress evidence but also to fabricate it.

Major (Lieutenant Colonel as he later became) Henry had come up the hard way in the army. Of peasant stock he had been commissioned from the ranks* and had seen action in Algeria and Indo-China where he had been wounded and decorated for valour. But he was not naturally suited for military intelligence; he spoke no foreign languages, was uneducated and lacking in finesse; he did have a degree of cunning and quickness of mind but was without profound judgement and the ability to foresee the consequences of his actions; he was also unscrupulous and mendacious. He had first been appointed to the SS in 1879, but the head of the department had dismissed him as being unsuitable for the type of work required. Due to the favour of a high-ranking officer, however, he was returned there in 1893 and became second-in-command to Colonel Sandherr, showing some aptitude for the more underhand aspects of espionage. It was he in 1894 who took delivery of the *bordereau* and soon afterwards became convinced of the guilt of Dreyfus; his lack of scruple became evident when at that time he secretly informed *La Libre Parole* of Dreyfus's arrest on a charge of treason, thus provoking a stream of anti-Jewish propaganda (see p. 15). From then on he and Du Paty de Clam led the investigation into Dreyfus and showed themselves determined to establish his guilt – despite the lack of hard evidence and the complete absence of motive. All Henry knew was that the high command wanted a conviction of someone, that Dreyfus aptly filled the bill and it was up to him to nail him. As has been seen at Dreyfus's

---

* During the Franco-Prussian War he held the rank of sergeant-major.

trial he had intervened dramatically to commit perjury, and this made it all the more necessary for him to obtain a conviction and see that it stuck. A retrial might well bring his perjury to light with fatal consequences.

When a few months after the Dreyfus trial the head of the SS, Colonel Sandherr, died suddenly, Henry might have expected to take his place, but he was passed over in favour of Picquart. If Henry felt any resentment at this he did not at first show it and relations between the two men were reasonably amicable, although there was not complete trust between them. In particular Henry regarded himself as the 'guardian' of the secret file on Dreyfus and did not show it to Picquart. It was only after a year, when Henry was away from the office for a long period, that it was brought to Picquart's attention.*

With the discovery of the *Petit Bleu* in March 1896 (see p. 90) and Picquart's growing conviction that Esterhazy was the real traitor, Henry became increasingly apprehensive: a retrial of Dreyfus was the last thing he wanted, both for his own sake and for that of the senior generals involved. He attempted to persuade Picquart to lay off: 'One doesn't make a nuisance of oneself to one's superiors,' he told him, but Picquart was not to be moved by such advice, and the relations between the two men became worse. At the same time Henry started resorting to dirty tricks. Although it cannot be proved it is likely that it was he who concocted the Weyler letter to Dreyfus on Devil's Island with a message in invisible ink. It is also probable that it was he who wrote or provided the information for the articles in *L'Eclair* and was responsible for the publication of the facsimile of the *bordereau* in *Le Matin*. What is known for certain is that from September 1896 he saw to the altering and forging of documents in the SS to implicate Dreyfus more fully. It has been seen (p. 92) how the reference to '*ce canaille de D*' in a letter from Schwartzkoppen to Panizzardi was changed from 'D' to Dreyfus in the *L'Eclair* article.† But more important than this was the document which came to be known as the *Faux Henry*. In this with the help of a skilled forger with a criminal record he took two letters from Panizzardi to

---

* Years later in court Henry accused Picquart of 'stealing' the file – an obvious absurdity as Picquart was his commanding officer.

† It has never been discovered for certain who was the real 'D'. It may have been a minor civil servant called Dubois, but it may have been another agent employed by Schwartzkoppen whose name did not necessarily have to begin with D.

Schwartzkoppen, which had come into the possession of the SS, and joined them together so that there was an empty space between them into which in the forged handwriting of Panizzardi was added a highly incriminating passage:

> I have read that a deputy is going to interpellate about Dreyfus. If new explanations are required at Rome, I shall say I have never had relations with this Jew. You understand. If you are asked, say the same thing, for no one must ever know what happened with him.

The forgery was carried out skilfully, but not skilfully enough; the papers joined together, although similar, were not identical, and two years later this was detected. In the meanwhile, however, the *Faux Henry* served its purpose all too well; it was shown to senior officers and the Minister for War who were confirmed in their belief that Dreyfus was guilty. At the same time Henry instigated a clandestine campaign against Picquart; he told the Chiefs of Staff that he had become obsessed with the Dreyfus Case and was neglecting his other duties; and with great audacity hinted that it was Picquart who was responsible for the articles in *L'Eclair* and the facsimile of the *bordereau* in *Le Matin*. Here too at first he had success; on 14 November 1896 the Chiefs of Staff decided that Picquart must go. They thought it would attract less attention if he were to be suspended from his duties rather than dismissed, so some mission was concocted for him on the German frontier and he was despatched there at a moment's notice. To extend his absence from Paris another mission was found for him on the Tunisian border (from which it was hoped, maybe, he would not return). With the departure of Picquart, Henry might seem to be triumphant, but he continued with his deceptions and in time these became so complex that he became enmeshed in them.*

Picquart was, of course, well aware of what was going on; he was being kept out of the way; more than that his life was in danger. And so in April 1897 he drew up a full statement of all he knew about the Dreyfus Affair with an instruction that it was to be delivered to the

---

* Among, his more improbable inventions were letters from Dreyfus to the Kaiser as well as a copy of the *Bordereau* with annotations by the Kaiser. These were said to have been photographs of documents stolen from the German embassy and then returned there. Although mentioned, they have never been discovered and it is possible Henry destroyed them when he realized he had gone too far.

President of the Republic in the event of his death. And soon afterwards, while on leave in Paris, he confided all to his lawyer and lifelong friend, Louis Leblois, leaving it to his discretion how he would make use of this information, but binding him to total secrecy as to its source. Revelation of this would mean his certain ruin or even death.

In order to maintain the case against Dreyfus it was necessary for Henry to cover up as much as possible for Esterhazy. As well as suppressing and distorting facts it was imperative that Esterhazy should be kept under some sort of control. All too easily he might do something insane. Henry was under no illusions as to Esterhazy's character. He had a police report on him which read: 'an adventurer and blackguard, a cheat, a swindler, a pimp, a pillar of the brothel and the bawdy house and he sweats vice, wickedness and treason'. It was also known that he was a compulsive gambler, permanently in debt and prepared to do anything for money. In the autumn of 1896 his situation was particularly desperate: he had been paid off by Schwartzkoppen and put on half pay by the French army due to 'temporary infirmities'. He had separated from his wife, most of whose money he had squandered and was being put up in the house of a common prostitute (known as 'Four-fingered Margaret'). Henry's great fear was that in such straits he would be driven to some reckless action; as the evidence against him mounted he might well commit suicide or flee the country, both of which would be taken as signs of guilt, and so lead to further pressure for a retrial of Dreyfus. Henry decided, therefore, that he must make contact with him and keep him as stable as possible; he should be warned of the dangers of his position but at the same time be assured that, provided he obeyed instructions, he would have the protection of the high command.

The events that ensued were past belief, more bizarre than any musical comedy. To establish contact Henry contrived that Du Paty (with false beard) and Gribelin, another member of SS, (with dark glasses) should meet him at a secret rendezvous in a deserted park after dark. A message summoning him there was conveyed to Esterhazy who immediately became panic-stricken. What happened next was later told by Panizzardi to Carlos Blacker (see p. 4) who described it vividly in a memorandum he wrote on the Dreyfus Affair:

> On October 23rd at about 3 in the afternoon Esterhazy suddenly appeared in Schwartzkoppen's rooms. He was livid, haggard and trembling with terror. He threw himself on a sofa, asked for brandy, and said that he had been found out. He rolled out imprecations of God, humanity and

himself and behaved like a creature from hell at bay.

Schwartzkoppen, who had not seen him since the publication of the *bordereau* in *Le Matin* in November of the preceding year, was dumb-founded. He asked what on earth had brought him to Paris, why he came to him again, and to steady him gave him brandy.

As soon as Esterhazy had recovered some composure he told Schwartzk-oppen that, being in the country, he had the day before received an anonymous letter warning him that he was going to be denounced as being the author of the *bordereau*, and urging him to come to Paris in order to be prepared to meet the charge. He said that on that very morning someone had called on him making a mysterious appointment for six o'clock at the Parc Montsouris and giving him a little slip of paper on which the hour and place were written down; this he showed to Schwartzkoppen. 'But,' he added, 'how do I know that this is not an ambush, and while I am speaking to some person in that remote place in the dark, other men do not come up from behind and seize me? You must help me out of the difficulty,' he said to Schwartzkoppen. 'You must go to the Dreyfus family and tell them that the *bordereau* was written by Dreyfus, that he was your informant and secret agent, and that it is futile trying to make anyone else responsible for the *bordereau*.'

Schwartzkoppen at this only shook his head, whereupon Esterhazy, suddenly pulling out a revolver, covered Schwartzkoppen saying: 'Unless you give me your word that you will do as I tell you, I will blow your brains out and mine afterwards.'

Schwartzkoppen with complete composure said: 'You tell me that you have an appointment and you fear an ambush. Since, however, you are so well armed, it will be more opportune for you to commence firing when you are quite convinced that you are lost. It may, however,' he added, 'be quite the contrary and you may find some friend or protector. Go there and come here afterwards to tell me the result.'

This quite disarmed Esterhazy and he said he would follow this advice. Then, as if nothing unusual had happened, he commenced to speak with his usual vivacity and fervour on the old theme of the stupidity and villainy of French officers, saying that anything might be expected of them.

He left at 4 – at 8 he returned.

This time he was radiant and almost beside himself with joy. 'I am protected,' he said. 'I hold them now. They are afraid of me. I have all those brutes in my hand. I can now sleep on both ears. They dare not touch me.' He could hardly contain himself with high spirits and added:

'I always told you they were a pack of cowards and scoundrels, and now you will see to what lengths they will go to protect me.'

He told him about the meeting; about the false beards and spectacles etc. He knew Paty du Clam from the first, though he did not recognise Gribelin and Henry who held themselves at a distance, Henry remaining in the cab in the dark.

He said that Paty du Clam had told him that he had nothing to fear, for even if Scheurer-Kestner or Picquart or Mathieu Dreyfus denounced him, the Etat Major (high command) would protect him through thick and through thin, and that he must avoid doing anything rash, and must do just as he was told for he would then be perfectly safe. He was assured that protection came from the highest quarters and that all would be well.

To this Schwartzkoppen said 'Well I congratulate you for you must consider yourself very lucky. As it is, though, I do not think there is any necessity for you to come here again. Adieu, Monsieur, *et portez-vous bien!*'

It was, of course, expecting too much that Esterhazy would do nothing rash and would behave calmly and sanely. Only two weeks later he was embarking on a dirty tricks campaign against Picquart, then in Tunisia. For this he emulated the tactic of whoever it was who wrote the 'Weyler' letter to Dreyfus (see p. 92) – that is of sending him conspiratorial communications which he knew would be censored and so fall into the hands of army intelligence. On 10 November (1897) he wrote him an anonymous letter which contained the words: 'Take care. Whole work discovered. Withdraw quietly. Write nothing.' And on the same day he sent two telegrams in similar vein one signed 'Speranza' and the other 'Blanche'. Nonsense as these were, Picquart could not afford to ignore them as he knew quite well what

Commandant Ferdinand Esterhazy

lay behind them. He reported them to the high command and they were not used in the proceedings which were later taken against him.

At the same time Esterhazy was active in another quarter, pulling every string to obtain a post in army intelligence, and writing menacing letters to the French President (Félix Faure) saying that he had in his possession a vitally important document, given to him by a veiled lady who had taken it from Picquart who in turn had stolen it from a foreign embassy, and if this document were ever to be published it would bring great humiliation to France and might cause a European war. Furthermore he would publish it unless he was given justice and full support by the French Government. Incredible as this braggadocio might be, even more incredible was it that President Faure took it seriously and ordered an enquiry to be set up into Esterhazy and all his doings. But at that time he was coming under pressure from another quarter.

At the end of 1896 Mathieu Dreyfus was still unaware of the machinations that were taking place in the War Office; of Picquart, Henry, the *Petit Bleu*, the *Faux Henry*, even of Esterhazy he knew nothing. When, out of the blue, in November 1896, the facsimile of the *bordereau* appeared in *Le Matin* he had been at first amazed and then full of hope. Surely it would be seen now that the handwriting was not that of his brother? And his first action was to employ a number of handwriting experts, French and foreign, to testify to the fact. He was also hopeful that someone might recognize the handwriting, but this was not to happen at once. For the time being all he could do was to continue his efforts to win support for his brother's retrial and in this he was making progress. As a result of the pamphlet of Bernard Lazare a powerful voice in the Chamber of Deputies had been won over, that of Joseph Reinach, a French Jew with a reputation for fiery eloquence and patriotism; he became convinced that in the Dreyfus trial there had been a flagrant abuse of individual rights and that the honour of the Third Republic was at stake to see that this should not be covered up. Like Mathieu he felt that, if the campaign for a retrial was to succeed, it was necessary to win support from people in high places, and there was one man in particular of whom he had great hopes.

Auguste Scheurer-Kestner was vice-president of the Senate (upper house), an elder statesman with a distinguished record who commanded great respect from men of all parties for his integrity and fairness of judgement. He had already been approached by Mathieu and had been greatly disturbed by what he had told him. He had then made enquiries in government circles about Dreyfus and had been urged to keep clear of the matter as there was no doubt that Dreyfus was guilty and the matter was *chose jugée*. He might have left the matter at that but for a chance meeting with Louis Leblois, the lawyer to whom Picquart had told all he knew. On the spur of the moment, it would seem, Leblois had told Kestner all that Picquart had told him on the understanding that he made cautious use of the information and bound himself never to reveal Picquart as being its source. This had caused Kestner deep unease. It seemed to him almost certain that an injustice had been done and was being covered up, that Dreyfus was innocent and the guilty man was at liberty and unpunished. But what was he to do? His hands were tied by his promise not to reveal the name of Picquart. Also he had a deep respect for the French army and hated the idea of causing it disgrace. For the time being he kept the information to himself, but he did have an interview with the War Minister and urged him to set up an enquiry; but Billot stuck to the usual government line of the certainty of Dreyfus's guilt and the matter being closed. Yet he also admitted that secret papers had been shown to the judges at the trial. Damaging as was this admission Kestner felt that for the present he could do no more than let it be known generally that he had become convinced of Dreyfus's innocence, which promptly drew on him furious and obscene abuse from *La Libre Parole* and other anti-Semitic newspapers.

In the autumn of 1897 Mathieu's campaign received another boost when the formidable Radical deputy, Georges Clemencau was won over to the cause. Clemencau had recently lost his seat in the Chamber and was turning to journalism, and in the newly founded newspaper, *L'Aurore*, was thundering out anti-government articles which included ones on Dreyfus. But the great breakthrough for Mathieu came in November 1897. He had organized the distribution in Paris of the facsimile of the *bordereau*, and almost exactly a year after its publication in *Le Matin* it fell into the hands of a banker, M. Castro who had had business dealings with Esterhazy and recognized his handwriting. He then made his discovery known to Mathieu who, in a state of some excitement, broke the news to Scheurer-Kestner. He, of course, already knew about Esterhazy from Leblois but had been keeping his promise to say nothing. However, now that the secret was out, he felt liberated, confirmed the facts about Esterhazy and advised Mathieu to write at once to the War Minister, charging Esterhazy with being the author of the *bordereau*.

The government was now beset on all sides. At the same time a letter appeared in *Figaro* from someone calling himself 'Vidi' who clearly had inside information making allusions not only to the secret file but also to 'the real traitor' who was not named but referred to as 'a titled officer in garrison not far from Paris, well known in the capital'. To top it all mention was also made of forged documents emanating from the Statistical Section. It later became known that this letter came from a deputy, Arène, but the source of his information has not been discovered. Inevitably it caused great excitement and was immediately answered by a letter in *La Libre Parole* signed 'Dixi' which was brought to the newspaper by Esterhazy but was probably written by Henry. This accused a high-ranking officer in the War Office referred to as 'XY' but clearly meaning Picquart, of being in league with a Jewish syndicate with the object of incriminating an 'innocent but somewhat wild officer'. It also stated that the case against Dreyfus rested not only on the *bordereau* but on a hundred other documents proving his guilt. To add to the general bewilderment Schwartzkoppen and Panizzardi took the occasion to state again that they had never had any dealings with Dreyfus.

In the midst of this turmoil the government of Félix-Jules Meline attempted to keep aloof, still maintaining that the judgement against Dreyfus was inviolate and could not be retracted and emphasizing strongly that any charges that might be brought against Esterhazy were completely separate and unconnected. The War Office, however, was becoming seriously alarmed by the ever more deranged behaviour of Esterhazy who was still threatening to reveal the document from the veiled lady and, in desperate need of money, was bombarding newspaper editors with fantastic and libellous articles. Something had to be done to calm him down and the War Office decided that the best course of action was to set up an enquiry into his conduct, at the same time letting him know that he had nothing to fear from it and that it was designed only to clear his name. The enquiry was entrusted to General de Pellieux, the youngest general in the army, to whom it was made clear what was expected of him. It lasted three days in the course of which the only matter of significance to emerge was that Kestner for the first time mentioned Picquart by name as being the source of his information, and Leblois revealed further information given him by Picquart which resulted later in the latter being convicted of disclosing secret military information. De Pellieux's report was predictable enough: no charges against Esterhazy had been substantiated whereas blame was to be attached to Picquart for indiscretion. At the time Picquart was still in Tunisia, but he was ordered back to Paris to face a reopened enquiry in which de Pellieux treated him with great harshness, and Henry, ever ready to bear false witness, testified that he had seen him and Leblois in the Statistical Section with secret documents in front of them.

It seemed, then, that the enquiry was achieving its object of white-washing Esterhazy, but suddenly there came a most embarrassing development. A bundle of letters written by Esterhazy to his one-time mistress, a Madame de Boulancy, was delivered to Scheurer-Kestner. These were highly compromising, showing a bitter contempt for the French army and the French people. Top-ranking French officers were described as 'ignorant poltroons who were not worth the cartridges to kill them'. And of Frenchmen he wrote: 'If I were told this evening that I could be killed tomorrow while putting Frenchmen to the sword as a Captain of Uhlans (a body of German cavalry), I should be perfectly happy ... I would not hurt a dog, but I would with pleasure have a hundred thousand Frenchmen put to death.' Nothing could be more explosive. Scheurer-Kestner took the letters to De Pellieux who dis-missed them as a fraud. But then some of them were published in *Figaro* side by side with a facsimile of the *bordereau* so that the handwriting could be compared. It seemed that Esterhazy's name must be for ever blackened, but, incredibly, he was to survive. He claimed at once that they were forgeries, and *La Libre Parole* declared that they were all part of a Jewish plot to make Esterhazy a martyr. And De Pellieux continued to treat them as of no importance. He had just been shown the *Faux Henry* which had convinced him of Dreyfus's guilt, and he was now prepared to go to any lengths to exonerate Esterhazy. In his report he stated that it was impossible to compare Esterhazy's handwriting with a mere facsimile, and when it was pointed out to him that it could be compared with the original, which was in the War Office, he said that use could not be made of this as the matter had been settled finally at Dreyfus's court martial.

Esterhazy had, however, been greatly alarmed by the de Boulancy letters, and had had thoughts of fleeing abroad which caused the government anxiety as it would have been tantamount to an admission of his guilt. The government also had fears that Esterhazy would bring a libel action against Mathieu Dreyfus which would have to be tried in a civil court where embarrassing and discreditable matters might be brought to light which might lead to legal action against senior officers. It seemed that further action was needed to calm Esterhazy down, and it was decided that a more exhaustive enquiry was needed; this time he would appear before a court martial which he himself would request in order to clear his name. Once again it was conveyed to him that he had nothing to fear provided be cooperated. To this Esterhazy agreed and on 10 January 1898 the court martial began its proceedings.

As before the judges were made aware of the verdict that was expected from them and after two days and only a semblance of a trial Esterhazy was acquitted of all charges and emerged from the court a popular hero, his actions vindicated and his honour intact. At the same time Picquart, who had tried to uphold the truth and had advocated the honourable course, was censored for divulging military information and put under arrest.

Once again it appeared that the government had been successful in its efforts to cover up for Esterhazy and maintain the conviction of Dreyfus. In the Chamber of Deputies and in the Senate it was supported by large majorities, and its great hope now was that the Dreyfus Affair would be heard of no more.

Chapter XI

Yesterday the French army won its first victory since its defeat in 1870–71 on the day after the conviction of Zola.
(Berliner Tageblatt)

Before all the honour of the army.
(Colonel Henry)

Your unlucky forgery will be acclaimed as your finest deed of war.
(Tribute to Henry)

Only two days after the acquittal of Esterhazy any hope the government had that the Dreyfus Affair had been laid to rest were shattered when the most powerful writer in France entered the fray and brought the matter to life in a way that it had never been before.

Since his meeting with Oscar Wilde in 1891 (see p. 3) Emile Zola had continued to pour out novels of great length and intensity. As has been seen these were not universally admired, many people regarding them as overlong, in bad taste and at times obscene. But they were widely read and in 1898 Zola was at the height of his powers. He had become interested in Dreyfus in the previous year and had been deeply shocked by what he had learned. In newspaper articles in December 1897 he had lavished praise on Scheurer-Kestner ('the most open, the most upright of lives, a life of crystal, not a blemish there, not the slightest weakness') while at the same time pouring bitter scorn on the idea promoted by anti-Semites of a sinister 'syndicate' bent on exonerating Dreyfus and bringing disgrace to the army:

> The syndicate? Yes, there is a syndicate. Men of good will, of truth and equity, in all quarters of the globe, working at a distance from and unknown to one another ... A syndicate to cure public opinion of the madness into which it has been driven by the shameless press ... a

syndicate to demonstrate that all judicial errors are rectifiable, a syndicate to conduct a campaign so that the truth may be made known, so that justice may be done in spite of all obstacles, even if it is necessary to fight for years. Yes, I am, indeed, a member of this syndicate as I hope all honest men in France intend to be.

These were ringing words but at the time they made no great impact,

Emile Zola

and it was borne in on Zola that when he next raised his voice on the subject it must be in stronger and more dramatic tones. An occasion for this arose a few weeks later with the court martial and acquittal of Esterhazy which he regarded as a shameless cover-up and an insult to justice. He was in no doubt that he must make a protest and in such terms that it could not be ignored. And so when it came it was passionate and libellous. It took the form of an open letter to the President of the Republic in the newspaper *L'Aurore* under the flaming headline of *J'ACCUSE*.

In this historic letter Zola showed himself to be well informed on every aspect of the Dreyfus Affair. He stated bluntly that the Esterhazy court martial had been rigged and that the judges, on orders from above, had given a false verdict and deliberately acquitted a guilty man. He then inveighed against the indictment of Dreyfus, saying that it rested on the *bordereau* alone on which experts had disagreed. As for the secret document which could not be revealed because it might cause a European war, he flatly denied that it existed. It was a monstrous iniquity that anyone should be condemned on such a charge, and he defied any honest man 'to read it without being filled with indignation and exclaiming in horror at the thought of the unbounded sufferings of Dreyfus on Devil's Island for a crime he did not commit'. The courts martial of Dreyfus and Esterhazy had resulted in false judgements which had stained the honour of the army, which he felt keenly as he had nothing but 'tenderness and respect' for the army, but this did not mean that he wanted to see it become a law unto itself and perhaps one day the master of the country. And could there be any doubt that the honour of the army was being better upheld by such men as Picquart and Scheurer-Kestner who were insisting on truth and justice rather than by those who were contriving an ignominious cover-up? And then came a string of personal accusations:

'I accuse Lieutenant-Colonel du Paty, a diabolical man with an extraordinary and demented imagination, of having been the instrument of the judicial error – an unconscious instrument, I am willing to believe – and of having subsequently defended his fatal deed, for the past three years by the most outrageous and wicked plots.'

'I accuse General Mercier of having been a party, through weakness in any case, to one of the greatest iniquities of the century.'

'I accuse General Billot of having had in his hands the sure proofs of the innocence of Dreyfus and of having suppressed them.'

'I accuse General de Boisdeffre and General Gonse of being parties to the same crime.'

'I accuse General de Pellieux and Major Ravary [prosecutor in the Esterhazy trial] of having conducted a villainous inquiry, by which I mean an inquiry of the most monstrous partiality, the report of which has afforded us an imperishable monument of naive audacity.'

'I accuse the three handwriting experts of having made untrue and fraudulent reports, unless a medical examination should prove them to be stricken with an affliction of the sight and judgement.'

'I accuse the officials of the Ministry of War of having conducted in the press an abominable campaign in order to lead the public astray and cover themselves.'

'Finally I accuse the first court-martial of having violated justice by condemning an accused man on a document which was kept secret, and the second court-martial of having, by order, sanctioned this illegality, and of having in its turn, committed the juridical crime of deliberately acquitting a guilty man.'

This was momentous language and Zola was well aware of what would be the consequences of it: he would be put on trial, found guilty of libel and be imprisoned. But so be it. If this was the only way for the truth to be made known, let it happen. 'Let them dare arraign me before the Court of Assizes and let the case be heard in the open. I am waiting.' There are cynics who have questioned Zola's motives in doing what he did, saying that what he did for Dreyfus was as nothing to what Dreyfus did for him. But this does not stand up. Zola had nothing to gain by his action. He already had fame and fortune and did not need publicity. He can only have been impelled by a burning hatred of injustice which would not allow him to remain silent.

The government's first reaction to Zola's outburst was to take no action and to dismiss it with contemptuous silence. The Prime Minister, Méline, knew that Zola was certainly guilty of libel, but it would be playing his game to bring a charge against him in a civil court where embarrassing and even incriminating matters might be brought to light. But he found that it was impossible to stand aside. The honour of the army had been impugned and he was expected to avenge it. In the Chamber of Deputies anger was so great that action had to be taken. And so on 18 January the government brought a prosecution for libel against Zola, but at the same time it sought to limit its scope by confining it to Zola's defamation of the Esterhazy court martial – that the judges had acquitted a criminal they knew to be guilty on orders from senior officers. His libels of individual officers were to be ignored lest awkward questions be asked about Dreyfus and Esterhazy.

Zola's defence counsel, Fernand Labori, wanted to call some two hundred witnesses of which the most important was Picquart who knew of all the behind-the-scenes goings on in the War Office and was known to believe in the innocence of Dreyfus. The government was aware of the danger to its case from Picquart and before the trial began did what it could to damage his reputation. On 1 February he was charged with disclosing secret military information and brought before a court martial. Strictly speaking this should have been before officers of the regiment in which he was serving, but to be sure of getting the verdict it wanted the government brought him before a court nominated by itself which in due course pronounced that Lieutenant Colonel Picquart had 'committed a gross offence while on duty' for which he was liable to be cashiered. The government, however, delayed carrying out this sentence in the hope that Picquart, under such a threat, would follow the official line in giving evidence at Zola's trial. But Picquart was not to be silenced in this way and answered all questions put to him fully and candidly. He was subjected to a rigorous cross-examination by Henry who became enraged at not being able to shake him and at one point accused him of being a liar. At this Picquart stiffened and it looked as if the two officers might come to blows, but the President of the Court made an emollient intervention and the moment passed (although subsequently the two men fought a duel in which Henry was slightly wounded and had to go to hospital where he was visited by most senior army officers).

Of the other witnesses sought by the defence the military officers who had been concerned in the cover-up – Mercier, Boisdeffre, Gonse, du Paty, Henry – at first refused to appear, but when ordered to do so by the Court, came into the witness box and refused to answer any question they found compromising, and in this they were supported by the judge of the Assize Court, Delegorgue, who showed himself to be a pawn of the government, disallowing any questions that had any bearing on Dreyfus or Esterhazy and clamping down instantly on any reference to a secret dossier on Dreyfus. He even refused to allow Scheurer-Kestner to read in court the correspondence between Gonse and Picquart, although this had just been published by *Le Siècle* on its front page. The witness with most to hide was Henry, and Labori was ready with some searching questions for him, but he avoided these by pleading a bout of fever which made him confused ('I have eighteen campaigns behind me and have every right to have a touch of fever'). When military officers gave evidence it was noticeable that they were given great freedom to say what they liked in contrast to other witnesses, including a former President of the Republic and a Vice-President of the Senate, who were constantly checked and silenced.

By the end of the trial the pressure on the jury had become intense; they had been made to realize that on their verdict depended the well-being of the army and the future safety of the country. It was left to the chief of staff, Boisdeffre, to employ the ultimate blackmail:

> You, gentlemen, are the jury; you are the nation. If the nation has no confidence in its Army's leaders, in those responsible for the national defence, they are ready to leave the heavy task to others. You have only to speak. I will say nothing more. I ask leave to withdraw.

In face of such a terrible threat – in effect a threat of strike action on the part of the General Staff – what could the unfortunate jurymen do? These were small tradesmen and petits bourgeois who were overwhelmed at the thought of being the arbiters of their country's fate. Since the beginning of the trial they had been subjected to every kind of pressure; their names and addresses had been published in the press and it was made clear that an acquittal of Zola would mean that they had been bought by the 'syndicate'. Every day large crowds, for the most part professional troublemakers whipped up by the anti-Dreyfusards, had gathered outside the courthouse, screaming anti-Jewish slogans and crude abuse of anyone who had given Zola support. The situation confronting the jurymen was a stark one: to acquit Zola and bring on themselves great odium and danger, or convict him and live with the charge that they had participated in a government fraud and condemned an innocent and, as they may well have thought, heroic man.

It seems that there was some hesitation and disagreement among them, but in the end they brought in a unanimous verdict of guilty. The court then imposed the maximum penalty of one year's imprisonment and a fine of 3,000 francs. This did not, however, conclude the matter as Zola's counsel immediately lodged an appeal, and a higher court decided that the trial had been illegal as an indictment for libel could be made only by the parties libelled – in this case the judges of the court martial. And so it was necessary for a second trial to be held three months later which resulted in the same verdict and the same sentence, but before this Zola had yielded to the urgent entreaties of his friends and taken refuge abroad; this he did with reluctance as he was bent on martyrdom, but he was persuaded that it was essential that he stay out of prison so that he would be available if there were developments in the Dreyfus Case. And so he spent the next months in England under the name of Doctor Pascal.

Once again it seemed that the government had triumphed: Zola had been convicted, the honour of the army had been upheld and the case against Dreyfus remained intact. In the Chamber of Deputies the government was supported in its handling of the matter by a large majority. But still the matter would not go away. The government's ham-handed methods both in the Esterhazy court martial and in the trial of Zola had caused deep unease in some quarters; more and more people were realizing that something shameful had occurred and was being covered up. And Zola's dramatic outburst had for ever changed the nature of the Dreyfus Case. No longer would it be a matter of discreet and cautious negotiations between a few people. From now on it would be a burning national issue. Passions were aroused which were to divide families and set friend against friend. In Paris angry mobs confronted each other and anti-Semitism reached a pitch equal to that in Nazi Germany thirty years later.*

On the one side in this conflict were the army, most of the Roman Catholic Church and those natural backers of the 'establishment' – fiercely patriotic but not deep thinking. They believed passionately that the honour and prestige of the army was paramount – especially with a European war in the offing – and compared with this the fate of an obscure officer, who was also a Jew, was of minor importance. They stated openly that in certain circumstances reasons of state should override personal rights and that social solidarity was of greater importance than justice to an individual. Ranged against them were those who believed equally passionately that in a democratic republic rights of the citizen were of essence and any government abusing them was fatally flawed and did not deserve to survive. Was not this what the French Revolution had been all about? Had not Frenchmen in 1789 proclaimed to the world freedom and justice for all? And were these ideals now to be set aside for reasons of political expediency? On this side were many intellectuals, writers (including Marcel Proust and Anatole France) and artists (including Monet and Pissarro); but there were also many more humble people who dared to stand up and be counted, and in doing so took great risks – teachers who might lose there jobs, small tradesmen who might be boycotted by their customers

---

* Except, of course, there were no death camps.

Les dîners : « A table, à Paris comme à la campagne, on ne parlait plus que de l'" Affaire" et bien heureux quand on ne se disputait pas... »

The Dinner Party
(Before and after talking of the Dreyfus Affair)

and numerous citizens who had the courage of their convictions and risked being threatened and set upon by raging mobs.*

With the Dreyfus Case being set ablaze by the intervention of Zola it was to be expected that the flames would spread to the outside world. The leaders of the French Revolution had insisted that liberty and equality were not confined by national borders and were for all nations. A hundred years later it was shown that this lesson had been learned and in many parts of the world passions were aroused by the fates of Dreyfus and Zola. Foreign newspapers, no doubt with some relish, inveighed against the French Government for dishonouring the principles Frenchmen had once championed so strongly. And in no country were the protests more vehement than in England. 'M. Zola's real offence,' thundered The Times, 'is that he has dared to stand up for truth and civil liberty at a moment when many saw the peril but no other was ready to brave the extremity of personal danger in order to aid in averting it. The civil trial, like the military ones, degenerated into a travesty of justice and the court ... administering the civil law was absolutely dominated by the military element and by military ideas as the courts martial themselves. That is the appalling outcome of the whole affair which must today cause the profoundest misgivings among all Frenchmen capable of serious reflections.' While the Daily Mail, then the leading organ of the popular press, declared: 'France drops out of the list of civilised countries until she awakens to the gross enormity of this judicial farce.' In America too voices were raised. Mark Twain likened the heroism of Zola to that of Joan of Arc, and the New York Journal of Commerce stated: 'The French Republic cannot and should not continue if a military caste, a few Jew haters or a mob of students can bring her to a state of hysteria which drives her to trample the liberty of her citizens underfoot.' In Germany there were outcries in the press and great concern and embarrassment in government circles, as it was a German agent who had been at the centre of the affair. Just before Zola's trial the German Foreign Minister, von Bülow, repeated what had been said before 'in the most formal and categorical terms that there had never been any relation or connection of any kind whatever between Dreyfus and any German agent of any sort. With regard to Esterhazy von Bülow was less emphatic, using a different form of words

---

* It seems to have been the case, and was remarked on by Clemencau, that Dreyfusards were drawn mainly from the middle and lower-middle classes. The working class seemed generally unconcerned.

and pouring scorn on the *bordereau*, saying that 'the tale of a letter found in a wastepaper basket would look well between the covers of a novel.' But, as before, the only people in France who believed him were those who wanted to believe him, the rest assumed he was only protecting his agents. And the government was quick to resent anything in the nature of foreign interference. 'We are,' declared the war minister, 'master in our own house, and will deal with our own affairs as we see fit.' In the Chamber of Deputies this was received with thunderous applause from all sides.

In the Dreyfus Case, as it unfolded, the role of the French army is not easy to defend, but it can be exaggerated and distorted. It is certain that several officers, including some very senior ones, connived at a cover-up and were ready to pervert the course of justice; but in doing so their motives, though mistaken and unworthy, were not wholly base. In acting as they did they were not out to save their own skins but those of others, particularly of senior officers; their fundamental duty, as they saw it, was to preserve the honour of the French army. To army officers (and none more so than Alfred Dreyfus himself) the traditions, disciplines and uniforms of the French army were a religion. Disloyalty was the ultimate sin, and their immediate reaction when confronted with hostility or any kind of intrusion from outside was to close ranks and support blindly their fellow officers. In the Dreyfus Case the correct action, of course, would have been, as Picquart recommended, to admit that a mistake had occurred and to give an assurance that amends would be made, in which case the matter would have blown over comparatively quickly. But instead the Army High Command stuck to its guns and became more and more entangled. Some officers may have believed genuinely that Dreyfus was guilty; others may have had doubts but suppressed them and blinded themselves to facts; while a few were prepared to go to any extremes to avoid a climb-down. One thing certain is that the Dreyfus Affair was not, as some alleged, part of a concerted plot to overturn the Third Republic and replace it with military rule. It was the case that most army officers had little love for Republican government and would have dearly loved a king or emperor; but basically the army was non-political and had no wish for a confrontation between Army and Nation. But it did seek to regulate its own affairs and to be master in its own house and to resist strongly any attempts at interference from outside.

Others besides the army were not seen in their best light in the Dreyfus Affair. Since the French Revolution relations between governments and the Roman Catholic Church had been sensitive and contentious. The clergy had been closely associated with the monarchy and were deeply distrusted by many Republicans and Socialists. Since 1892 Pope Leo XIII had been trying to establish a sounder relationship with governments of the day by a *Ralliement* of sympathetic people, but this had had a mixed response; the situation was still delicate and he had no wish to put further strain on it by taking sides over Dreyfus. And so on the great principle that was at stake between individual rights and political expediency the hierarchy of the Church either held aloof or gave support to the anti-Dreyfusards.

On the political scene few emerged with credit. After Zola's conviction, the government was supported in the Chamber of Deputies by a large majority which included Radicals and Socialists who might have been expected to be strong in their support of individual rights. But only the Socialist leader, Jean Jaurès, and a few others spoke out about the threat of military law overriding civil law and the danger to a Republic of an over-powerful army. For the wrongs of Dreyfus, a well-to-do Jewish officer, they found it hard to sympathize; he was hardly an archetypal working-class hero; if he had been impoverished and under-privileged it might have been different, but as it was they were ready to use him as a whip with which to chastise the government and as an opportunity to rant against 'the Jesuitical-militaristic cabals', but their support for him was seldom wholehearted.

After the conviction of Zola there was a succession of Republican governments whose handling of the Dreyfus Affair brought them little credit. That of Méline lasted only a few more months during which there were some discreditable incidents, notably the ousting of Scheur-er-Kestner from the vice-presidency of the Senate and the persecution of Picquart – placed on half pay after unwarrantable investigations into his private life and the spreading of untruthful rumours about a close friendship with Schwartzkoppen. There was also the suspicious incident of the suicide of Lemercier-Picard, the criminal forger who had been employed by Henry to do his dirty work for him. In March 1898 he was found hanged in his lodging; although suicide was pronounced by the police there were those who thought that he had been 'taken out' as a potentially dangerous witness. On the matter of Dreyfus, Méline and his War Minister, Billot, continued to maintain the same position as before – that the government could not interfere with the verdict of a court martial subsequently confirmed by the Court of Appeal.

But the case against Dreyfus was crumbling. A vitally important development was the publication in *Le Siècle* of what came to be known as 'Letter from a Diplomat'. This emanated from Berne and was signed only by the pseudonym 'Diplomat'. The letter and the circumstances surrounding it will be examined in detail in a later chapter. Here it will be said only that the writer appeared to be a confidant of Schwartz-koppen and told of his dealings with Esterhazy – the first time these had been mentioned in public. At the time it caused a furious outburst from the anti-Dreyfusards and a counter-reaction from their opponents but, surprisingly, in the general election which was held a month later the Dreyfus Case was not an issue between the parties. The election brought no great surprises but it did lead to the resignation of the Méline government and its replacement by another Republican government under Henri Brisson in which the dominant character was Godefroy Cavaignac. Cavaignac was a civilian but an ardent supporter of the army and totally convinced of the guilt of Dreyfus; he had been strongly critical of his predecessor, Billot, for his handling of the Affair. More was needed, he had declared, than just saying that the matter was closed and could not be touched. Why did Billot not prove Dreyfus's guilt beyond doubt by publishing some of the documents from the Dreyfus dossier, in particular the confession he was alleged to have made on the day of his degradation? Now that he himself was War Minister he found himself hoist with his own petard. He discovered that the evidence of Dreyfus's confession was, to say the least, insubstantial. It seems to have originated with gossip in *Le Moulin Rouge* when an officer who had accompanied Dreyfus to his degradation ceremony, Lebrun-Renault, talked loosely of Dreyfus having confessed his guilt to him. This was spread abroad and a few days later the words alleged to have been used appeared in *Le Temps*.

> I am innocent. If I have given documents to the foreigners, it was only as a bait to tempt them into giving up more important ones. In three years the truth will be known, and the Minister of War himself will take up my cause.

Subsequently, however, Lebrun-Renault's memory proved uncertain, at one time being clear that Dreyfus had confessed, at another denying it. Cavaignac saw that, if he was to make a convincing case, he needed more than this, and so in his first speech in the Chamber of Deputies after taking office (7 July) he also read out the letter from Schwartz-koppen to Panizzardi referring to *ce canaille de D* (see p. 92) and the *Faux Henry*. This was very rash as it constituted an official recognition that in Dreyfus's court martial there were documents shown to the judges and not to the defence. But in the Chamber Cavaignac's speech was received with enthusiasm by all parties and it was immediately voted with a large majority that copies of it should be put on display all over the country. Surely now, the government hoped, the dreaded Dreyfus Case would disappear, but a few days later Picquart, now in retirement, and therefore with greater freedom of speech, wrote an open letter to the Prime Minister, Brisson, stating that he was in a position to prove that because of its dating the letter to Panizzardi could not possibly refer to Dreyfus and that the *Faux Henry* bore all the characteristics of a forgery. At the same time Maitre Demange wrote an open letter saying that none of the documents read out by Cavaignac had been communicated to him or Dreyfus at the time of the court martial. These letters were received with delight by the Dreyfusards who immediately opened a fund so that they too could be put on public display.

Cavaignac's initiative had clearly backfired, and it must have occurred to him that Méline's policy of silence, which he had strongly attacked, was the best one; but instead of holding back he embarked on a course of action which was to land him in even deeper waters. In the first place he sought to silence Picquart by ordering his arrest (on the old charge of disclosing secret military information), and at the same time ordered an enquiry into the behaviour of Esterhazy. Both of these actions might have been justified, but it might have occurred to Cavaignac that they were likely to result in the exposure of unwelcome facts. But what proved his most damaging move was to order the chief of his military secretariat, General Roget, and his aide, Captain Cuignet, to make a thorough examination of all the documents in the Dreyfus Case, now amounting to nearly four hundred. This, indeed, proved calamitous as Cuignet, working through the papers laboriously, eventually came to the *Faux Henry* and noticed that this consisted of bits of paper joined together and that the faint lines on the top part were of a different colour to those on the bottom. After further examination he had no doubt that the document was a forgery and reported the matter to Roget who informed Cavaignac who was then faced with the fact that one of the documents being placarded all over France had been forged. He had certainly paid the price for his openness.

In his predicament Cavaignac could have chosen to hush the matter up and turn a blind eye to the forgery, but to his credit he did not do so. He decided that the matter must be thrashed out and by himself. And so on 30 August, in the presence of Boisdeffre, Gonse and Roget, he submitted Henry to a rigorous cross-examination at the end of which he confessed to forgery. On Cavaignac's orders he was put under arrest and sent to the fortress of Mont-Valérien. On the next day he was found dead in his cell with his throat cut. The official verdict was suicide, but there were those who suspected that he had been murdered; it was certainly unusual for a prisoner to be left alone in his cell with a razor.

Henry is one of the more mysterious characters in the Dreyfus Affair. That he played a nefarious part in it is certain, but his exact role is less clear. Was he, as some averred, just a simple soul of peasant origin with a blind devotion to the army and ready to do anything, including forgery, on orders from above? Or was there, as others thought, a more sinister explanation of what he did? Was he in league with Esterhazy in his treasonous activities? He certainly went to great lengths to shield him, but this may again have been on orders from above to cover up the mistakes and indiscretions of senior officers. Perhaps the most significant clue to the question is his last pathetic cry before going into Mont-Valérien: 'What do they want of me then? ... It is madness on their part ... My conscience reproaches me with nothing ... What I did I am ready to do again ... It was for the good of the country and of the army. I have always done my duty.'

The news of Henry's confession and death was welcomed with jubilation by the Dreyfusards who thought that the case would now be brought to a rapid conclusion. But to the anti-Dreyfusards it made no difference at all. *La Libre Parole* stressed strongly that a forgery committed in 1896 could have no bearing on a judgement passed in 1894. It also lost no time, as did other organs of the anti-Semitic press, in proclaiming Henry a martyr, a victim of the secret Jewish syndicate. One writer referred to 'this disciplined soldier who had wanted to save the army with his patriotic forgery'. 'Your unhappy forgery,' wrote another, 'will be reckoned among your finest deeds as a soldier.' Another could even bring himself to write of the forgery as 'an act of intellectual and moral nobility'. In his native village the mayor opened a fund for a memorial to him, and subscriptions poured in from all over the country. The death of Henry did, however, bring about the immediate resignation of Boisdeffre, the Chief of Staff, and Gonse, his Deputy, who were implicated with him, also that of De Pellieux who wrote an angry letter to Cavaignac saying that he had been 'the dupe of dishonourable people'. It also resulted in the hurried exit from the country of Esterhazy.

It has been seen how, after his court martial and again after the trial of Zola, Esterhazy had emerged a popular hero, and this despite the publication of the very damaging letters he had written to Madame Boulancer (see p. 106), his scandalous private life and his alleged admission that it was he who had written the *bordereau* (see below p. 124). A few months later he was again in trouble when his nephew Christian Esterhazy, who had been his accomplice in some of his underhand activities, threatened to sue him for money which he had misappropriated. The matter was brought to the attention of Judge Bertulus who had been commissioned by the government to enquire into all legal matters arising from the Dreyfus Affair. He at once ordered the seizure of all Esterhazy's papers and then his arrest as well as that of his mistress, Marguérite Pays.* As a result he was ordered by Cavaignac to appear before yet another court of enquiry which, in spite of some damning evidence, acquitted him of 'failure to respect the honour and discipline of the army', but by a majority of 3–2 found him guilty of 'habitual private misconduct' ('moral degradation incompatible with the dignity of an officer'). A finding of this sort with such a small majority might in normal circumstances have been overlooked, but Cavaignac was convinced of his criminality and wanted to be rid of him and ordered his dismissal from the army forthwith. At the same time Esterhazy was advised, in his own interests, to leave the country, but this he did not do at once as he was convinced that he would always be protected. After the death of Henry, however, he lost no time in getting out first to Belgium and then to England. The following year he was found guilty of embezzlement on the charge brought against him by his nephew and was sentenced *in absentia* to three years imprisonment, which kept him out of France for the rest of his life.

As well as despatching Henry and Esterhazy, Cavaignac also sought to bring down another leading character in the Dreyfus drama. Picquart had long been a thorn in the side of the military establishment. But for him the Dreyfus Case would, in all likelihood, have been buried long ago. He had already been treated with great harshness by his superiors and after the Zola trial had been retired on half pay. But this had not silenced him, and Cavaignac had been enraged by the letter he had written after his speech in the Chamber, exposing the documents he had quoted as being either fraudulent or irrelevant. As has been seen he had him arrested, and as he had now retired from the army, he was

---

* Later Bertulus was to tell Cavaignac that he had arrested an army officer without other domicile than the bed of a prostitute.

held in a civil prison, where it was intended at first to bring him before a civil court. Later, however, with the arrival of a new War Minister (Chanoine) he was transferred to military justice with an additional charge against him of forgery – of the *Petit Bleu* (see p. 90). This outraged him and before being removed to the Cherche-Midi he was able to make a moving and forceful public statement:

> I absolutely oppose my being surrendered ... It is only here, and a few moments ago, that I learned the reality of the abominable plot, in which this morning I still could not believe ... I shall perhaps this evening go to the Cherche-Midi; and now is probably the last time, prior to the secret trial, that I can say a word in public. I would have people know, if there be found in my cell the rope of Lemercier-Picard or the razor of Henry, that I have been assassinated. For a man like myself cannot for an instant think of suicide. I shall face this accusation erect and fearless, and with the same serenity with which I have ever met my accusers.

The high command had been warned in ringing tones that it must not resort to foul play. Picquart was, however, kept in solitary confinement, without access to his lawyer, for seven weeks, and was in detention for nearly a year. At the end of that time, with a change of government and crucial developments in the Dreyfus Case, he was released with no charge being brought against him (9 June 1899).

One of the most bewildering aspects of the Dreyfus Affair is the way that apparently honourable people, despite overwhelming evidence to the contrary, believed unshakeably in Dreyfus's guilt. Four successive ministers of war, who had access to all the papers, were convinced of it, as also were the two men responsible for uncovering Henry's forgery, Roget and Cuignet. When Cavaignac reported Henry's suicide to the cabinet and someone remarked that revision of the Dreyfus Case was now irresistible, his reply was 'Less than ever'. But he was to find that he had stirred up forces he could no longer control; more and more people were coming to believe that revision was inevitable, and these included the Prime Minister, Henri Brisson. At first Brisson had played a somewhat passive role in the matter, giving Cavaignac his head and supporting him, although often against his better judgement; but after the Henry debacle he took a line of his own, albeit a somewhat weak one. Like his predecessors he longed to be rid of the Dreyfus Affair and thought he saw a way of doing this by transferring responsibility for it to the civil judiciary. And so he conveyed a message to Lucie Dreyfus that she should lodge a formal appeal for the retrial of her husband which the government would then pass on to the Court of Criminal Appeal, a civil court, which would then judge the matter. This attitude brought about the resignation of Cavaignac and, in quick succession, of his two successors as War Minister. But on 26 September (1898) the cabinet decided by a majority of 6–4 that Lucie's appeal should be forwarded to the civil court which, three days later, agreed to accept it, and started work at once on its investigations.

It did not take long for the judges of the Court of Criminal Appeal to realize that the case against Dreyfus, which legally rested solely on the *bordereau*, was a very thin one. They heard evidence that the language of the *bordereau* was unlikely to have been that of an artillery officer such as Dreyfus, that the handwriting was that of Esterhazy and that the paper on which it was written was identical to that used by Esterhazy on other occasions. At the same time Esterhazy in England was reported to have told a journalist that it was he who had written the *bordereau*. Subsequently he denied this and sued for damages, but he was not generally believed. Later, with a promise of safe conduct, he gave evidence to the Court of Criminal Appeal, but said nothing of significance, refusing to answer questions on the *bordereau* and saying merely that everything he had done was supported by the General Staff. The judges also lost no time in discounting Dreyfus's alleged confession to Lebrun-Renaud. Their application to see the secret dossier was at first refused by the high command and then, when they insisted, only parts of it were shown to them with misleading explanations and comments from Cuignet. By the end of 1898 the movement for Revision was gaining in strength all the time, and once again it seemed that the Dreyfus Affair must soon be brought to an end. But this was to underestimate the fanaticism of the anti-Dreyfusards. For them the matter was one of faith rather than of reason, and nothing could disenchant them of their obsession with secret Jewish syndicates and malevolent plots to undermine the army and corrupt the French way of life. The more the case against Dreyfus collapsed, the more hysterical and obscene became their abuse of his supporters. Brisson was 'a smooth lackey of the Prussian Syndicate'. Scheurer-Kestner, the much venerated vice-president of this Senate, became 'a scoundrel, now a nonentity, a piece of human rubbish'. There were open calls for Jews to be lynched and for their property to be destroyed. Their fury was particularly directed against the judges of the Court of Criminal Appeal when it seemed that they were moving towards a judgement favourable to Dreyfus; and in this they had support from an unexpected quarter.

At that time the Appeal Court (Cour de Cassation) consisted of three chambers – that of Criminal Appeal, Civil Appeal and Petitions. It had been assumed that the Dreyfus Case would be solely in the jurisdiction of the first of these, but while it was making its enquiries the President of the Civil Court, Quesnay de Beaurepaire, made a slanderous attack on some of its members, accusing them of partiality and improper conduct; and soon afterwards he gave up his post in order to lead a crusade 'to save the army'. His behaviour then became more and more outrageous and in newspaper articles and by word of mouth he spread scurrilous and mendacious stories about his fellow judges. He then went on to devise a scheme whereby responsibility for delivering judgement on Dreyfus should rest not with the Criminal Court alone but with a United Court drawn from judges of all three chambers. To achieve this would require a law passed by Parliament with retrospective effect, in effect disqualifying the Criminal Court and assigning its authority to the United Court. In face of such unwarranted interference with the judicial system and such monstrous attacks on judges of high reputation the government should have stood firm, but instead it was weak and temporizing, and in the end agreed to bring in an act which it called 'a law of necessity and alleviation', relieving the Criminal Court, so it was claimed, of an intolerable responsibility. Few were deceived by this and both in the Chamber of Deputies and the Senate there were strong protests at such an insult to the judiciary and the craven way in which the government was yielding to 'threats and calumny and a kind of secret inquisition'. But in spite of these the deputies heeded the demagogic advice of the Justice Minister to 'consider their constituencies', and this shameful piece of legislation was passed by both the Chamber and the Senate.

While this had been going on Paris had been in a state of turmoil. In the ten months following the death of Henry there had been a confusion of events. These included three changes of government and the appointment in quick succession of six different ministers of war. There had also been a threat of a general strike as well as an unfortunate confrontation with England which nearly got out of hand and might have led to war. This concerned a village in the Sudan on the banks of the Nile called Fashoda. In 1898 this was occupied by a small French expedition after a march of some 2,800 miles from the other side of Africa; the French flag was then hoisted and the district claimed for France. But strong objection to this was made by the British who had recently assumed the government of Egypt and was in the process of extending their rule into what came to be called the Anglo-Egyptian Sudan. A military force under General Kitchener arrived on the scene to order the French to go, which in face of superior force they were obliged to do; but it caused furious resentment in Paris.

There was too all the clamour surrounding the persecution of Picquart and the flight of Esterhazy to England. And then there was the somewhat farcical incident of the death and funeral of President Faure. Félix Faure was not a politician of great stature and owed his election to the presidency, according to one deputy, to 'the affability of his approach, his incontrovertible mediocrity and his tailor'. He also prided himself greatly on his gallantry, and when death came to him, which it did suddenly in the form of a cerebral haemorrhage, he was in the arms of his mistress. An attempt was made to cover up these embarrassing circumstances, but not entirely successfully, and various reports of it with differing interpretations appeared in the press. As he was a mild anti-Dreyfusard he was in favour with *La Libre Parol* who saw foul play and proclaimed that he had been brought down by a Jewish Delilah, although he himself scarcely bore comparison with Samson. As a matter of custom he was accorded a state funeral and a right-wing group decided to make this an occasion for a military *coup de force* by which the Republic would be overturned and the Duc D'Orléans, waiting expectantly on the Belgian frontier, would be proclaimed king. Several generals were approached as they rode solemnly in the funeral procession and implored to come to the rescue of France; but they proved unresponsive and the affair ended in fiasco with the conspirators being rounded up by the police and being charged with nothing more serious than trespass.

The act disqualifying the Court of Criminal Appeal from being the final arbiter of the Dreyfus Case and transferring the responsibility to the United Court meant that Lucie's application for a retrial had to be heard all over again, this time in front of no less than forty-six judges. By the time these began their proceedings the judges of the Criminal Court had completed their report which had been printed but publication of it was strictly prohibited; the forty-six judges were allowed to see it but no one else. However, Mathieu Dreyfus already had in his possession much of the evidence which had been presented which he contrived to have published, illegally, in *Figaro*; and this had great effect on public opinion.*

---

* Getting the documents to *Figaro* involved a complicated clandestine operation as the police were on guard to prevent it. It was only achieved, it seems, by the use of yet another veiled lady.

Almost at once the United Court demanded to see the secret dossier on Dreyfus and, like its predecessor, found nothing in it definitely incriminating of Dreyfus, but it did discover some gross distortions, notably in the translation of a telegram from Panizzardi to his chiefs in Rome at the time of Dreyfus's conviction. This should have read:

> If Captain Dreyfus has had no relations with you it would be advisable to instruct the ambassador to publish an official denial so as to prevent comments in the press.

But the translation made, it seems, by Du Paty and passed on to the chiefs of staff ran:

> Captain Dreyfus has been arrested. The Minister for War has proof of his relations with Germany. Every precaution has been taken.

Perhaps the most important new evidence heard by the United Court was that given by one of the judges at Dreyfus's court martial in 1894, Captain Freystaetter. He had since become greatly troubled by the verdict in which he had concurred, and wanted to explain to the Court about the evidence given to the judges at that time in secret by Henry. The direct question as to whether secret documents had been shown to them was not allowed to be put to him, but the implication in his answers was obvious. By the end of May (1899) the majority of the judges had come to the conclusion that the *bordereau* had been written by Esterhazy, and as this was the only admissible evidence against Dreyfus, he must be acquitted. Two courses of action were now open to the Court: either it could quash the verdict of the court martial and set Dreyfus free without retrial, or it could order a retrial by court martial without formally finding him innocent. After four and a half years incarceration on Devil's Island there would seem to have been much to be said for the former, but Lucie decided that her husband would want to be declared innocent by his fellow officers and that the victory then would be all the more emphatic. And so on 3 June this judgement was given. On the same day, by a curious coincidence, a report appeared in *Le Matin* that Esterhazy in London, and desperate for money, had given an interview to its correspondent and told him that it was he who had written the *bordereau*, but it was part of a counter-espionage operation and he had done it on the orders of Sandherr, the chief of the Statistical Section, and that Billot, the War Minister, Boisdeffre, the Chief of Staff and Gonse, his Deputy, had all known of it. Also on 3 June a cruiser was despatched to Devil's Island to bring Dreyfus back to France to face his second court martial. Soon afterwards Picquart was released from prison, Zola returned from exile and the Chamber of Deputies voted that the judgement of the United Court should be put on exhibition all over the country. Again it seemed that the Dreyfus Case was coming to an end, but it was to be seven years yet before it was finally laid to rest.

While all this was going on Alfred Dreyfus, alone on his 'rock tossed in the sea', continued to drag out his tortured existence. For four and a half years he had somehow managed to survive, racked with stomach pains and malaria, infested with vermin, glared at night and day by hostile eyes and subjected to every kind of barbarity and indignity inflicted on him by Deniel, the sadistic Governor of Guiana. In the early part of his imprisonment it had been his 'supreme comfort' to look out to sea, watching for the twice-monthly steamer from Europe and praying that it brought news of justice having been done to him. But for the last two years even this had been denied him when the Minister for the Colonies, the manic André Lebon, had ordered a high palisade to be built round his hut.

Of the commotion in France of which he was at the centre, he knew nothing. Newspapers were banned and Lucie's letters were censored if they contained any news of developments. Anxiously he would scan these letters for any hint of hope and occasionally these did occur. In the spring of 1897 Lucie wrote: 'If you only knew how our burden is less heavy.' And in the autumn: 'We have definitely found our way.' And early 1898 she managed to get past the censors: 'We are in full possession of the truth.' These words gave Dreyfus hope and the courage to keep going, but still the months passed and his condition grew weaker all the time. But at last in October 1898 came the word he had been waiting for so desperately for so long. It came in the form of a tersely worded telegram handed to him by the odious Deniel:

> You are informed that the Criminal Court of Cour de Cassation has formally declared admissible the request for revision of your trial and decreed that you should be advised of this decision and invited to provide means for your defence.

Little more information was vouchsafed to him in the following months during which judgement of his case was transferred from the Criminal Court to the United Court. In December a commission, sent by the Criminal Court, arrived to question him about his alleged confession to Lebrun-Renaud which he indignantly denied. And then silence again for another six months during which Deniel saw to it that the conditions of his imprisonment became ever more brutal. It was not until 3 June 1899 that the United Court finally gave its verdict, and this was conveyed to him two days later when he was handed a document by the chief guard:

> The court rescinds and annuls the judgement proclaimed on 22nd December 1894 against Alfred Dreyfus, and remands the accused to a court martial ... As a result of this decision Captain Dreyfus ceases to be subjected to the regime of deportation and becomes a simple prisoner.

This news which, he later recalled, caused him 'immense unutterable joy' meant that he was no longer a convict and his rank was restored to him, but he had not yet been acquitted and he was still in custody. Four days late he boarded the cruiser *Sfax* where he was lodged in a special cabin with barred portholes and an armed guard and a regime of silence still persisted. His homecoming to France could not have been less spectacular; for security reasons he was landed on a deserted beach at the dead of night and hustled into a special train in which there were thirteen policemen and four detectives, and taken to Rennes where it had been decided his second court martial was to be held.

Chapter XII

The cruelty of a prison sentence starts when you come out.
(Oscar Wilde)

*Something is killed in me and I feel no desire to write. I am
unconscious of power.*
(Ibid.)

*The fact that he wrecked my life makes me love him . . . I love him
as I always did with a sense of tragedy and ruin.*
(Ibid.)

When Oscar Wilde came out of prison on 18 May 1897 Alfred Dreyfus
was barely halfway through his stint on Devil's Island. Prison regulations
required that a prisoner had to be released from the prison in which he
was first held and so it was necessary for Wilde to travel from Reading
to Pentonville outside the gates of which he was met by More Adey
and the Rev. Stuart Headlam. They then went to Headlam's house in
Bloomsbury where they were joined by Ada Leverson who reported that
she found Wilde his usual self, full of wit and good humour and looking
markedly better, slighter and younger. It was assumed that he would go
abroad as soon as possible, but there were no definite plans and,
apparently on the spur of the moment, he sent off a message to the
Jesuits in Farm Street asking if he could go into retreat with them. But
the brothers felt that this was too sudden and sent back a message that
more deliberation and preparation were necessary. This seemed to have
upset him unduly and caused tears, but plans then went ahead for him
to take the next boat to Dieppe where Robbie Ross and Reggie Turner
were waiting to meet him. The meeting with Ross (as with Adey) might
have been awkward, as only a week before in a letter written in prison
he had lambasted them for mismanaging his financial affairs and causing
discord between himself and Constance. But all appeared to be forgiven

now; it seemed that this letter, like *De Profundis*, was an example of 'the passing delirium of gaol moral fever'. 'You must not mind foolish, unkind letters,' he told Ross.

In France, with the help of money collected from friends, he set about rebuilding his life, but soon found that Dieppe was not the ideal place for this. He was living under the assumed name of Sebastian Melmoth (a martyr and lone wanderer in a story written by his great-uncle), but he was soon recognized and had to suffer numerous rebuffs and insults, particularly from English visitors there who included old friends, and he never knew when he went into a restaurant whether he would be welcomed or asked to leave. After a week, therefore, he decided to move to the little fishing village of Berneval, some five miles along the coast. Here at first he was content and thought he had found somewhere which would afford him what he sought – 'a quiet mode of living with isolation for thought and freedom from the endless hunger for pleasure that wreck the body and imprison the soul'.

He was still hopeful of a reconciliation with Constance. It has been seen that relations with her had been badly set back when Adey, backed by Ross, had bought from the Official Receiver on his behalf but against his wishes his life interest in her marriage settlement. This had seemed to her a breach of faith, and at the same time as making a new financial arrangement she had compelled him to sign a Deed of Separation whereby he assigned guardianship of his two sons to herself and her cousin, Adrian Hope; and the family name was changed from Wilde to Holland. She had also laid it down that payment of the allowance was conditional on his leading 'a respectable life' and would be cut off if he was guilty of any 'immoral misconduct or notoriously consort with evil and disreputable companions', her solicitor to be the sole judge in this matter. Wilde later described these conditions as 'insulting and painfully humiliating'. However, soon after his arrival in France he wrote Constance an impassioned letter 'full of penitence' and begging for a reunion. But although deeply touched, Constance, prompted by her advisors who always presented Wilde in the worst light, would not agree to a visit from him for the time being; it would seem that she wanted to be reassured about the sort of life he was going to be leading. But this stalling was to have ill-fated consequences. It made it almost certain that Wilde would come together again with Bosie.

It was the hope of Wilde's friends that he would emerge from prison, chastened and disabused and, at the age of forty-two, still capable of great literature. Wilde too was at first optimistic. In a letter to Will Rothenstein he wrote:

> I have not come out of prison an embittered and disappointed man. On the contrary: in many ways I have gained much. I am not really ashamed of having been in prison: I often was in more shameful places: but I am really ashamed of having led a life unworthy of an artist ... I know simply that a life of definite and studied materialism, and a philosophy of appetite and cynicism, and a cult of sensual and senseless ease, are bad things for an artist: they narrow the imagination, and dull the more delicate sensibilities. I was all wrong, my dear boy, in my life. I was not getting the best out of me. Now I think that with good health and the friendship of a few good simple nice fellows like yourself ... I think I may do things yet that you all may like.

In his first weeks out of prison, Wilde wrote a number of letters to friends, as well as a long and passionate one to the *Daily Chronicle* on the iniquities and follies of the prison system. In particular he inveighed against the treatment of children who were shut up alone, cold and hungry, in a dark cell for twenty-three hours a day. This he described as 'an outrage on humanity and common sense', and recalled how he had seen a small child in prison whose face was like 'a white wedge of sheer terror'. He also recalled his horror when he had heard the cries of a mentally defective prisoner being given twenty-four lashes for 'malingering'. His conclusion was that people were 'utterly contaminated' by prison life, and it was not so much the prisoners who needed reformation as the prisons themselves.

While Wilde was at Berneval several people came to him with ideas about what he might write. At one time he undertook to write the libretto for an opera, but it must be doubtful if he ever intended to carry this out, even though he accepted an advance for it. He was more interested in writing another Biblical play, possibly about Pharaoh or Ahab and Jezebel. Two things he ruled out definitely: he would not write newspaper articles about his prison experiences, however highly paid, and he would write no more light comedies. He was not in the mood for these: 'I would rather stitch sacks,' he told a friend. In the event he was to write only one more work of any note. The *Ballad of Reading Gaol* told of the brutalities and stupidities of prison life and in particular, of the death sentence carried out on Trooper Aldridge for the murder of his unfaithful wife. The theme of betrayal had long been a favourite with him, and the Ballad was partly poetry and partly propaganda: cruel as had been the murder, the execution was even more horrible. One theme which obsessed him and to which he kept returning was that 'man kills the thing he loves'. Later he was evasive as to what he meant by this, but when asked by Bosie replied: 'You should know.' Publication of the poem posed problems as all the main publishers still shied away from him. Eventually, however, the work was accepted by Leonard Smithers, who prided himself on publishing 'anything that others are afraid of '.* But even so the first editions did not bear Wilde's name, only C.3.3., his number in Reading Gaol. When it was published, in February 1898, it had a mixed reception from the critics: some found it impressive and moving, but some were doubtful about the quality of the poetry. 'A jumble of excellence and rubbish,' said one. More brutally another said that 'the trail of minor poet is over it all.' The consensus was that it was good if not great literature. Inevitably the identity of the author soon became known and this may have prevented objective criticism, but it did not affect the sales, and the first editions were soon sold out. This might have encouraged him to further writing, but ill health, unhappiness and a return to his old ways had their effect, and soon afterwards he wrote in a letter: 'I feel no desire to write. I am unconscious of power.'

It was perhaps inevitable that at some time Wilde and Douglas would be reunited. In spite of misunderstandings, violent disagreements and furious outbursts the love of the two men for each other had not died. In their hearts they longed to be together again. At first the initiative came from Douglas who had not yet read Wilde's bitter condemnation of him in *De Profundis* and was confident he could soon re-establish his hold on him. At first Wilde was resistant and before leaving prison he told Ross to be sure that Douglas was not waiting to meet him in France, and two weeks after his release was reiterating the language of *De Profundis*: 'I feel him as an evil influence, poor fellow. To be with him would be to return to the hell from which I do think I have been released. I hope never to see him again.' At the time he was pleading with Constance for a family reunion, and he knew that this would be impossible if she became aware of any contact between him and Douglas. But, as has been seen, Constance prevaricated, and the longer she did so the unhappier Wilde became and the greater the temptation for him to find consolation elsewhere.

Constance has been blamed by some for her hesitation, it being

---

* He also ran a profitable sideline in pornography.

maintained that if she had received Wilde back at once he might have been saved. But it must be that she was justified; she needed to be sure that he had put aside his old ways and that she and her children would not again be embroiled in scandal. And all too soon it became evident that he had not put aside his old ways. Only three weeks after his arrival in France he had become intimate with a young poet, Ernest Dowson, and was writing him letters praising his 'dark hyacinth looks' and asking him why he was 'so persistently and perversedly wonderful'. At first he had been well pleased with Berneval: he made friends with the *curé*, joined in village activities and gave a children's party to celebrate the diamond jubilee of Queen Victoria.* But boredom soon set in. It was not likely that he would for ever be content with the simple pleasures of a French fishing village; he would soon be longing for a livelier, more sophisticated existence; more than anything he craved for love, and it seemed that this could only come from Bosie. Only two weeks after settling in Berneval he was writing to him almost every day, at first quite temperately, addressing him as 'my dear boy' and signing himself 'ever yours'; but this soon changed to 'my own dear boy' and then 'dear honey sweet boy'. For a time he continued to hold out against a meeting, saying that although he loved him more than anyone else, 'our lives are inseparably severed'. But this too changed. By 15 June a meeting was agreed, but two days later had to be cancelled when Wilde realized what the consequences might be – the loss of friends, the stopping of his allowance by Constance, as well as some madcap action on the part of Lord Queensberry. He had already become aware that Queensberry had set detectives to watch him, and had declared that if ever Wilde and Douglas were to meet, he would be over to France at once with a revolver. 'I think of you always,' he wrote to Douglas, 'and love you always but chasms of moonless night divide us. We cannot cross it without hideous and nameless peril.' But this in time he was prepared to risk as his loneliness and boredom became unbearable. On 28 August they met for a day and a night at Rouen. It was an emotional reunion, both men declaring undying love for the other and agreeing that somehow they must live together for the rest of their lives. In a letter soon afterwards Wilde wrote: 'I feel that my only hope of again doing beautiful work in art is being with you. It was not so in the old days,

---

* For whom he had an unbounded admiration. He had once declared (perhaps extravagantly) that she, Victor Hugo and Napoleon were the three outstanding personalities of the nineteenth century.

but now it is different, and you can really recreate in me that energy and sense of joyous power on which art depends.' Only a few months earlier he had written in *De Profundis*: 'While you were with me you were the absolute ruin of my art.'

As was to be expected their reunion proved fatal. It has been described by Richard Ellman as 'a second fall for Wilde'. From then on redemption for him became impossible. It was downhill all the way to an early death. In his heart Wilde knew what would be the consequences. To Robert Ross he wrote: 'The fact that he wrecked my life makes me love him ... I love him as I always did with a sense of tragedy and ruin ... My life cannot be patched up. There is a doom on it.'

They decided that they would make a home for themselves in Naples where the climate was warm, costs low and morals lax. Almost immediately, however, there was hesitation on the part of Douglas who insisted on a delay of six weeks which drove Wilde almost to the point of suicide, as life in Berneval had become intolerable to him. When eventually they reached Naples in September they were desperately short of money – Wilde had had to borrow the fare there from a friend in Paris – but this did not stop them from running up a bill of £60 (equivalent to at least £3,000 today) at a leading hotel. Subsequently they rented an attractive villa* complete with four servants, and for a time led an amiable, easy-going life, Wilde revising and adding to the *Ballad of Reading Gaol* and Bosie writing some verses of poetry. But it could not last. Before the end of September Constance became aware of what was happening and wrote Wilde a furious letter: 'I forbid you to see Lord Alfred Douglas. I forbid you to return to your filthy, insane life.' And she was in a position to enforce these commands. She lost no time in invoking the clause in the financial settlement by which Wilde's allowance would be cut off if he associated with disreputable persons. Whether or not Bosie fell into this category was left to her lawyer who had no hesitation in declaring that he did. And so at the end of November the allowance was stopped. At the same time Lady Queensberry was equally appalled to hear that Bosie was once more living with the man she regarded as her son's corrupter. She too wrote stating plainly that unless she had a pledge in writing from both men that they would never again live together Bosie's allowance from her, his only means of support, would be cut off. This brought the two men

---

* At first plagued by rats, but was rid of them with the help of incantations from a bearded witch.

to heel; it meant that they would have virtually nothing to live on, and they had no alternative but to comply, especially as Lady Queensberry undertook to pay off their debts in Naples, to make a down payment to Wilde of £200,* and to pay a further three months rent of the villa for Wilde alone.

Bosie capitulated at once and left Naples at the beginning of December. It appeared that he was not altogether sorry to go. Life with Wilde had begun to pall. It had not been the same as before. Wilde had been less fascinating and he himself less youthful. Before leaving he wrote to a friend: 'The whole thing has been a hand to mouth struggle, kept up by desperate telegrams to reluctant relations, and pawning of pins and studs.' To his mother, a few days later, accepting her terms, he wrote: 'I am glad, O so glad to have got away ... I wanted to go back to him, I longed for it and for him, because I love him and admire him and think him great and almost good, but when I had done it and when I got back, I hated it, I was miserable. I wanted to go way. But I couldn't. I was tied by honour.'

Left alone Wilde was desolate. To his publisher, Smithers, he wrote: 'I am very sorry, but I really am a wreck. I don't eat or sleep and I live on cigarettes.' To Robert Ross he reverted to the sentiments of *De Profundis*:

> The facts of Naples are very bald and brief. Bosie for four months, by endless letters, offered me a home. He offered me love, affection and care, and promised that I should never want for anything. After four months I accepted his offer, but when we met at Aix on our way to Naples, I found he had no money, no plans, and had forgotten all his promises. His one idea was that I should raise money for us both. I did so to the extent of £120. On this Bosie lived quite happily. When it came to his having to repay his own share, he became terribly unkind and penurious, except where his own pleasures were concerned, and when my allowance ceased, he left ... The bald fact is that I accepted the offer of the home, and found that I was expected to provide the money, and when I could no longer do so I was left to my own devices. It is, of course, the most bitter experience of a bitter life. It is a blow quite awful and paralysing. But it had to come, and I know it is better that I should never see him again. I don't want to, he fills me with horror.

---

* This Wilde had no qualms in accepting as he regarded it as part payment of a debt of honour from the Queensberry family for his legal expenses which it had guaranteed but never paid.

As in *De Profundis* this was unjust to Bosie who, when later he read the letter, described it as 'one of the most astonishing products that the history of literature had ever recorded'. It took little account of the sacrifices he had made and of the financial provisions of his mother.

After Bosie left Wilde lingered on in Naples for a few weeks during which other misfortunes crowded in on him. He went away on a week's visit and arrived back to find a servant had stolen all his clothes. For a time he was occupied with correcting the proofs of *Ballad of Reading Gaol*, but then he could not wait to get away and, even though the rent of the villa had been paid for a further month, he left for Paris in the middle of February.

Chapter XIII

*We are the two greatest martyrs of humanity, but I have suffered the
most.*

(Esterhazy to Wilde)

*The interesting thing surely is to be guilty and wear as a halo the
seduction of sin.*

(Wilde to Esterhazy)

*When the triumph comes I know that Carlos's name will transpire
and be in the mouths of thousands of French people as that of one
who . . . did not pass by on the other side of the road.*

(F.C. Conybeare)

*Oscar Wilde was one of the direct instruments in the freeing of
Dreyfus.*

(Christopher Healy, confidant of Zola)

Oscar Wilde arrived in Paris on 13 February 1898, by chance a week
after his old friend Carlos Blacker. It has been seen (Chapter 1) that
Blacker had once been Wilde's greatest friend, but following his infatu-
ation with Bosie the two men had drifted apart, and Blacker was
completely taken by surprise when Wilde was put on trial. It seems he
had no inkling of Wilde's homosexuality, and this in spite of his close
and much-vaunted friendship with Douglas, as well as the strong homosexual undertones in *The Picture of Dorian Gray*. Like many Victorians
it was a subject he could not comprehend. In 1898 the two men had
not met for three years since when the fortunes of both of them had
plummeted. For a brief time they were to come together again with
fateful consequences.

Carlos Blacker was a richly gifted man. He had a first-class mind and
a wide range of interests including Hellenism and comparative religions.

He had a prodigious memory (knowing the whole of Dante by heart) and a special aptitude for languages, learning a new one every year (including in his last years Hebrew so that he could, as he hoped, converse with God in his own language). But above all he had 'a genius for friendship'. Wilde described him as 'the truest of friends and most sympathetic of companions', and George Bernard Shaw had written how much he enjoyed his 'very congenial company'. And his friends came from many countries. Descended on his mother's side from a Spanish-Peruvian family, he was by nature cosmopolitan, and was deeply absorbed in the whole of European civilization.

The fates had, indeed, endowed him amply but, as is often the case, certain gifts had been withheld, notably any kind of business sense. This would not have mattered greatly if he had left well alone; he had an adequate private income and there was no need for him to put this at risk. But unfortunately he was disposed to speculate and on a visit to America in 1891 he became deeply involved in the affairs of the North Alabama Land Development Company. Not only did he buy a large number of its shares but he also underwrote its debentures so that if these remained unsold, as they were, he would be responsible for them. He thus found himself landed with an unmanageable debt and to pay it off he gambled on the Stock Exchange and, inevitably, lost. Then in desperation he raised a loan from an insurance company guaranteed by two close friends, the Duke of Newcastle and his younger brother, Lord Francis Hope.

Compared with other holders of the title the seventh Duke of Newcastle was sane and well intentioned. Essentially he was a pathetic character. As a baby he had been dropped by a careless nurse so that he was crippled for life and could not take part in any strenuous activity. He inherited the dukedom at the age of fourteen and found himself confronted with a devastated estate, his father having run up racing debts of some £230,000 (some 11½ million by present day values).* By nature the young duke was quiet and retiring and deeply religious, his main interests in life being Anglo-Catholicism and the rebuilding of the Newcastle fortunes. Sadly he was not blessed with a happy marriage,† and he once described life at Clumber, his ancestral home, as 'a cave

---

* Hereafter present-day values will be placed in brackets after any sum mentioned.

† Partly perhaps because of his habit of reading his wife a sermon every night at bedtime.

of horror'. In this dismal life one of his few joys had been a close friendship with Carlos Blacker whose brilliant gifts dazzled him. But, as will be seen, this for a time was to fall apart grievously. Lord Francis Hope, his younger brother, was cast in a different mould. Attractive, exuberant and recklessly irresponsible, he inherited at the age of twenty-one a fortune of some £20,000 (£1,000,000) a year, and was bankrupt by the time he was twenty-eight with racing bills of £70,000 (£3,500,000). He had also, to his brother's fury, married a penniless music hall star known as 'Madcap May Yohe'.

It is appreciated that May Yohe plays only a peripheral role in this history, but it is difficult to pass by a life story so romantic and variegated. May was born in America, the daughter of an ironworker of German origin. When still a child it became apparent that she was gifted with a very remarkable deep contralto voice; and at the age of thirteen she was put on the music hall stage where she became known as 'the girl with the foghorn voice'. At the age of eighteen she appeared in London where she was a sensation and was besieged by hosts of admirers. Most of these might have been content to drink champagne out of her slipper, but not Lord Francis Hope who insisted on marrying her immediately. For a time May was numbered in the ranks of the aristocracy and, with more stability, would in due course have become Duchess of Newcastle; but after a few years she became restless and made off with the son of the Mayor of New York. But this too proved transitory, and she was subsequently heard of in a rubber plantation in the East Indies with the Sultan of Johore, in South Africa during the Boer War working as a nurse, and in Seattle during the First World War earning a few dollars cleaning offices, before finally coming to rest on a chicken farm in New Hampshire married to a South African, Jan Smuts, a distant cousin of the famous general and prime minister. Truly a unique odyssey.

The loan from the insurance company proved of little permanent benefit to Carlos Blacker; with mounting losses on the Stock Exchange he soon defaulted on the terms, and with Lord Francis Hope recently declared bankrupt, the unfortunate Duke of Newcastle found himself liable for a sum in excess of £10,000 (£500,000). This appalled him. After years of trying to put the Newcastle estate in order it was a bitter blow. What happened next is obscure and ludicrous if it were not tragic; it seems that the Duke exploded with rage in the Savile Club and in front of witnesses poured abuse on Blacker and made a totally unwarrantable accusation that he had cheated at cards. This was a very serious matter, at that time one of the most deadly accusations one gentleman could make against another. A few years earlier there had been a great furore when a charge had been levelled against Sir William Gordon Cumming, a lieutenant colonel in the Scots Guards, a pillar of society and a close friend of the Prince of Wales. After a lawsuit for slander, which he lost, Cumming was dismissed from his regiment, expelled from his clubs and driven into exile in a remote part of Scotland (Gordon-stoun). With ominous undertones of this case and of the Wilde case, Blacker proceeded to sue Newcastle for slander and so became involved in an action which dragged on for several years and which was to blight his life. It might have been settled sooner, but Newcastle denied ever having made the accusation and maintained that there was therefore no need for an apology.

This was not the end of Blacker's misfortunes. Earlier in 1893 he had become engaged to Caroline Frost, the daughter of a wealthy, if some-what choleric, American general, while she and her mother were on a tour of Europe. Caroline had since returned to America, and in 1894 Carlos set out to St Louis for the wedding. However, he was intercepted in New York, for the general had come to hear reports of Newcastle's accusation and sent his son to say that the marriage could not take place until the matter had been cleared up. Blacker was therefore obliged to take a ship back to England, and in the course of the voyage word came to him that Newcastle had instituted bankruptcy proceedings against him. This was the nadir of his fortunes: his honour questioned, his engagement broken and impending bankruptcy. That his life did not end in total disaster was due to Caroline Frost. A lady of great character, she refused to accept the parental ban on her marriage, and in company with an old nurse ran away from home and made her way to England where her engagement to Blacker was restored, and the two were married soon afterwards in Paris. In spite of many vicissitudes the marriage was happy and lasted for over thirty years during which, it was said, they never spent a night apart. Caroline lost no time in repairing the ruins of her husband's life: he was made to give up opium which he was taking to relieve deep depression, his drinking was curtailed and gambling banned, as also was fencing to which, for some reason, Caroline had a strong aversion. But in 1895 it was necessary for Carlos to return to London to face the ordeal of appearing in the bankruptcy court. And so they were there in February at the time of Wilde's greatest success, the opening of *The Importance of Being Earnest*. They returned to the Continent just after Queensberry left his fatal card at the Savile Club.

For the next years the Blackers were to live mainly in Freibourg in

Germany and it was from here that they were to hear of the dreadful developments of Wilde's action against Queensberry. During the time of his imprisonment there was nothing they could do to help Wilde, but they did give great support and comfort to Constance and her two sons, taking them into their home and giving help and advice on such matters as suitable schools. After Wilde's release Carlos re-established contact with him by letter (Caroline forbade a meeting), and Wilde was effusively grateful for this:

> I need not tell you with what feelings of affection and gratitude I read your letter. You were always my staunch friend and stood by my side for many years.
>
> Often in prison I used to think of you: of your chivalry of nature, of your limitless generosity, of your quick intellectual sympathies, of your culture so receptive, so refined. What marvellous evenings, dear Carlos, we used to have! What brilliant dinners. What days of laughter and delight!

For a time Blacker acted as intermediary between Wilde and Constance and seemed to be on the point of bringing them together; but this ended abruptly when Wilde went back to Bosie. To Blacker this was unforgivable and he broke off all relations and urged Constance to do the same, but this Constance, furious as she was, could not bring herself to do. She continued to think of him as weak rather than wicked and capable of redemption. She may also have felt some guilt that she had not been more responsive to his overtures. She had been delighted when he sent her a copy of *The Ballad of Reading Gaol* which she described as 'exquisite'. After Wilde and Douglas had broken up in Naples it was her great hope that Wilde would embark on a major work of literature and when she heard that he was in Paris, asked Blacker to visit him and urge him to start writing again. This, eventually, Blacker agreed to do, but had no success. As will be seen, Wilde could not be persuaded to write anything and Blacker's visit had tragic consequences ending in the final rupture of their friendship with bitter recriminations and ill-feeling.

At the time when Blacker and Wilde arrived in Paris the trial of Zola had just begun and the city was in a ferment; feelings about the Dreyfus Case were more passionate than ever, and almost at once Blacker became deeply involved. This arose from his friendship with Alessandro Panizzardi, the Italian military attaché who was at the centre of the Affair. At the time of Dreyfus's conviction in 1894 he and his close friend and colleague, von Schwartzkoppen, the German military attaché, were unaware that Dreyfus was innocent. They knew that they had had no dealings with him but, as the trial was in camera, they did not know what other evidence there might be against him. But when two years later there appeared in *Le Matin* a photostat of the *bordereau*, which they knew originated from Esterhazy, they were convinced of Dreyfus's innocence. The thought of an innocent man sweating it out on Devil's Island greatly disturbed them and they issued further statements that they had never been in communication with Dreyfus but, as before, these were regarded with cynicism.

In the months that followed as the net was drawn closer around him, Esterhazy became more and more unbalanced and on 23 October (1897) he had a hysterical interview with Schwartzkoppen (described in Chapter X) as a result of which the latter became convinced that French military intelligence was on Esterhazy's tracks. The accepted practice at that time was that if one of his agents was detected a military attaché should relinquish his post, and Schwartzkoppen decided that the time for this had come. And so a few weeks later he left Paris, having first been decorated by the French President with the Legion of Honour. With him he took a bag containing some 140 documents which Esterhazy had supplied to him during the last three years.

Left in Paris without Schwartzkoppen, Panizzardi became increasingly distraught. He was tormented by the thought that Dreyfus had been wrongly convicted and that it was in his power to save him. By the time Blacker reached Paris three months later he was on the verge of a nervous breakdown. In a memorandum drawn up later Blacker described the situation:

> I immediately went to see my old and intimate friend Panizzardi, knowing that I would learn the whole truth from him, for it was obvious that three beings alone knew the whole and entire truth, namely God and the two military attachés.
>
> I found Panizzardi very excited and distressed. He seemed aged and worn and he unbosomed himself to me without hesitation, seeming to find comfort in so doing. He told me at once that Esterhazy was the guilty man and that Dreyfus was wholly innocent.

In the weeks that followed Panizzardi's position in Paris became increasingly stressful; he was treated with coldness and suspicion by French officers and, as Blacker recalled, was under permanent surveillance:

Panizzardi constantly dined with us, and he was always shadowed and watched. We could see the men in the street watching the house and waiting for him to leave, when they would jump on their bicycles and follow him as soon as he took a cab.

Much as Panizzardi would have liked to help Dreyfus, he knew that if he attempted to do so openly he would bring on himself a storm of troubles and his military career might be brought to an end. Blacker by then had become an ardent Dreyfusard and wanted to do everything in his power to see that justice was done; but he too realized that he must walk warily; all too easily he (and his family) could become engulfed in terror and violence. And so the two men thought up a plan whereby the truth would be made known but their tracks would be covered. This involved the publication in England of some of the documents which Esterhazy had passed to Schwartzkoppen. For this Blacker invoked the help of a great friend of his in England, Frederick C. Conybeare. At first this might seem a curious choice. Conybeare was a gentle, unworldly academic, specializing in Armenian and Georgian manuscripts bearing on the early history of Christianity. However, he responded at once to Blacker's call, and in time became as deeply obsessed by the subject of Dreyfus as he was. Later he was to write: 'I feel morally the better somehow for having done what I could, and I am very grateful to yourself for having inspired me and set me on to a task which more than any other I have engaged in has lifted me out of myself and I hope contributed to further the cause of humanity.' And so his patristic studies were put aside and in the following months he was to write a book and newspaper articles on Dreyfus and Zola which were to have great impact. He also prepared the way for the publication in the *Daily News* of the Esterhazy documents. But this plan was to miscarry.

It was recounted in Chapter XI how on 4 April (1898) there was published in *Le Siècle* a long letter originating in Berne signed 'Diplomat' which told in detail of Schwartzkoppen's dealings with Esterhazy. This 'Letter from a Diplomat' has received scant attention from historians; it is hardly mentioned in G. Chapman's *Dreyfus Case* nor even in Joseph Reinach's five-volume history. But its importance can be judged from the storm of fury it stirred up in the anti-Dreyfus press; and this was intensified four days later by another article in *Le Siècle* by the Italian journalist, Casella, who told much the same story based, as he claimed, on an interview with Schwartzkoppen. In neither of these articles was there significant mention either of Panizzardi or of Blacker, but a few days later yet another article appeared this time in the *New York Times* by its Paris correspondent, Rowland Strong, which, besides affirming the innocence of Dreyfus and the guilt of Esterhazy, alluded to a plan that was afoot to prove the matter by publishing relevant documents. It also mentioned by name both Panizzardi and Blacker as being involved in the matter. This article was subsequently reprinted in French newspapers, and from then on the situation of the two men became mortally dangerous; both were suspected of being the author of 'Letter from a Diplomat' and both were subjected to a frenzied hate campaign, as Blacker later recalled:

> Then commenced my troubles. I was attacked by the low and infamous press and for days my family and I were insulted and dragged through the most filthy dirt. Anonymous and foul letters were addressed threatening me with assaults and death to myself and my family. I was followed and tracked without intermission for a month and it was only on the frontier when I left France that I finally saw two men leaving the train who had been watching me from the next carriage ...
>
> Then Panizzardi's fate was sealed as far as remaining in Paris was concerned. The low press attacked him, anonymous letters poured in threatening to attack him and spit in his face in public, and even his ambassador was molested. He dined with us every night during this last week of his stay in Paris. He wished to entrust me with all his documents and papers, as he was afraid that they might in some way be got hold of, but I could not accept the responsibility.
>
> At length on the 15th April his position having become quite untenable, he left Paris for Berne on the plea of a mission there. Eventually without being officially recalled from Paris he was given a regiment of Bersaglieri in Rome where he now is.

At this point it is necessary to examine all the known facts about 'Letter from a Diplomat' which caused such a sensation. It became known later, and is stated in Reinach, that it was written by two journalists on the staff of *Le Siècle*, Yves Guyot and Francis de Pressensé. But from where did they get their information? Reinach states that it came from Zola and that it was he who instigated the letter. But who told him? There has been a presumption that it was the journalist, Rowland Strong who in his article in the *New York Times* seemed to be fully apprised of all the facts. But from whom, then, did he discover them? And it is here that the trail leads to Oscar Wilde.

When Blacker wrote to Wilde proposing to visit him in the hotel where he was staying, Wilde had been overjoyed:

> I cannot express to you how thrilled and touched by emotion I was when I saw your handwriting last night. Please come and see me tomorrow ... I want particularly to see you, and long to shake you by the hand again, and to thank you for all the sweet and wonderful kindness you and your wife have shown to Constance and the boys ... I am living here quite alone: in one room, I need hardly say, but there is an armchair for you. I have not seen Alfred Douglas for three months: he is, I believe, on the Riviera. I don't think it probable that we shall ever see each other again.

When the two men met Blacker lost no time in urging Wilde to start writing. Since coming out of prison Wilde's only writing had been a poem and a newspaper article on the iniquities and cruelties of the penal system and the need for greater mercy and understanding of the weak and oppressed. It seemed to Blacker, therefore, that the plight of Dreyfus would surely arouse Wilde's compassion and be a suitable subject for his great literary gifts. Accordingly he confided to him all that Panizzardi had told him, withholding only the name of Panizzardi as his source. Unfortunately, however, Wilde failed to respond: he could feel little sympathy for the dour, upright, innocent military officer. More than that he failed to honour the pledge of secrecy he had given on the matter.

Since coming to Paris Wilde had fallen into disreputable company, perhaps inevitable as most reputable people still shunned him, and among his new associates was the newspaper reporter, Rowland Strong. Strong was the black sheep of a well-to-do English family (his brother was Bishop of Oxford) and was Paris correspondent of the *New York Times* and the London *Observer*. He was also a heavy drinker, a strong anti-Semite and a practising homosexual with a taste for 'the rough'. In the hope of getting a newspaper coup he had cultivated the acquaintance of Esterhazy whom he introduced to Wilde. The two men established rapport at once. 'We are the two greatest martyrs of humanity,' Esterhazy told Wilde, 'but I have suffered the most.' 'No,' Wilde replied. 'I have.' Wilde became fascinated by the wickedness and panache of Esterhazy – so much more attractive than the drabness and innocence of Dreyfus. 'The innocent always suffer,' he told Esterhazy. 'It is their métier. Besides we are all innocent until we are found out. It is a poor common part to play and within the compass of the meanest. The interesting thing surely is to be guilty and wear as a halo the seduction of sin.' During their drinking bouts the two men and Rowland Strong talked wildly. On one occasion Esterhazy freely admitted what he had done: 'Why should I not make a confession to you?' he said. 'I will. It is I, Esterhazy, who alone am guilty. I put Dreyfus in prison, and all France cannot get him out.' For his part Wilde talked recklessly about what Panizzardi had told Blacker and the plan of Blacker and Conybeare for establishing Dreyfus's innocence. This must have been the source of Strong's information for his article in the *New York Times*, but it does not account for the information reaching Zola who then made use of it to instigate the writing of 'Letter from a Diplomat' which preceded Strong's article by a week. Zola's informant was certainly not Wilde as there had been no contact between them. It was thought by some to have been Strong, but this is unlikely as there was little sympathy between him and Zola and Strong had no reason for doing so. It would seem to be more or less certain that Zola was informed by a young, none too respectable journalist-cum-poet, Christopher Healy. Healy was a secretary and intimate companion of Strong and was also an intimate of Wilde. When Wilde arrived in Paris he wrote to Ross: 'I see no one here but a young Irishman called Healy, a poet.' Much later (1906) Healy in his memoirs, *Confessions of a Journalist*, gave his version of the events of the summer of 1898 and of his association with Zola (between his first trial in February and his second in July):

> It was my very good fortune at that time to see Emile Zola often when all newspapers were filling their columns with his adventures, and I had ample opportunity to see and study the peculiarities of the Dreyfus Affair. And if the secret history of this is ever written, I claim the right to contribute two or three chapters at least.

He then went on to recount what he described as 'the extraordinary role played by Oscar Wilde in the liberation of Dreyfus' – how Wilde had told him all he had learned from Blacker and how he had passed this on to Zola who had made use of it to stir up the pro-Dreyfusard agitation. He also told how Zola had wanted to meet Wilde, but this did not happen. Since their first meeting in 1891 relations between the two men had cooled considerably. About a year later they had come together at a dinner in Paris where they were both guests of honour, and Zola in his speech had referred, somewhat offensively, to Wilde as an Englishman who would soon, no doubt, be addressing them in his 'barbaric tongue'. To which Wilde replied that he was not an Englishman but an Irishman and could quite easily address the company in French, but that evening he did propose to speak to them in the language of Shakespeare. And later, when Wilde was in prison, Zola had refused to sign the petition for his early release, of which Wilde must have been aware. And so in 1898 Wilde refused to meet Zola on the grounds that he wrote 'immoral novels', coming strangely from one who had once declared that there was no difference between moral and immoral books, only between books that were well written and those that were badly written. In spite of this, according to Healy, Zola had affirmed that Wilde was one of the instruments which brought about the liberation of Dreyfus, and how this opinion was backed up later by Labori (Dreyfus's counsel) and Mathieu Dreyfus. It is necessary to regard the testimony of Healy with some reserve as he was not altogether wedded to the truth and he was deeply devoted to the memory of Wilde whom he regarded as 'an artist of perfect erudition and a great gentleman whose heart was a mine of generosity'. But if it is the case that Wilde was one of the links in the chain which led to the acquittal of Dreyfus, it should be stressed that he was an unwitting one. In revealing what he knew to Healy and Strong it was not with the liberation of Dreyfus in mind.

Very different to Wilde's was the viewpoint of Carlos Blacker. His commitment to Dreyfus was total. 'There is nothing that has ever excited me like this Zola affair,' he wrote to Conybeare. His plan to publish Esterhazy's communications to Schwartzkoppen in an English newspaper had had to be abandoned when it was revealed by Strong in his *New York Times* article. Later in his book on the Dreyfus Affair Conybeare alluded to this without giving details: 'The project unhappily fell through at the last moment because the conditions of secrecy under which alone we could work were menaced by the rashness of outsiders.' But he and Blacker had no intention of withdrawing from the struggle. During the month of May, when a general election was being fought, the Dreyfus Affair faded from the forefront of the political scene, but it came back strongly when on 1 June Conybeare, primed by Blacker but not mentioning his name, published in the *National Review* in England an article 'The Truth about the Dreyfus Affair'. Like 'Letter from a Diplomat' this set out forcefully and in detail the weakness of the case against Dreyfus and the overwhelming evidence against Esterhazy. A few days later it was reproduced in *Le Siècle* with a supporting commentary by Joseph Reinach in which he pointed out the dangers of the Esterhazy documents being at the disposal of the Kaiser who could release them at a moment of crisis or on the outbreak of war, and so shatter public confidence in the French high command. 'How long will it be,' he asked, 'before

William II draws tight the noose into which all the leading French generals and colonels and nearly all the leading politicians, save the Socialists, have so obligingly adjusted their necks?' Predictably this brought forth howls of rage from *La Libre Parole* and other anti-Dreyfus organs, and the government felt obliged to take some sort of action against Reinach. It was discovered that he was a captain in the territorial army, although long since out of active service; and so he was arraigned before a court martial and formally expelled from the army for 'grave offences against discipline'. It was believed at the time that, as well as writing the commentary to the article in *Le Siècle*, he was also its author as Conybeare had not signed it but used the pseudonym 'Huguenot'. But when Reinach was court-martialled Conybeare wrote a letter in which he admitted his authorship as well as restating powerfully the case against Esterhazy. The letter was read out in court where it was ignored; but it was printed in some 200 newspapers and had considerable influence;* and the mild-mannered academic suddenly found himself the target of the most scurrilous abuse. *La Libre Parole* declared that he was a member of the secret Jewish Syndicate; it discovered that the father of his first wife was called Müller who, of course, was Jewish and so was Conybeare himself, his real name being Koenigsberg. In the safety of North Oxford Conybeare could smile at this nonsense, but for Blacker and his family life was much more hazardous. After the uproar caused by 'Letter from a Diplomat' (which many people continued to believe had been written by him) Blacker had left Paris for Boulogne where for a time there was some reprieve from persecution, but with the publication of Conybeare's article in the *National Review* it flared up again, more violently than before and more personally. It was this which led, amid great rancour to the final rupture of his friendship with Wilde.

At first the rapprochement between the two men had seemed to be heartfelt, but it was not long before it came under strain. It soon became evident to Blacker that Wilde had not mended his ways. He was seeing a lot of a character called Maurice Gilbert, a young soldier who could only be with him for one purpose, and he had not broken off relations finally with Bosie; also he was drinking more heavily than ever. Blacker soon realized that his efforts to make Wilde start writing again had been in vain and he was deeply shocked by his offhand attitude to the Dreyfus Case. This was a subject on which Blacker felt passionately strongly and

---

* Described by a contemporary writer as 'the terrible letter from Oxford which sealed Esterhazy's doom before the bar of the world's educated opinion'.

he was outraged by Wilde's association with Esterhazy and his quip that Esterhazy, who was guilty, was more interesting than Dreyfus who was innocent. For his part Wilde became aware that Blacker was becoming cold and disapproving and resented this deeply from his oldest and greatest friend. The breach between them widened considerably when Blacker suspected that Wilde had passed on the information about the Dreyfus Affair which he had given him in confidence, and it came to a head with the bitter personal attacks on Blacker in the anti-Dreyfusard press. These mentioned certain incidents from Blacker's past life, including the Duke of Newcastle affair, for which, he was convinced, Wilde must have been the source; and there was one abusive article which he believed Wilde had written himself. What happened next is not entirely clear: there was an angry exchange of letters between the two men but these have not survived; there is only an account of them, not altogether reliable, in two letters from Wilde to Ross. These show Wilde to have been deeply embittered as he poured out his rage against Blacker in the same way as he had done against Douglas in *De Profundis*. In the first of these he wrote:

> C. Blacker has behaved like a hypocritical ass to me – and finally wrote me a letter accusing me of having written some attack on him that appeared in some Paris paper! I need hardly say I never read the paper, or saw the attack, and that I never write anonymous attacks on people anywhere. I was so angry, I wrote him a very strong letter ...
>
> The comic thing about him is the moral attitude he takes up. To be either a Puritan, a prig, or a preacher is a bad thing. To be all three at once reminds one of the worst excesses of the French Revolution. I see no difference between him and Bill Nevill; they both got £10,000 out of a young man of unbusinesslike character, but Carlos was cunning enough to keep within the letter of the law, and his refusal to take any action when he was accused of cheating Newcastle at cards, or conniving at the fraud, shows how little he really cares about his character. He came down to see me about a fortnight ago, enquired affectionately into my financial position, actually wept floods of tears, begged me to let him pay the balance of my hotel bill, a request that I did not think it right to refuse, and left me with violent protestations of devotion.

It seems that in this matter the faithful and devoted Robbie Ross had taken the side of Blacker. For Wilde then wrote:

> It is a curious thing, dear little absurd Robbie, that you now always think

that I am in the wrong. It is a morbid reaction against your former, and more rational, estimate of me ...

Why not sometimes think that I may be in the right? Why, at once, take the side of 'le triste individu' [Blacker]? I often wonder what would have happened to those in pain if, instead of Christ, there had been a Christian.

A few weeks later he wrote Robbie an even more venomous letter:

With regard to Blacker you must not think I quarrelled with him. Far from it. Although he treated me with utter indifference, never invited me to have a bite or sup with him at a café or elsewhere, and in the course of five months only came four times to see me, I never quarrelled with him. But three weeks ago he wrote me a letter breaking off our friendship – ugly things cannot be done prettily, in life at any rate. And what he said was: 'I have no further interest in you or in your affairs.' To this letter I made no reply at all, though, considering our ancient friendship and how I stuck to him in his trouble – one, of course, gravely affecting his position as a gentleman, or his claim to be one – I might have written him a letter that would have made him writhe like an adder in a fork, with grotesque outraged contortions and ineffectual venom ...

A week later he wrote me a Nonconformist conscience letter in which he said that as he did not approve of my knowing Bosie he thought it would be morally wrong of him to help me in any way except by advice! He also added that his wife disapproved of my knowing Bosie. So Tartuffe* goes out of my life.

Of course the fact of his being a Jew on his father's side explains everything.

I hope on the day of St Hugh of Lincoln† there will be a general massacre – but I don't known when the day occurs – Do you?

This is a shameful letter. As in *De Profundis* Wilde pours forth his pent up rage in a volley of abuse regardless of truth. Of course Blacker did take action against Newcastle concerning his accusation and the matter

---

* A pious hypocrite from a play by Molière.

† St Hugh (the younger) was a boy of nine whose mutilated body was found at the bottom of a well in Lincoln (c. 1255). According to local mythology he had been abducted by the Jews and ritually murdered after being scourged and crowned with thorns. In retribution eighteen Jews were said to have been executed.

was finally settled amicably between them; and there was never any question of fraud. And to compare Blacker's strictures on his homosexual way of life with the worst excesses of the French Revolution is, to say the least, ridiculous. His grudging concession of Blacker's financial assistance is unattractive and his anti-Semitic swipe is odious – particularly so as, when his affairs were at their worst, two of his greatest benefactors were Jewesses, Ada Leverson and Adela Schuster. In fact Blacker had no known Jewish blood in him although this was being shrilly maintained at the time by the anti-Dreyfusard press. It seems that here Wilde was weakly following the crowd.

Without knowing full details final judgement should perhaps be withheld, but it is noteworthy that several of Wilde's friends, besides Ross, thought him to have behaved badly. And Blacker, the most urbane and charitable of men, wrote later that Wilde 'had treated him with gross cruelty and injustice and that he would finish in the gutter as he deserved'. The two men never met again, but on Wilde's death Blacker felt constrained to visit his deathbed where bitterness gave way to tears of pity and regret. 'When I saw him on his bed,' he wrote, 'and considered the old days and the sufferings he had endured and had caused others to suffer, I broke down and cried as I am almost ashamed to have cried.'

There can be no gainsaying the part Blacker played in the Dreyfus Affair. He was directly or indirectly responsible for the agitations during the summer of 1898 which culminated in the suicide of Henry, the flight of Esterhazy, the release of Picquart and the consent of the government to Lucie Dreyfus's appeal going to the Court of Criminal Appeal. But because he abhorred the limelight and shunned all publicity he has never been accorded the honour which is his due. Joseph Reinach had been informed by his brother Salomon, a close friend of Blacker, of the role he had played, but was sworn to secrecy which he observed so scrupulously that in his massive five-volume history of the Dreyfus Affair Blacker's name appears only once in a footnote. And Conybeare too in his much shorter work, which owed everything to Blacker, never mentioned him by name. But in a private letter he made his opinion clear: 'Whenever the triumph comes I know that Carlos's name will transpire and be in the mouths of thousands of French people as that of one who, though he was an Englishman and had not the same interest and duty in the matter as a Frenchman has, yet did not pass by on the other side of the road.'

Chapter XIV

Dying beyond my means.
(Oscar Wilde)

My life has been full of perverse pleasures and strange passions.
(Ibid.)

When I saw him on his bed and considered the old days and the suffering he had endured and had caused others to suffer, I broke down and cried as I am almost ashamed to have cried.
(Carlos Blacker)

After his return to Paris in February 1898 Wilde was to live for a further two years and nine months. For most of this time his life was seedy and unhappy, as a friend later put it, 'keeping disreputable company in disreputable places'. His only chance of leading a contented life depended on Constance taking him back into the family, but after his return to Douglas there was little likelihood of this, although Constance's love for him never died completely. She told Carlos Blacker that if she ever saw him again she would forgive him everything; and to her younger son at boarding school she wrote movingly: 'Try not to feel harshly about your father; remember that he is your father and that he loves you. All his troubles arose from the hatred of a son for his father, and whatever he has done he has suffered bitterly for.'

She also added a codicil to her will to ensure that Wilde's allowance from her would continue after her death. And this was to happen all too soon. She had never recovered from her fall downstairs at Tite Street which had caused spinal paralysis; and this had become increasingly painful so that an operation became necessary. It was not expected that this would be particularly dangerous, but on 7 April 1898 she died as a result of it – at the age of forty. Wilde seems to have reacted to the tragedy with mixed feelings. He wrote to Robert Ross that he was in great grief, but when Ross arrived in Paris to comfort him he found him in 'good spirits' and 'did not seem to feel Constance's death at all'. He said that the night before she died he dreamed she came to see him and he kept saying: 'Go away, go away, leave me in peace! One result of Constance's death was that there was now no chance of Wilde seeing his sons again. It is possible that in time Constance might have relented on this, but the children's guardian, Adrian Hope, was rigidly opposed to it, and did everything he could to eradicate all connections between the boys and their father (including even preventing them from bene-fiting from royalties on his plays).

It is possible that Wilde might have made something of his last years if he could have started writing again, but to those who urged him he said that the intense energy of creation had been kicked out of him. 'Something is killed in me and I feel no desire to write. I am unconscious of power.' And he told Blacker that *The Ballad of Reading Gaol* was his *chant de cygne*.

More and more his life became void and dissipated. He might have lost his power to write, but he could still enthral with his talk; but he lacked a worthy audience. Most of his English friends fell away, particularly after his quarrel with Blacker, and even among the supposedly liberal and tolerant French he was kept at a distance. Company was hard to find and it usually came from the rebellious or the depraved. In spite of squalls he still saw something of Douglas. The anger he felt when Douglas left him in Naples had subsided and the two men did meet again and seemed to be still quite fond of each other, but their relationship was different; the passion had gone. To his mother Bosie wrote that he had lost 'that supreme desire for Wilde's society', and he kept his promise to her that he would never again live under the same roof as Wilde. But he still enjoyed his company and seems to have felt towards him an obligation of an old friend. At the beginning of 1900 he inherited quite a large sum of money on the death of his father. The 'screaming scarlet marquess' had never been reconciled to his third son, but he did not cut him out of his will. In view of the fact that the Queensberry family had never honoured its pledge to pay his legal expenses, Wilde asked Douglas to make over some money to him but, according to Wilde, this was refused indignantly, causing another outburst of rage in a letter to Ross. But Douglas did, nevertheless, make money over to him (which he later proved to the disbelieving by printing in his autobiography letters from his bank certifying the fact). 'Gilded pillar of infamy' though Douglas might have been, in some ways he did not entirely forsake Wilde in hard times.

There was, indeed, much suffering in Wilde's last years. As he sadly remarked: 'The cruelty of a prison sentence starts when you come out.' Always he had to expect snubs and insults when people turned their backs on him or markedly failed to recognize him, and when barmen refused to serve him and restaurateurs asked him to leave. Outwardly he seemed to bear these blows with indifference. Although capable of outbursts of rage which were soon forgotten, he was incapable of lasting malice and it always surprised him to find it in others, regarding it as silly rather than wicked. Similarly he regarded himself as being mainly responsible for his downfall. He might have felt great bitterness towards England for the way he had been treated but, to the contrary, he was always strongly patriotic, as was shown on such occasions as Queen Victoria's diamond jubilee and the outbreak of the Boer War. It is possible, however, that the insults he received hurt more than he showed. Vincent O'Sullivan, an Irish journalist who came to know him well in his last years, wrote after his death: 'Wilde endured too much cruelty in the Paris of his time; he received too many wounds, hardly ever resented them openly, but finally died of them.'

In his letters during his last years Wilde dwelled much on his financial straits. To a friend he wrote: 'Like dear St Francis I am wedded to poverty, but in my case the marriage is not a success. I hate the bride that has been given to me.' Certainly money was short, at times desperately so, but perhaps he protested too much. With his allowance from Constance, gifts from friends and other sources (including some royalties and advances on books he never wrote) he had enough to live on provided he exercised reasonable economy; but this he was never able to do. Money flowed though his hands. Whenever he had it, and when he didn't, he spent recklessly, usually on inessentials, or helping out a stray acquaintance with a hard luck story. Of saving or budgeting he had no conception, and he saw nothing wrong in building up debts which he was unlikely to be able to repay. He was also quite ready to beg a loan or a gift.* To him money had always been something to be

---

* Nellie Melba, the famous opera singer, recounted how she was approached in Paris by a large man with upturned collar. 'Madam Melba,' he said, 'you don't know who I am, I'm Oscar Wilde and I am going to do a terrible thing. I'm going to ask you for money.' She gave him what she had in her purse and he muttered his thanks and went on his way.

shared, and just as he was ready to part with it, so he was also ready to accept it.

Wilde's daily round in Paris was unattractive. He lived in a shabby hotel room, sparsely furnished.* He seldom rose before noon and then went out to see what he could find – perhaps a free drink, more or less agreeable company, a sexual partner, dinner sometimes paid for sometimes on tick. He did not go to bed before two or three o'clock. But there were breaks in this routine, notably when he travelled abroad. In December 1898 Frank Harris gathered him in and bore him off to the Côte d'Azur where he was in the process of buying a hotel. This meant that for much of the time Wilde was left on his own, and at La Napoule near Cannes he found consolation with the young fishermen who, he was delighted to discover, 'have the same freedom from morals as the Neopolitans have'. At La Napoule he also made the acquaintance of a wealthy homosexual, Harold Mellor, who invited him to stay at his house in Switzerland. This he did for a month, but it was not altogether a success. He found that he had little love for either Switzerland or the Swiss. The country was, undeniably, beautiful but 'the chill virginity of Swiss Alps and snow' did not appeal to him. For the Swiss people he felt contempt – 'nothing but theologians and waiters'. 'Shapeless, colourless, grey of texture and without form, they lacked physical beauty.' And, in addition, they tended to be chaste. To make matters worse he did not get on at all well with his host whom he found mean, even niggardly. 'Too repulsive for anything', he wrote, nor did he feel any more warmly towards him when, on his departure, he wept profusely with 'protestations of admiration and remorse'.

In spite of his distaste for Mellor, Wilde agreed a year later to accompany him to Italy. After visiting several Italian cities including Naples, where Wilde found most of his friends of two years ago in prison, they arrived in Rome during Holy Week. As always Wilde was deeply impressed by 'the only city of the soul' and not least by the Vatican and the Holy Father by whom he contrived to be blessed seven times. Since university days he had had strong leanings towards the Roman Church and had once declared: 'Much of my moral obliquity is due to the fact that my father would not allow me to become a Catholic.' And it has been seen that his first thought on coming out of prison was to

---

* Of the wallpaper in his room he wrote before he died that he was fighting a duel with it to the death and that 'one or other of us has to go'. It would appear that the wallpaper won.

enter a Catholic retreat. He was not ready for a complete conversion, but he was moving in that direction. After leaving Rome he stayed again in Switzerland with Harold Mellor who then drove him to Paris in his automobile – 'a nervous, irritable, strange thing, more wilful than animals' he remarked of it after one of several breakdowns.

Back in Paris Wilde had only six months to live. He resumed his old lifestyle which Douglas later described as 'openly notorious' and of which he himself said that he preferred to be bad than bored. As before he suffered many slights and insults, but he also received some great kindnesses, in particular from Jean Dupoirier, proprietor of the Hotel Alsace. To him Wilde owed a large sum of money and because of this he did not return there but went to other small hotels until his credit ran out. One of these impounded all his clothes and refused to release them until he paid up. From this extremity he was rescued by Dupoirier who paid his bill and brought him back to the Hotel Alsace where he died a few months later. During that time he never pressed for payment of his ever-increasing debt, and when Wilde was dying brought him at his own expense many little luxuries including champagne. Ross later wrote that he could 'scarcely speak of the magnanimity, humanity and charity of Dupoirier'. All Dupoirier said was that M. Melmoth* told such wonderful stories. Before his last illness Wilde's life was much enlivened by the Paris Exhibition of 1900 which he visited many times. This brought a large number of visitors from England, some of whom were kind and provided him with the company he craved. One of these, William Rothenstein, a well-known painter, noticed a difference in him: 'He made himself very charming, but his gaiety no longer convinced; there was a stricken look in his eyes, and he plainly depended on drink to sustain his wit.'

For some time Wilde had had a premonition of death and was ready for it. He knew his health was deteriorating and was not prepared to arrest this by changing his lifestyle. In September he became bedridden, and received a number of visits from the British Embassy doctor (sixty-eight in all) who did not seem to understand the nature of his illness and to whom Ross referred as 'a silly, kind, excellent man'. He called in a specialist who recommended an operation on his ear which had been giving trouble ever since his fall in the prison chapel. This took

---

* Wilde still used this pseudonym although nearly everyone knew his real name. When he died it was to cause great complications with the authorities concerned with granting burial certificates.

place on 10 October and Ross, who arrived in Paris a week later, described him as being in good spirits and full of laughter. But he said his sufferings were acute. 'My throat is a lime-kiln, my brain a furnace and my nerves a coil of adders.' During the next weeks his ear became increasingly painful and it was found that meningitis had set in. The great fear was that this would spread to the brain which it did soon afterwards so that he became delirious. From cerebral meningitis there was no chance of recovery,* and it was at this point that Ross decided to call in a Roman Catholic priest. Ross, who was himself a Catholic, had up till then been discouraging of Wilde's leanings towards his Church; he felt that he was not serious and would have long, frivolous arguments with any priest who came to oversee his conversion. But now, when he was unable to speak and clearly dying, he thought the time had come for a priest to administer Conditional Baptism, Extreme Unction and Absolution. For this it was necessary that Wilde should be aware of what was going on and this was not easy to determine as he could not communicate and showed few reactions. However, when offered a cigarette he took it into his fingers and raised it to his face (but not his lips), and this was considered sufficient evidence of his awareness.

Wilde died on 30 November 1900. Robert Ross and Reginald Turner were with him at the end. Between them they had seen to it that all medical and nursing attention that was necessary had been provided; his death had certainly not been free from pain but everything possible had been done to alleviate it. Carlos Blacker arrived from Germany the morning after his death with flowers on behalf of his two sons to go into his coffin; and Douglas arrived from England a day later, and at once agreed to pay all funeral expenses. At the funeral, which took place in a neighbouring church, there were some fifty people present including some ladies veiled. A temporary burial place had been obtained at Bagneux cemetery where there were twenty-four wreaths including one from Ross inscribed 'A tribute to his literary achievement and distinction' with the names of all those who had shown kindness to him since his downfall.

---

* It seems probable but not certain that this was syphilitic in origin.

Chapter XV

The transcript of the Rennes process, when published in full, will stand as the most execrable monument of human infamy.

(Zola)

The right of an innocent man is not clemency; it is justice.

(Dreyfus)

My heart will not be eased until there is not a single Frenchman left who could impute to me a crime committed by another.

(Ibid.)

When Dreyfus arrived in France on 30 June 1899 he was still in almost complete ignorance of the events of the last five years; he was one of the few Frenchmen who knew nothing of the Dreyfus Affair. On the voyage from Devil's Island he had read of the suicide of Henry and the arrest of Du Paty,* but he was unaware of their significance. Of the efforts on his behalf by Picquart, Scheurer-Kestner and Zola he knew nothing; and he had only five weeks before the beginning of his trial to find out about all that had been going on. And he was in no condition to do this. His long ordeal had taken its toll. He was beset by malaria and rheumatism and, occasionally, hallucinations; his digestion was such that he could take only milk and biscuits; and his voice from long disuse had become no more than a strangled croak. His appearance, it was remarked at the time, was 'numb and dejected and revealed depths of unspeakable suffering'. His mental condition too was unsound; he was easily confused and soon lost the thread of what was being said to him.

---

* Du Paty had been put on trial following the verdict of the United Appeal Court for forgery of documents including the *Blanche* and *Speranza* telegrams and the *Faux Henry*, also of communicating the *canaille de D* letter to *L'Eclair*. But these charges could not be substantiated and he was released.

It was going to be a desperate struggle to get him through the impending trial.

Although his conviction by the court of 1894 had been set aside, Dreyfus was still under arrest awaiting a second trial, and in Rennes he was lodged in the local jail. Here after a few hours he had an emotional reunion with Lucie and later with Mathieu who began the difficult process of enlightening him about what was happening. Rennes had been chosen by the government as the location for the trial because it was a quiet provincial town, within easy reach of the sea and, it was thought, at a safe distance from the noise and turbulence of Paris. But it was expecting too much that this turbulence would not spread there: pressmen by the hundred poured in from all over the world, as did groups of anti-Semites bent on making trouble as well as passionate Dreyfusards, eager to give their hero an effusive welcome. The peaceful country town soon found itself crowded out and in the throes of violent agitation so that hundreds of extra police had to be drafted in.* Normally the inhabitants of Rennes were not vehemently political, but, fomented by anti-Semites spreading scare stories of secret Jewish plots, the atmosphere became highly charged and anti-Dreyfusard, so that Lucie and well-known Dreyfusards were being harassed and having difficulty in finding lodgings.

After a few days Dreyfus was visited by his lawyers: Edgar Demange, who had defended him at his first trial, had been retained as also had Fernand Labori who had defended Zola so zealously. This looked a formidable combination, but had a weakness in that the two men differed strongly as to how the defence should be conducted: Labori wanted a great showpiece full of drama and eloquence with Dreyfus held up as the noblest of martyrs; while Demange maintained that, while these methods might succeed in a civil court, they were unsuitable for a court martial where histrionics would be unsuitable and counterproductive; they would put up the backs of the military judges whose instincts would be to rally to the support of the honour of the army; better far to rely on quiet persuasion and unostentatious exposure of fallacious evidence so that doubts were sown in the minds of the judges. In the event it was the latter view that prevailed which must have been the right one if only because Dreyfus himself was incapable of drama and unwilling to act the part of a great wronged hero. In spite of all he had been

---

* This was just as well as some anti-Dreyfusards were openly proclaiming that if Dreyfus was acquitted, it would be the duty of every patriot to kill him.

through he remained still the dour, disciplined officer, strongly patriotic and totally loyal to the army which he had no wish to denigrate or embarrass. Towards those who had condemned him he felt no bitterness; he would have done just the same himself in their place.* At no time during the trial did he make any reference to his sufferings; his sole aim remained to clear his name and reveal the true culprit with as little agitation as possible. During the trial, then, he was to be a disappointment to some of his supporters who were looking for emotion and strong words; throughout he sat cold, rigid and apparently unmoved.† When his letters to his wife were read out tears were brought to many eyes but not to his.

It was thought by some Dreyfusards that the second court martial would be no more than a formality; the Dreyfus Case had just gone before the highest judges in the land who in ordering a retrial had indicated by implication their belief in Dreyfus's innocence. But once again this was to underestimate the obduracy of the Army high command. Senior officers were well aware that Dreyfus's acquittal might mean their indictment. This applied particularly to General Mercier, the War Minister who had instituted proceedings against Dreyfus and had then, with the help of Henry, rigged the court martial by showing secret documents to the judges and not to the defence counsel. Already after the verdict of the United Appeal Court there had been a call for his prosecution and this would became much more insistent if Dreyfus were acquitted. And so at Rennes Mercier played an active part, overseeing the military witnesses and making sure they adhered to their original stories. And it was not only the witnesses to whom it was made clear what was expected of them. As senior officer present he contrived to overawe the middle-ranking judges of the court martial and saw to it that they realized that it was up to them to uphold the honour of the army, and that the choice that lay before them was the guilt of Dreyfus or himself – the Jew or the General. It is likely too that he was responsible for rumours circulating at Rennes that in 1894 he had been in possession of momentous information which might have had catastrophic consequences, and these were only avoided by his deft handling of the situation. The nature of this information was not revealed but

---

* It has been said with some aptness that if his name had not been Alfred Dreyfus he would have been a strong anti-Dreyfusard.
† In contrast to Esterhazy, who was guilty and who at his trial had been overwrought and uncontrolled.

reports were renewed of a copy of the *bordereau* annotated by the Kaiser and mentioning Dreyfus by name. It cannot be proved that Mercier was the source of these rumours but he certainly did nothing to deny them. At the same time he could bring himself to declare in court: 'If the slightest doubt had entered my mind I should be the first to declare and say before you, to Captain Dreyfus that I was mistaken in good faith.' Even for Dreyfus this was too much and for the only time in the trial he showed signs of excitement and cried out in a hoarse voice: 'That's what you ought to do. It's your duty.'

The proceedings of the court martial proved to be more of a spectacle than a trial, one observer going as far as to describe it as a 'harlequinade'. More than a hundred witnesses, mainly for the prosecution, were lined up to give evidence which in some cases had already been given several times before in other trials. But the key figures were absent: Esterhazy because he was in exile, Du Paty because he was allegedly too ill and Henry because he was dead. There was also a mountain of documents – now over 400 – many of which had been dismissed at the trials of Esterhazy and Zola and later by the United Appeal Court, but they were brought out again and it was up to the unfortunate judges, who had little experience of legal matters, to decide whether or not they were admissible. Most of the evidence covered well trodden ground. Once again the graphologists wrangled among themselves and gave conflicting and in some cases bizarre evidence, one of them going so far as to say that because some of the words in the *bordereau* were identical to the handwriting of Esterhazy, they could not have been written by him because no one ever wrote the same word in exactly the same way, and so they must, therefore, have been a copy or tracing by someone else. Once again the argument raged as to whether Dreyfus had been in a position to deliver the documents listed in the *bordereau* and whether this was in the language to be expected of an artillery officer. There was also dispute about the date of the *bordereau* which was of importance as it had been dated originally in the summer of 1894 in which case it would not have been possible for Dreyfus to be 'just off on manoeuvres' as was stated in it. So it had been attempted to backdate it to the spring of 1894 when it might have been possible. Also brought up again was the question of Dreyfus's moral character, and on the flimsiest of evidence he was portrayed as a womanizer and gambler.

The witnesses for the prosecution included a number of eminent figures. General de Boisdeffre, one time Chief of Staff, who had resigned under a cloud following the uncovering of the *Faux Henry*, came and testified to his complete conviction that Dreyfus was guilty – a particularly hard blow for Dreyfus who had once been on friendly terms with him and regarded him as his patron. General Roget and Captain Cuignet, who together had brought to light the forgeries of Henry, might have been expected to be convinced of Dreyfus's innocence, but to the contrary they denounced him with great virulence. Another active and unscrupulous anti-Dreyfusard at Rennes was Quesnay de Beaurepaire, the one-time judge and president of the Civil Court (see p. 125) who seems to have put aside all judiciousness and to have allowed himself to become obsessed with rabid anti-Semitism. It was he who produced a particularly disreputable new witness, one M. Cernusky who claimed to be a retired officer of aristocratic descent in the Austrian army and who had heard of Dreyfus's espionage from senior officers and had seen written evidence of it. On investigation, however, it emerged that he had a history of mental instability, was heavily in debt and had a record for fraud. At Rennes, faced with the prospect of cross-examination, he

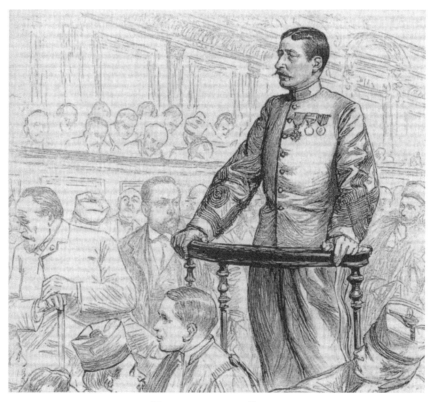

Picquart in court in Rennes

disappeared suddenly. The defence counsel had, however, been disturbed by Cernusky's fabrications, and to counter them they attempted to obtain fuller and more definite clearance of Dreyfus from the German and Italian governments, perhaps by the production of some of the correspondence between Esterhazy and Schwartzkoppen; but here they were rebuffed. The Kaiser affirmed that his foreign minister had already stated plainly on several occasions that no German officer had had any communication with Dreyfus, but this had apparently not been believed by the French Government and he was not prepared to do anything further. A much more important witness than Cernusky, but who was given much less freedom to speak, was Captain Freystaetter, one of the judges at the 1894 court martial who, following the suicide of Henry, had become convinced of Dreyfus's innocence and wanted to give evidence about the secret documents shown to the judges; as with other defence witnesses, he was constantly interrupted and cut short by the President of the Court, as well as being brutally reviled by Mercier.

After the witnesses had been heard it had to be decided which of the two defence counsel would make the final summing up. Halfway through the trial Labori had been shot while walking in Rennes, but the injury was slight and he was ready and eager to make a powerful, declamatory oration. It was decided, however, (principally by Mathieu) to rely on Demange with his quiet, compelling reasoning. He spoke for seven hours and at the end there was little left of the case against Dreyfus. It had to be certain that the *bordereau*, on which alone Dreyfus had been convicted, had been written by Esterhazy who, it was reported, in the safety of England had admitted as much. As to the 'secret dossier' it could no longer be denied that documents had been shown to the judges in 1894, but of these the only one to have been made public was the one alluding to *ce canaille de D*, and it had been demonstrated by Picquart that it was impossible that this could refer to Dreyfus. Any civil court would have been bound to bring in an acquittal. But this was a court martial and the stark fact confronting the seven judges was that the honour of the army required the conviction of an innocent man. Military chiefs and politicians had become so steeped in falsehood and evasion that the situation was unavoidable. Desperately the judges looked for a way out, and the solution they found was, indeed, desperate: by a majority of five to two Dreyfus was found guilty of treason but with 'extenuating circumstances'. What extenuating circumstances there could be for treason was never explained. The sentence of the Court was ten years imprisonment less the five already served.

Moves were then made to obtain a presidential pardon. The Prime Minister at that time was René Waldeck-Rousseau, a brilliant lawyer who, while maintaining strict neutrality during the court martial, was believed to have wanted an acquittal. Like others before him his over-whelming wish was for the Dreyfus Affair to be laid to rest and to be heard of no more, and he thought that a pardon, which would mean Dreyfus's immediate release, might achieve this. And so President Loubet was advised to grant one which he was ready to do. But the hope that this would bury the Dreyfus Affair was in vain. What Dreyfus sought was justice and the clearing of his name, not an act of clemency for a crime he had not committed. And it was borne in on him that accep-tance of the pardon would be taken as a tacit admission of his guilt. His first reaction, then, was to reject the pardon and fight on, and in this he was vehemently supported by the more ardent Dreyfusards. But his family and close associates knew that he had reached the limit of his endurance; no way could he survive another spell on Devil's Island. To reject the pardon would mean certain death. In the end Dreyfus was persuaded when it was pointed out to him that he could carry on the fight more effectively if he was at liberty rather than in jail. However, he insisted on issuing a proud and defiant statement:

> The government of the Republic have given me my liberty. It means nothing to me without my honour. From now onward I shall persistently seek to obtain reparation for the frightful judicial error of which I am still the victim.
>
> I wish all France to know that I am innocent through the promulgation of judgment to that effect. My heart will not be eased until there is not a single Frenchman left who could impute to me a crime committed by another.

The reaction of the anti-Dreyfusard press to the Rennes verdict was, predictably, loud and obscene. 'France is saved,' blazoned *L'Intransigeant* and went on underneath: 'What ecstasy there is in all French hearts and what rotten luck for the hook-nosed Yid ... finding himself down on his immense *derrière* among all the Yids who will be yelling their heads off, clamouring for their money back.' At the same time large, excited crowds gathered outside the offices of *La Libre Parole* which flaunted huge banners proclaiming 'France for the French' and 'Death to the Jews'. The Dreyfusard press was also vehement but without the obscenity. 'The Innocent Condemned,' declared *L'Aurore* and went on to revile 'this abominable judgment'. 'We know that this judicial lie is not the last word of the affair, and that the forgers, victorious today, have only put off the hour of their own imprisonment. We count on tomorrow. France cannot let itself be dishonoured in the world by five officers, Jesuits and idiots, who aimed to cover up the crimes of their chiefs.' And with regard to the 'extenuating circumstances' in the verdict: 'Do they imagine that we will accept their vile poison just because they serve it up with a bit of honey?' Zola too, as might be expected, surged in: 'The transcript of the Rennes process, when published in full, will stand as the most execrable monument of human infamy ... The ignorance, the folly, the madness, the cruelty, the lies, the crime, will have been exposed with a shamelessness that will make future generations tremble from shame.'

It was not only in France that there were feelings of outrage. The German *chargé d'affaires* in Paris wrote to the Kaiser: 'It will always be regarded as a monstrous thing, and as such the judgement will be condemned by public opinion in the whole of the civilised world, with the exception of France, who has thus cut herself off from civilised nations.' In America there was widespread indignation, one newspaper declaring that 'the most celebrated perjurers in history were models of sincerity compared with those at Rennes'. In no country was there more moral outrage than in England, never entirely unhappy at French misfortunes. *The Times* lost no time in loosing its thunder: it had 'no hesitation in affirming that the sentence ... constitutes in itself the grossest and ... most appalling prostitution of justice which the world has witnessed in modern times ... Never before has a nation which claims to march at the head of civilisation so flagrantly, so deliberately, so mercilessly trampled justice, honour and truth under foot!' The Dreyfus Affair even caught the attention of Queen Victoria who despatched the Lord Chief Justice to Rennes as her special observer, and when she heard the verdict let it be known that she regarded it 'with profound sorrow and that it was in defiance of good sense'. Moderate words but from that source carrying great weight.

The French Government, while strongly resenting any interference in the country's domestic affairs, could not but be disturbed by such violently hostile feelings. For these were not confined to newspaper articles. Demonstrations were staged, French consulates were stoned and there was talk of blacklisting French goods. More potent still were threats to boycott the great Paris Exhibition of 1900 in which millions of francs had been invested. This must certainly have had an influence on the French Government in granting a pardon to Dreyfus and later in the declaration of an amnesty. If the acceptance of the pardon saved Drey-fus's life, it also created a lasting rift among the Dreyfusards, some of whom regarded it as an unforgivable betrayal. Men who had made great sacrifices for the cause, incurring danger and compromising their liveli-hoods, could not be satisfied with anything except complete victory. 'We might have died for Dreyfus,' one of them proclaimed, 'but Dreyfus has not died for Dreyfus.' And Clemencau declared: 'After having roused whole populations in defence of justice, it is immoral to ask them to be content with the pardon of one person.' To these men the cause was everything, Dreyfus was secondary, no more than a symbol.

This rift was further widened when in December 1900 the government passed a Decree of Amnesty for all crimes and misdemeanours connected with the Dreyfus Case and at the same time suppressed all pending legal actions connected with it. This caused great bitterness as guilty and innocent were treated alike, the heroic and the righteous with the forgers and the perjurers. Picquart was pardoned for a crime he had not com-mitted while Mercier was let off for those that he had; and while enabling the guilty to escape punishment it deprived those most wronged, notably Dreyfus himself, of means of redress. When the Amnesty Bill came before the Senate Dreyfus made a strong protest:

> The amnesty puts an end to the lawsuit by means of which I had hoped revelations would be made enabling me to bring the matter before the Cour de Cassation … No one desires peace, the reconciliation of honest Frenchmen and the termination of the dreadful passions of which I was the first victim, more ardently than I do. But only justice can bring peace. The amnesty strikes me to the heart. It can benefit no one but General Mercier.

For a time after Dreyfus had accepted the presidential pardon it seemed that the government might have succeeded in ridding itself of the everlasting Affair. With a large majority Parliament passed a reso-lution urging the government 'energetically to oppose a resumption of the Dreyfus Affair from whatever quarter the proposal might come'. And there were many signs that public interest was subsiding: people had heard enough of Dreyfus and were not prepared to feel as sorry for him now that he was living comfortably at home as when he was sweating it out on Devil's Island. To Mathieu and other members of the family the thought must have occurred to call it a day: Alfred was on the point of collapse and in desperate need of rest and recuperation; and the pardon carried with it an implication that the government disagreed with the verdict of the court martial and had gone as far as it could to show this. Still the fact remained that Dreyfus had been pardoned not acquitted. Officially he was still a traitor and, as long as this was so, he was determined that the struggle had to continue. But this had to be on his terms: he was not prepared to join in turbulent demonstrations or head political movements; under no circumstances would he appeal for pity for the sufferings he had endured; and he firmly put aside all ideas of financial compensation. Since he had consecrated his life to his country, he maintained, the country had a right to dispose of him and to inflict unmerited suffering on him. Despite over four and a half years on Devil's Island and two courts martial with flagrant miscarriages of justice, his devotion to the army remained intact and he had no wish to humiliate it. All he sought was calmly and logically to assemble evidence that would overturn his conviction, and so restore his honour and enable him to resume his rank. Of course such coldness and precision widened the gap between him and the ultra-Dreyfusards who were eagerly seeking some sign of warmth and humanity – what one of them called 'a cry of a wounded bleeding animal'. Some of them, including Picquart, became bitterly hostile – more so, it seemed at times, than the anti-Dreyfusards – and accused him of 'ingratitude, lack of feeling and indifference'. But he was not to be deflected. After the Rennes verdict there was a period of several years before the Dreyfus Affair again made its way into the political arena. This was due partly to the distraction caused by the Great Exhibition of 1900 and partly to the determination of successive parliaments not to allow the subject to be brought up. During this time, however, Mathieu and Alfred Dreyfus were not inactive. In order to obtain a retrial it was necessary that new evidence be found which had not been available to the judges at Rennes, and with nearly all doors closed to them, following the amnesty, this was going to be difficult. For a time it seemed that their best hope lay in tracking down the so-called *bordereau annoté* (see p. 99). At Rennes there had been much talk of this, but no one ever claimed to have actually seen it, although Mercier gave credence to it by putting it about that he had 'irrefutable proof' of Dreyfus's guilt. If such a document did exist Mathieu was confident that it was a forgery and could be exposed as such. Also if at the court martial it had been shown to the judges and not to the defence counsel, this was illegal and should invalidate the verdict. The Dreyfusards were eager to bring the matter up in the Chamber of Deputies, but for three years this was blocked. In 1903, however, the Socialist Leader, Jean Jaurés managed to introduce it in a debate on a different but related subject. It has been seen that some Socialists were not zealous Dreyfusards, looking on the Affair as a dispute between rival bourgeois groups in which they need not become involved. Jaurés, however, thought otherwise: to him Dreyfus was the victim of an unjust system and deserved support, whatever his background or class. After a very long speech in the chamber he proposed an official inquiry into the *bordereau annoté* which was rejected, but the new War Minister, General André, a staunch republican bent on curbing the powers of the army, agreed to a 'personal investigation'.

Once again, then, a War Minister, with the assistance of an aide-de-camp, set out to examine the entire Dreyfus dossier in the expectation and hope of finding incontrovertible proof of Dreyfus's guilt, and once again, instead of this, finding documents that had been tampered with and others that had been suppressed, and all pointing towards Dreyfus's innocence. Being an honest man, André made no attempt at a cover-up but made a report to the Prime Minister (Emile Combes) of 'discoveries of a serious nature'. From then on the wheels turned inexorably but inconceivably slowly towards retrial and acquittal. On 26 November (1903) Dreyfus petitioned formally for a revision of the Rennes verdict on the false testimony given by Cernuski and a statement by the German ambassador for the first time naming Esterhazy as Schwartzkoppen's agent. Three months later the petition was accepted and referred to the Criminal Court of Appeal to decide whether there was a case for revision. For five months the court, yet again, ploughed through all the Dreyfus documents and again heard all the witnesses who had given their evidence so often before. It heard the more bizarre theories of the handwriting experts debunked, it could find no trace of the *bordereau annoté*, it found the evidence of Cernuski worthless and most of the other evidence against Dreyfus inapplicable. By a unanimous decision the Court then decided that there was justification for revision, and the case was referred to the highest court in the land, the United Court of Appeal (where it had been five years before, see p. 125).

There was then an unaccountably long delay of two years before the United Court began its deliberations (18 June 1906). It then took five weeks to decide that 'condemnation was erroneously and wrongly given' and that Dreyfus was innocent. The judges were, however, divided on an important matter – as to whether their judgement was final or whether Dreyfus should face another court martial. Dreyfus himself was ready for this and Clemencau, among others, maintained that for full justice to be done the Rennes verdict should be rescinded by a military court. But there were strong arguments against this: the Dreyfus Affair had been dragging on much too long and everyone was longing for it to come to an end. Also the United Court was the highest in the land and overrode all others, civil and military; and there was something ridiculous about the matter having been settled by the country's top judges for it then to go before a third court martial presided over by youthful, inexperienced and possibly biased army officers. And so the ruling of the Court (by 31 to 18) that its judgement was final and irrevocable was accepted.

This time the verdict was received comparatively calmly – no angry street scenes, no threats to the judges nor frenzied abuse of leading Dreyfusards. The Dreyfus Affair was no longer a burning issue; it seemed to be generally accepted that the judgement was inevitable and right; even *La Libre Parole* sounded deflated. It then behoved the government to make amends: substantial financial compensation would have been in order, but Dreyfus had always disclaimed this; he was reinstated in the army but only with the rank of major, not that of colonel which he would have attained in the normal course of his career. He was, however, appointed a Chevalier of the Legion of Honour (4th class), and a quiet, dignified ceremony for this took place in the grounds of the Ecole Militaire where twelve years before he had undergone the ordeal of degradation. And so the Dreyfus Affair at last came to an end. It had spanned nearly twelve years. At times it had divided and embittered the French people, had taken up much time of public figures and diverted their attention from more pressing matters at home and abroad.

Ceremonial reinstatement of Dreyfus

It had given rise to both heroism and villainy, and the changes it brought about, or helped to bring about were almost entirely beneficial. Changes in the army were overdue: there was no place in a democracy for an army which was a law unto itself or, as it was described, 'a state within a state'. It had not come well out of the Dreyfus Affair, senior officers having shown themselves capable of mendacity and equivocation and being prepared to see an innocent man condemned to a fearful punishment. It may be true that they acted not for their own benefit but for that of the army but, as was said at the time, the honour of the army should not require the conviction of someone for a crime he had not committed. Some Republicans and most Socialists had long regarded the army with fear and suspicion, and even before the end of the Dreyfus Affair some army commanders (although not Alfred Dreyfus) had become convinced of the need to 'republicanise' the army or, as General André the new War Minister put it, 'to adapt the army to modern ideas, modern manners and modern institutions'. And so measures were taken to ensure the subordination of the army to the civil power: promotion of senior officers was to rest no longer with the high command but with the War Minister; some of the responsibilities of the SS (intelligence service) were taken away and transferred to the police force; conscription was reduced from three years to two; and action was taken to reduce the allegedly pervasive influence of the Roman Catholic Church in the army.* The results of these changes, however, were in some ways detrimental. They caused rancour and division so that the army's efficiency was impaired. It could be that it would have been more ready for war in 1914 without them.

Another important change, which was helped on its way by the Dreyfus Affair, was the separation of Church and State which came about formally in 1905. This had been coming for some time, but the anti-Dreyfusard stance of the Roman Catholic Church and the unpopularity it incurred thereby exacerbated relations with Republicans and Radicals and hastened the process. But the great and abiding benefit arising from the Dreyfus Affair lay in the field of human rights where it was established that they predominated over all other considerations – the honour of the army, political expediency, public security – and in this the lonely, stoical figure from Devil's Island, however unwittingly, had had a vital role.

---

* Army officers were interrogated unduly intrusively, some thought, on their religious proclivities.

Postscript

Chapter XVI

He gave an impetus to the conscience of mankind.
(Anatole France on Zola)

On Wilde's behalf I suffered exile, obloquy and disgrace.
(Alfred Douglas)

Rather a humorous stroke of Fate's irony that the son of a Marquess of Queensberry should be forced to expiate his sins by a succession of blows beneath the belt.
(George Bernard Shaw)

There's no smoke without fire.
(Alfred Dreyfus)

Dreyfus remained in the army for only one year after being reinstated. He had not been well treated. In his *History of France* the distinguished French Historian, André Maurois wrote: 'It has been said that in no other country would such an injustice as the Dreyfus Case have been possible, but that in no other country would the injustice, once committed, have been fought with so much courage or redressed with so much generosity.' But this is not sustainable. The fight against injustice was fought by very few people against overwhelming odds and it took them twelve years to gain their ends. And the redress of the injustice, considering how monstrous it had been was far from generous. The very least the army could have done was to confer on Dreyfus the rank he would have attained in normal circumstances and which had been reached by most of his contemporaries – that of lieutenant-colonel. Instead of which he was accorded the lower rank of major. Then, when he requested retirement he was relegated to captain with a captain's pension and no allowance made for his four and a half years on Devil's Island. And this in spite of the fact that he and his family had spent over a million francs on legal fees and other expenses and had never claimed a centime in compensation. The army had, indeed, little to be proud of in the Dreyfus Affair.

In the years between the presidential pardon and his final acquittal by the Court of Appeal Dreyfus had become a worldwide celebrity, especially after the publication of his book *Five Years of my Life*, a factual, impassive account of his years on Devil's Island. Letters poured in from all over the world including lucrative offers for newspaper articles and lecture tours, even of new homes. But he was not interested: at first he concentrated on building up his strength in the healthy mountain air of Switzerland; but later he realized that if he was to carry on the fight for his acquittal he must return to Paris. This involved great risk as there were still many desperadoes imbued with the idea that it was their patriotic duty to assassinate him. Predictably he found it difficult to find accommodation as few people wanted him as a neighbour and when he did, it was necessary to spend most of his time behind closed shutters and barred doors. There were, however, certain occasions when he felt bound to emerge and make a public appearance; one of these was for the ceremony attending the transfer of Zola's ashes from Montmartre to the Panthéon, the historic resting place of distinguished Frenchmen. As was to be expected this stirred up great emotion. Old memories were revived and violence was threatened. Dreyfus must have known that if he made an appearance he would be a prime target, but he was not to be put off. He owed too much to Zola. Already he had received innumerable threats to his life which had come to nothing, but this time he came within an inch of being killed. A half-crazed elderly journalist managed to get close to him with a revolver and fired. Fortunately his arm was deflected at the last moment so that Dreyfus was wounded relatively harmlessly in the arm. The would-be assassin was arrested and brought to justice but was fortunate enough to appear before a strongly anti-Dreyfusard jury which acquitted him on the grounds that he was overwrought and not responsible for his actions. And *La Libre Parole* at once opened a subscription for his benefit.

Those Frenchmen who had accused all Jews, and the Dreyfus family in particular, of being unpatriotic and in league with the country's enemies were totally belied with the outbreak of the First World War when Jews of military age, and conspicuously from the Dreyfus family, rushed to enlist. In the course of the war Alfred's eldest brother Jacques was to lose two sons in action, and Mathieu was to lose a son and a son-in-law, while Alfred's son, Pierre, was to fight in the front line throughout the war, somehow surviving the carnage of Verdun and the Somme, rising from the rank of corporal to that of captain and being awarded three citations for bravery. Alfred himself, being in the reserve, was called up immediately after the outbreak of war; his first assignment was as artillery officer in the garrison of Paris in an organizational rather than a combative role. But he longed to be in battle. When on Devil's Island he had written home: 'When I am finally leading my brave soldiers again, I will forget everything, the suffering, the torture, the outrageous insults. May God and human justice make that day come soon.' The moment was delayed but did eventually come in 1917 when, partly because of the death of so many younger officers, he was sent at the age of fifty-seven to the front line. Here in spite of the squalor, the danger, the vile weather and endless bombardments he was happier than he had ever been. Someone who saw him at the time said that he seemed to be more revitalized by active service than by the judgement of the Court of Appeal. All reports were that he served with bravery and efficiency, so much so that the army was at last prompted to promote him to his rightful rank of colonel. After the war, however, with great meanness, it withheld what he craved and was clearly his due, a 'Carte de Combattant' testifying to his service in action, on the grounds that he had not been in the front line long enough and had not been wounded.

After the war Dreyfus was to live a further seventeen years. During this time he led a quiet, retiring life, seldom, if ever, 'coming out of his shell'. His son later wrote of him that 'he lived an intense interior life but no longer knew how to externalise his feelings.' But his sufferings were not yet over: in his last years he fell ill of what was described as 'infirmities of an interior type' which caused him great pain. According to his son 'for a long year his poor body suffered horribly'. But suffering was something to which he was inured. He died in 1935 at the age of seventy-five. After his ordeal on Devil's Island few people would have expected such a life span.

Outside the family no one had done more to obtain justice for Dreyfus than Emile Zola. It was he who transformed the matter from a low-key private action into a burning national issue. When he returned from his enforced exile in England in June 1899 he made contact with Dreyfus and the two men became firm friends, Zola not only giving him strong support in his continuing struggle to clear his name but also defending him against the Dreyfusards who wanted him to refuse the presidential pardon and lead a more dynamic and populist campaign.

Three years later in 1902 Zola died suddenly as a result of a domestic accident when carbon monoxide fumes escaped from a fire. He was only sixty-two and at the height of his powers. Dreyfus was deeply saddened and went round at once to his house and sat for several hours with his body. As has been seen he insisted on attending the funeral where he heard Anatole France say of Zola that 'he gave an impetus to the conscience of mankind.' Six years later Zola's ashes were transferred to the Panthéon where Clemencau, then Prime Minister, gave a moving address:

> Men have been known to oppose the most powerful kings; few men have been known to oppose the multitude, to stand alone face to face with the misguided mob, excited to the worst excesses of fury; to challenge implacable rage, weaponless and with folded arms; to dare, when a 'Yes' is demanded, to raise their heads and utter 'No'.

Of the army officers involved in the Dreyfus Affair Georges Picquart alone emerged with honour. If his advice had been taken and a mistake had been admitted at an early stage, then matters would never have escalated into a great national scandal.

As has been seen, he received no thanks for his pains: first sent off to a colonial frontier, then arrested on a trumped-up charge and kept in solitary confinement for many months. Reinstated in the army in 1906, after the final acquittal of Dreyfus, he was then treated with some generosity – promoted to general, two ranks above that which he had held previously. Soon afterwards, when Clemencau became Prime Minister, he was appointed Minister for War, a post for which he was ill-fitted partly because of his lack of ability and partly because of his unpopularity in the army. Although this unpopularity was due in the main to his role in the Dreyfus Affair, it was also because he was not a very likeable person; he was ungenerous, self-righteous and strongly anti-Semitic. He had been angry when Dreyfus accepted the presidential pardon, believing that the principal at stake in the Affair was of greater importance than the welfare, or even, the life, of Dreyfus himself. Later, when he was Minister for War, he had the opportunity to redress the wrong done to Dreyfus when he was reinstated in the army and given a rank lower than that which he might justifiably have expected. But when Dreyfus's plea for promotion came before him, he turned it down.

In 1914 he was given command of an army corps, but died as a result of a fall from a horse before the outbreak of war.

Few bore so much responsibility for the Dreyfus Affair as General Auguste Mercier. As Minister for War it was he who first instituted proceedings and who then stuck to his guns, maintaining to the bitter end, despite all evidence to the contrary, that Dreyfus was guilty. Mathieu Dreyfus once called him 'a hardened criminal'.

In 1900 he was elected to the Senate as a deputy on the extreme right wing. When the bill reinstating Dreyfus in the army was introduced he sought to speak against it, but was shouted down. He remained in the Senate until 1920 when he retired at the age of eighty-seven. He died the following year.

Another who had had an ignoble role in the Affair was Du Paty de Clam. Of him Zola wrote that he was 'the entire Dreyfus Affair'. But later in the First World War he was to atone for his misdeeds on the battlefield, dying of wounds at the age of sixty-three.

A more infamous career awaited his son who at the time of the Vichy Government in the Second World War became Commissioner for Jewish Affairs and was responsible for the deportation to Germany of thousands of French Jews including, in all likelihood, two members of the Dreyfus family – Alfred's nephew Julien and his granddaughter Madeleine, both of whom disappeared into the gas chambers of Auschwitz.

The most vicious anti-Dreyfusard of all, Edouard Drumont, editor of *La Libre Parole*, lived to see both his cause and his newspaper collapse. He died in poverty in 1917.

And what of the villain of the piece – Major Marie-Charles-Ferdinand Walsin-Esterhazy? The prison sentence passed on him for defrauding his cousin (see p. 122) kept him out of France, and he finally came to roost in England in the village (as it then was) of Harpenden where he was sometimes heard of living with a woman who kept a *maison de rendezvous* and sometimes making a living of sorts by trading in foreign tinned foods. He died in 1923.

Two central figures in the Dreyfus Affair who knew most of the secrets (although not all) were the German and Italian military attachés, von Schwartzkoppen and Panizzardi.

It has been seen (p. 143) that von Schwartzkoppen asked to be withdrawn from Paris in 1897 when Esterhazy was brought to trial, and soon afterwards he was assigned to the command of an infantry regiment. At the same time he was given strict orders that he was to make no comments on Dreyfus, and all attempts to draw him out on the subject were rebuffed. He retired from the army in 1908 but was recalled on the outbreak of the First World War. In 1914 he was to be found in command of a brigade on the Western Front and in 1916 in command of a division on the Russian Front. He died in 1917 and on his deathbed his last words were said to have been 'Frenchmen, listen to me. Dreyfus is innocent. All the rest was forgeries and lies.' In 1930 the German Foreign Office allowed the publication of some of his notebooks and correspondence which attested that he had had no dealings with Dreyfus but many with Esterhazy. When Dreyfus read of this he wrote to a newspaper that 'although Schwartzkoppen had acted as an honest man in revealing all he knew, it is profoundly regrettable that he did not fulfil his duty on the day he realised that a judicial crime may have been committed.'

When in 1898 Panizzardi was at length allowed to leave Paris after the torments he had been through at the hands of the anti-Dreyfusards, his one idea was to dissociate himself with anything to do with Dreyfus, and he refused to be drawn into any discussion of the matter. He had already said what he knew and had been disbelieved and abused. So why say it again? For a time he kept up an amiable correspondence with Carlos Blacker, but this came to an end in 1905. During this time he had been receiving promotion and just before the outbreak of the First World War he was about to take command of a division. But then, tragically, he was struck down by a stroke which left him crippled. He met up with Blacker again in Rome in 1916 when the two had a moving reunion.

The part played Carlos Blacker in the deliverance of Dreyfus has been known to only very few people. In all the main histories his name is hardly mentioned. Both F.C. Conybeare and Joseph Reinach were aware of what he had done but were sworn to secrecy and kept their pledges. Partly aware of it was the journalist, Chris Healy (see p. 147) who in 1902 published an article in the English magazine *Today* in which he stated that Oscar Wilde was 'one of the direct instruments in freeing Alfred Dreyfus'. This may have been so, but it would have been more fitting to have ascribed it to Carlos Blacker from whom Wilde had his information and whose plan for revealing Dreyfus's innocence was thwarted when Wilde broke his pledge of secrecy.

For various reasons Blacker went to great lengths to cover up what he had done. At the time there were good reasons for this: his promise of secrecy to Panizzardi as well as the obloquy and danger it would have brought to himself and his family. But for some reason the secrecy was maintained later, and his confidants were never released from their pledges.

After being hounded out of Paris in 1898 by the anti-Dreyfusards it might have been expected that Blacker and his family would return to England, but this he was reluctant to do; the country had too many unhappy memories for him, notably his bankruptcy and the acrimonious legal action against the Duke of Newcastle. Instead for the next years he led a somewhat itinerant life, sometimes in France and sometimes in Freibourg in Germany where he was close to his sister Carmen to whom he was devoted. But in time the question arose as to the schooling of his two sons, and he and Caroline decided this should be in English boarding schools, and so in 1908 in order to be near to them they took a house in Torquay; and it was here that the family was living when the First World War broke out.

For Carlos this was a traumatic event. He had a great love for both England and Germany. England was the land of his birth and now again his home, but some of his happiest years, unclouded by disaster, had been spent in Germany. In Freibourg he had received great kindness and had come to have great respect for German culture, science and way of life. To him, a liberal cosmopolitan, it was appalling that two civilized countries should be at war and, as he considered it, for no good reason. He refused to believe the propaganda being put about in England that Germany had always wanted war and had deliberately engineered it for the purpose of world domination. In Freibourg he had seen few signs of this either among ordinary people or even among the military garrison there. They liked to put on splendid parades and to sing loud patriotic songs, but only a small minority of militarists and intellectuals had serious ideas of a war of conquest. Nor did he believe the stories appearing in the British press about German atrocities in Belgium; he could not believe that the Germans he had known were capable of such things. In 1914, however, such views were rare and highly unpopular, and to no one more so than his wife. In contrast Caroline, despite her long residence in Germany, was caught up in the wave of anti-German hatred which swept England in 1914. She accepted unquestioningly the current dogmas that Germans glorified war and had been preparing for it for years, together with all the horror stories of German atrocities. This division of opinion between Carlos and Caroline became at times acute and put a strain on their relationship.

One eminent man who shared the views of Carlos was George Bernard Shaw. By chance the two men met on the beach at Torquay and soon became firm friends. Shaw listened with much sympathy to what Carlos said, and it is probable that he was influenced by him in the inflammatory book he wrote at the end of 1914, *Commonsense about the War* which he dedicated to Carlos and which brought him such furious unpopularity. The Blackers' elder son, C.P. Blacker (Carlos Paton but always known as Pip) has recalled a conversation between Shaw and his mother:

> They were sitting on the lawn at Vane Tower in 1914. Shaw sat in a wicker chair. He listened intently without moving, his right elbow on the arm of the chair, his chin in his right hand and his index finger against his cheekbone. It struck me that, as he listened, he was asking himself how my mother's tirade could be put into the mouth of a character in a play about the war. When she had finished, my mother asked him what he thought. He replied that there was little basic difference between Germany and other continental powers. All were suspicious, unscrupulous and ruthless. All had conscription, war offices, war plans and general staffs. All talked as if they hated war; yet all played power politics.

Later Carlos was to make a detailed study of the events leading to war based on such official documents as were then available. His conclusion was that no European country wanted war or expected it at that time. Both the Czar and the Kaiser made desperate last minute efforts to avoid it. The Austrian Government wanted a local war with Serbia to teach the country a lesson but had no wish for it to spread. In France the lost provinces of Alsace-Lorraine still rankled but there were not many who thought of regaining them by war. And England had nothing to gain from a European war. It seemed that a chain reaction had been set in motion which European rulers were powerless to contain. Some facts were certain: it was Germany who first declared war – on Russia and then on France, and by the invasion of Belgium made certain of Britain's entry into the war, thus converting a minor local war into a full-scale European conflict. But Blacker was inclined to put the main blame for this catastrophe not on Germany but on Russia which over-reacted to the Austrian treatment of Serbia. The order for first a partial mobilization and then a general one was unnecessary and fraught with danger; it ought to have been realized how provocative this would be and how Germany would be bound to react.

Whether or not Carlos was right in this judgement there was another matter in which his opinion has surely been borne out by history – that the war should be ended by a negotiated peace rather than by a peace dictated by a victorious power to a prostrate foe. Such a peace made under duress would, he was certain, lead inevitably to disaster and another war.

During the war Carlos and Caroline suffered as much or more than most British families. Their younger son was killed in 1915 and they suffered agonies of anxiety about Pip who served with the Coldstream Guards on the Western Front for four years. In addition Carlos had great worries about his sister Carmen, living in Germany with a German husband and a son in the German Army. In 1916 the Blackers moved from England to France and eventually settled in Dinard. In 1919 Carlos fell victim to the deadly flu' epidemic which spread over the world, claiming millions of victims. From this he never completely recovered.

He died in 1928, his part in the Dreyfus Affair still not fully recognized, but he left behind him a carefully worded memorandum describing his conversations with Panizzardi in 1898 and his subsequent actions. This was preserved by his son but kept from public view until the purchase of the Blacker papers by Robert Maguire in 1986. Even then, however, historians have not given him full recognition.

Lord Alfred Douglas has been much maligned by posterity. He is an easy target: selfish, wayward, tempestuous, and a lord. In *De Profundis* Wilde described him as 'a gilded pillar of infamy', and most people since have agreed and had no hesitation in writing him off as Wilde's *amour fatale* and the principal cause of his downfall. But this is not the whole truth: those who have readily excused Wilde's aberrations on the grounds of his genius have not extended the same tolerance to Douglas who, if not a genius, was a considerable artist with an artist's temperament. And if it is the case that Wilde's life was ruined by their friendship, so too was Douglas's and at a much earlier age. There is some justification in his plea that on Wilde's behalf he suffered 'exile, obloquy and disgrace'.

After the death of Wilde, Douglas seemed to have become a reformed character: he abandoned his homoerotic ways, settled down to marriage and was received into the Roman Catholic Church. His marriage came about as a result of a fan letter from one, Olive Custance, a poetess of moderate talent and the daughter of a somewhat crusty colonel in the Grenadier Guards. Their wedding took place secretly (at St George's, Hanover Square) as Olive was engaged to someone else at the time and her parents had no wish for Douglas as a son-in-law because of his association with 'a great and notorious scandal'. However, they adjusted to the situation and for a time relations were reasonably amicable.

Others, notably Douglas's mother, were delighted by the marriage as it showed that he had, indeed, 'turned over a new leaf'. Soon afterwards a son was born and there was reason to hope that they would live happily together. But this was not to be: much turmoil lay ahead.

One of the troubles that beset them was finance. The money Douglas had inherited from his father had been dissipated in horse racing and gambling and he had to rely on allowances from his mother and father-in-law as well as some earnings from his literary works. At times he was editor of various literary magazines, but never for very long. His life was always stormy: he was for ever writing angry and abusive letters, often to complete strangers,* and taking out writs for libel, especially against those who made any mention of his relationship with Wilde. In most cases these were settled out of court and, as he wrote in his autobiography, made a useful addition to his income.

His turbulent affairs came to a crisis in 1913. In January he was made bankrupt; in April he brought a costly and unsuccessful action for libel against Arthur Ransome (see below p. 189); and this was immediately followed by a libel action brought against him by his father-in-law Colonel Custance, as well as a suit in Chancery concerning the custody of his son. At the same time his wife left him. The marriage had been under strain for some time, and breaking point came with Douglas's libel of her father. Relations between the two men had always been prickly and had been greatly inflamed when Douglas became a Roman Catholic. The colonel had strong anti-Roman prejudices and was dismayed at the thought of his grandson being brought up a Catholic. He became determined to obtain guardianship of the boy and to this end applied financial pressure on his daughter. Douglas's reaction was predictably vituperative, describing his father-in-law as 'a despicable scoundrel and a thoroughly dishonest and dishonourable man', and threatening to send this description to the colonel's club, bank and the tenants on his estate. In response the colonel took out a writ for criminal libel and at the same time started an action to obtain custody of his grandson. When the libel case came to court, only days after the Ransome case, Douglas was found guilty and was lucky to avoid a prison

---

* One of the more outrageous of these was to Arthur Conan Doyle who had offended him by some remark about the Roman Church. In true Queensberry fashion he berated him as a 'disgusting beast who ought to be horsewhipped'. Doyle's reply was a masterpiece of terseness: 'I am relieved to get your letter. It is only your approval that could in any way annoy me.'

sentence, being merely bound over to be of good behaviour for six months. The case concerning the custody of his son came up soon afterwards and it was laid down that he spend three-fifths of his school holiday with his grandfather (and probably his mother) and two-fifths with his father. But this was not the end of the matter. Douglas took him off to Scotland where he hoped he would be beyond the jurisdiction of English courts; but Colonel Custance then arranged to have him abducted and brought to England in which, it appeared, he had the cooperation of the boy with the result that Douglas took great offence and had nothing more to do with him for ten years.

More lawsuits were to come Douglas's way. In 1914 he had to confront Ross (see p. 190) and in 1918 came the Billing Affair (see p. 192). In 1921 he suddenly found himself reading in the *Evening News* a notice of his sudden death accompanied by an unflattering obituary notice which described him as 'violently eccentric and showing marked signs of degeneracy'. He at once took the newspaper to court and in his most successful legal action won damages of £1,000 – no mean sum at that time. Very different was the outcome of an action in the following year when he was sued for libel by Winston Churchill. This arose from an article he had written in a magazine he was editing about the nefarious activities of Jewish bankers and businessmen. In particular he recounted how Jews had been responsible for the death of Lord Kitchener in the Great War when he had been drowned on his way to Russia in HMS *Hampshire*. Why international Jewry should have been so anxious to prevent Kitchener from reaching Russia was not adequately explained. A more fantastic and grossly libellous story was that Churchill had connived with Jewish financiers by issuing a misleading report of the Battle of Jutland, while it was still being fought, which caused British stock on the New York Stock Exchange to fall unduly, thus enabling profiteers to make a quick killing.* When the case came to court the jury had no hesitation in declaring the story a criminal libel, and Douglas was sentenced to six months imprisonment – a harrowing and humiliating experience but relieved by spending most of the sentence in the prison hospital.

By 1923 Douglas's fortunes had reached their nadir, but then the

---

* Churchill was not First Lord of the Admiralty at the time of Jutland but he was a member of the government and, at the invitation of the First Lord, wrote an assessment of the battle before it was over which gave an erroneous picture of its final outcome.

Fates began to relent. When he left prison, which he later came to regard as a stroke of good fortune and where he wrote one of his best poems, *In Excelsis*, he began to mellow. Writs ceased to flow in such numbers, as too did offensive letters. The gentler, kindlier side of his nature came to the fore, and this was shown in his attitude towards Wilde. In all he wrote three works of autobiography. In the first of these, *Oscar Wilde and Myself*, written mainly by a colleague on one of his magazines soon after the Ransome case, he was very bitter; but later he regretted what had been written and retracted much of it. The two later volumes were more temperate. Wilde was no longer 'the greatest force for evil in Europe during the last three hundred and fifty years', but 'a dear friend and considerable artist' and 'a great genius and a cruelly treated and injured man'.

During his last years his family affairs too were less turbulent. He remained deeply devoted to his mother, with whom he lived for several years in Hove and was heartbroken when she died. He was never completely separated from Olive and saw a certain amount of her, although relations always blew hot and cold. He also re-established relations with his son Raymond who, tragically, had to spend much of his life in a mental hospital. Quarrels did still occur but there were always good friends who visited him and corresponded with him. And his literary reputation remained high – there were those who regarded him as the greatest living English poet – and a number of young writers sought to talk to him about life and literature. If these had misgivings about their reception, bearing in mind Douglas's embattled past, they were unnecessary. They found an amiable old gentleman – talkative, alert, occasionally indignant (especially on the subject of modern poets), but always courteous and considerate. They also found an old man in whom there were no traces of his youthful good looks. Like the picture of Dorian Gray his face had been transformed.

One of the more unexpected of his new friends and admirers was Marie Stopes, authoress of a famous and controversial book, *Married Love* and described by Bernard Shaw as 'the high priestess of birth control'. They were to remain in close contact, he helping her with her poetry and she giving him moral and sometimes financial support. A less beneficial friendship was with an exceedingly nefarious young Wykehamist, one Adrian Earle,* who prevailed on him to make him his heir

---

* Subsequently imprisoned for fraud and extortion. For the full extent of his villainy the reader is referred to *Tricks of Memory* by Sir Peregrine Worsthorne.

and literary trustee with all copyrights. Fortunately, however, he became aware of his true nature and revoked the arrangement.

During the Second World War he became increasingly frail and impecunious, and in his last days kind neighbours, Sheila and Edward Colman, took him into their farmhouse in Lancing where he died in 1945.

At the time of Wilde's downfall no one had stood by him more steadfastly than Robbie Ross. He had been with him at the time of his arrest, had visited him in prison and had attempted to raise funds to avert his bankruptcy. After Wilde's release he continued to do all he could to smooth his path, taking in hand his meagre finances and trying to prevent his more reckless extravagances. It seemed never to have occurred to him to dissociate himself from Wilde, even though their continued relationship brought him disrepute and some danger, so much so that he had felt it necessary at times to take refuge abroad in case proceedings should be brought against him. And yet, in spite of his loyalty and care, there was something uneasy in the relationship of the two men. Ross was once quoted as saying that he thought Wilde had never really liked him, and he himself sometimes seemed ambivalent in his feelings. Perhaps there was some truth in what was once said about Wilde that he was incapable of true friendship. However this might be, when crisis loomed and Wilde fell mortally ill, Ross, at inconvenience and expense, was immediately at his bedside, taking upon himself all the final arrangements about Wilde's funeral and his acceptance into the Roman Catholic Church.

This solicitude was to continue after Wilde's death. On his own initiative he assumed the role of Wilde's literary executor and set about rescuing his estate from bankruptcy for the sake of his sons. Seven years later this was achieved following the publication of De Profundis which might have been a significant step in the rehabilitation of Wilde, but, as will be seen, this was set back by a succession of lawsuits.

It was always likely that in time Ross and Douglas would clash. But at first, after Wilde's death, relations between them were reasonably amicable. Ross contributed to Douglas's magazine, The Academy, and even attended his wedding; but then sourness crept in. Following his conversion to Rome Douglas became increasingly homophobic while Ross's private life remained all too evidently unreformed, and Douglas was writing to him: 'I do not care to meet those who are engaged in active propaganda of every kind of wickedness from anarchy to sodomy.'

Matters came to a head when Ross gave Arthur Ransome vital help in the libel action brought against him by Douglas. After that his hatred of Ross became ever more intense and his behaviour even more manic than that of his father in the pursuance of Wilde. He abused him in the most obscene language in the hope of provoking him into a libel action and when he succeeded in doing this and Ross subsequently felt obliged to withdraw his suit, he still did not let up on his vendetta.

Rather strangely Ross seems to have been taken under the wing of the Prime Minister, Herbert Asquith and his somewhat capricious wife, Margot, and had been entertained by them at 10 Downing Street.* This so infuriated Douglas that he proceeded to write an angry letter to the Prime Minister, threatening that unless he stopped seeing Ross, he would 'reveal all'. He also wrote to King George V, urging him to dismiss the Prime Minister and to Winston Churchill, telling him to be ready to take over the leadership of the Liberal Party. But to his dismay the results of all this agitation was not the disgrace of Ross but a public testimonial signed by many eminent people including the Prime Minister, other members of the government and various noblemen and bishops, praising Ross for his services to the arts and presenting him with a cheque for £700 (which he gave to charity). This was a notable tribute and shows the high regard in which Ross was held in spite of his murky reputation in some matters. He did not, however, live long to enjoy this acclaim. He died suddenly three years later in 1918 with the substantial estate of £20,000 and leaving in his will a wish that his ashes be laid alongside Wilde's remains in La Père Lachaise, a wish that was to be fulfilled some thirty years later.

Oscar Wilde's brilliant gifts and flamboyant personality, combined with an aura of martyrdom, made it likely that in time he would become a cult figure. But for several years his name caused a shudder in most circles, his works were taboo, and children were punished if they were caught reading them. Seven years after his death an attempt was made to revive *The Importance of Being Earnest*, but it was too soon and it was not until seven years later that the respectable felt that they could be seen at his plays without impropriety.

Before this, however, there had been signs that his rehabilitation was

---

* Strangely because Ross was a known homosexual and because he had delivered himself of opinions which could be interpreted as anti-war and even pro-German.

beginning. In 1905 Ross published an expurgated edition of *De Profundis* (without the tirade against Douglas) and it was favourably received. This was followed three years later by an edition of his complete works and this too was acclaimed and celebrated by a prestigious dinner for 160 guests. Then in the following year there was a ceremony when his remains were moved from Bagneux cemetery to Père Lachaise to lie beneath an Epstein sculpture alongside other famous artists and writers (and where for several years his tomb attracted most visitors). It seemed that people were beginning to become more interested in his literary works and less blinded to their merits by his sexuality. But interest in this was to be stirred up by a series of contentious and, in most cases, unnecessary, lawsuits.

In 1912 there appeared a life of Oscar Wilde by Arthur Ransome (later a world-renowned writer of children's stories). In this he was given much help, and possibly some prompting, by Robert Ross who showed him the full version of *De Profundis* as well as some letters from Douglas to Wilde of which he had taken possession when he made himself Wilde's literary executor. In his book Ransome made only guarded references to these; he did not mention Douglas by name but he did reveal that *De Profundis* was a letter addressed not to Ross but to 'a man to whom Wilde felt he owed some, at least, of the circumstance of his public disgrace'. And he went on to say: 'it was begun as a rebuff to this friend whose actions, even subsequent to the trials, had been such as to cause Wilde considerable pain.' There could be little doubt to whom he was referring. Certainly Douglas had no doubt, and it was the first time he became aware, so he claimed, that *De Profundis* was a letter addressed to him and was, therefore, by rights his. This was denied by Ross who said that Wilde had entrusted it to him with instructions only to give Douglas a copy, which he had done; but this was denied by Douglas. Whatever the truth, for which neither man had a scrupulous regard, Douglas, headstrong as ever, issued a writ for libel against Ransome although, as he wrote to Ross, the action was really directed against him as he looked on Ransome as no more than a catspaw.

The action proved to be a disastrous mistake, one which Douglas might have avoided if he had known of the full contents of *De Profundis*. When the case came up in the High Court the real issues at stake were whether Douglas was the cause of Wilde's downfall and whether he lived on him and then deserted him in his last years. Douglas actually had quite a strong defence against these charges as he was able to prove from his bankbooks that he had made Wilde substantial payments and, for as long as was possible, had provided him with a home in Naples; and had then arranged that his mother should make Wilde a further payment. And even then relations between them were not broken off completely; they were to meet amicably in Paris on a number of occasions. But when Ransome's counsel read out in court the outpouring against Douglas from *De Profundis* it had deadly effect. Douglas was so overcome by it that he did not return to the court, and in due course the jury had no hesitation in returning a verdict in favour of Ransome.*

The effect on Douglas of this failure was to inflame his hatred of Ross. 'I swore that day after the Ransome trial,' he wrote, 'that I would never rest till I had publicly exposed Ross in his true colours.' This he proceeded to do by emulating the tactics of his father in his feud against Wilde. He issued a number of obscene and libellous broadsides which he sent to eminent people, accusing Ross of sodomy and blackmail. At first Ross, with the example of Wilde in mind, ignored them, but there came a time when he felt he could be inactive no longer; and so brought a charge against Douglas for criminal libel. The trial opened at the Old Bailey a few months after the outbreak of the First World War. Like his father before him, Douglas, in order to plead justification, had had to delve deep in the mire to find witnesses to attest to Ross's malpractices. This in the end he was able to do, and the similarity to the Wilde case continued when in the first trial the jury disagreed, and in the second Ross gave up and withdrew his prosecution, agreeing to pay Douglas's legal fees. But unlike as with Wilde this was not followed by a criminal prosecution.

Both Douglas's case against Ransome and Ross's case against him did much to muddy the waters surrounding Wilde's reputation, and this was done even more sensationally by the so-called 'Black Book Trial' of 1918. More bizarre than any opera bouffe this affair concerned a maverick member of parliament, an erotic dancer, Maud Allan, and her relationship with an ex-prime minister's wife,† and a German prince

---

* Ransome was deeply disturbed by the case, so much so that he insisted that in future editions of his book the offending passages be omitted. It was also one of the reasons why soon afterwards he left the country and settled in Russia for a number of years.

† Margot Asquith delighted in the company of the way-out, what she called 'oddities', and had once invited Maud Allan to 10 Downing Street where she had performed a relatively decorous dance but in bare feet, which not only caused shock but gave rise to the absurd notion that Margot had lesbian tendencies.

(once king of Albania) who was said to possess a 'Black Book' containing the names of British citizens, including the highest in the land, whose sexual irregularities exposed them to blackmail.

The story began in February 1918 when N. Pemberton Billing, an independent member of parliament, printed in a magazine he owned and published an extraordinary and startlingly explicit article in which he revealed the existence of a book which had been compiled by German secret service agents who in the past twenty years 'had been spreading much debauchery and such lasciviousness as only German minds can conceive and only German bodies can execute'. The book was said to contain no less than 47,000 names of men and women who were 'practitioners of vices all decent men thought had perished in Sodom and Lesbos'. Because of these malpractices of top people and the hold thereby established over them vital secrets of state were being betrayed to the enemy. Sensational as the article was, however, it prompted little serious reaction; it resulted in no libel suits and was regarded generally as beyond the pale and treated with ribald hilarity.

But Billing was not to be put off. He proceeded to change the name of his magazine from *The Imperialist* to *The Vigilante*, announcing that its object in future would be to 'preserve purity in public life'. It was not long before he had an opportunity to demonstrate this intention. A Dutch theatrical director, J.T. Grein, had started a private theatre club in London for the production of *avant garde* plays which would not be passed by the Lord Chamberlain for public performance; and in February 1918 he decided to put on Wilde's *Salome* (see p. 25). For the leading part he chose a classical dancer, Maud Allan, who had attracted considerable notoriety in recent years with a dance, *The Vision of Salome*, based on Wilde's play; the performance of this, together with the severed head of John the Baptist, had been described as 'a delicious embodiment of lust'. The play, complete with the dance of the seven veils, promised to be a great attraction; but it also provoked frenzied opposition, notably from Pemberton Billing to whom it seemed a flagrant example of the moral malaise which was afflicting the country at that time – a cult of decadence and decay, basically foreign in nature but originating from Oscar Wilde. To him it was appalling that at the supreme crisis of the greatest war in history a degrading and disgusting play should be performed, and he was determined to put a stop to it. This he attempted to do by libelling Maud Allan in the columns of *The Vigilante*. Under a heading 'The Cult of the Clitoris' he intimated that she was a lesbian and that the names of everyone attending her performances would certainly be found in the pages of 'The Black Book'. When their attention was drawn to this monstrous assertion Maud Allan and H.T. Grein felt they had no option but to take out a prosecution for criminal libel against Billing.

The case came to court on 29 May 1918 at which time the German armies in their last great offensive were in striking distance of Paris. But the British press found plenty of room for 'The Black Book Affair'. The trial soon turned into something of a charade. It was presided over by Mr Justice Darling, an idiosyncratic judge (known to the irreverent as 'Little Darling') with a penchant for *bons mots* and witty asides, but not always impartial and at times manifestly incapable of keeping order in court. Although with little legal experience Billing decided to conduct his own defence which, predictably, he did unconventionally. He called a strange assortment of witnesses the first of whom, a Mrs Eileen Villiers-Stuart, was a lady enshrouded in mystery who, it seems, was at first a government *agent provocateur* bent on discrediting Billing, but was then won over to his cause and became one of his strongest supporters. In court she stated that she had seen 'The Black Book' and had read in it some of the names which included members of the government and other famous people including, no less, Mr Justice Darling. Mrs Villiers-Stuart was playing a dangerous game. Only a year before Mata Hari had been executed for espionage activities. But Eileen's fate was to be less drastic; it was discovered that she had committed bigamy and so it was possible to get her out of the way with a nine months' prison sentence for this.

As the trial progressed it became evident that it was having less to do with the libel of Maud Allan and more with the depravity of *Salome* and the pernicious influence of Oscar Wilde. Billing called witnesses who vied with each other to revile the play. He himself in his justification of libel had described it as 'an open representation of degenerated sexual lust, sexual crime and unnatural passion and an evil and mischievous travesty of a biblical story'. A drama critic was brought in to describe it as 'a bizarre melodrama of disease', and a Father Bernard Vaughan declared it to be 'an abomination and a constructive treason against the majesty and sanctity of God'. But the most vitriolic of all witnesses in condemning *Salome* and the 'cult of Wilde' was Lord Alfred Douglas, and this in spite of the fact that he had once at the behest of Wilde translated the play from French into English. At the time his hatred of Wilde was at its height; and in the witness box he gave full vent to his venom. He said he regretted ever having met Wilde and that Wilde was a diabolical influence on everyone he met. As for Salome 'normally healthy-minded people would be disgusted and revolted by it while sexual perverts would revel in it'.

Douglas was, of course, in a highly vulnerable position; his past was by no means unblemished. The prosecuting counsel did not scruple to read out in court Wilde's letters to him referring to his 'roseleaf lips and slim gilt soul'. They also produced a letter Douglas had written to the editor of *Truth* on the subject of homosexuality saying that he knew personally some forty to fifty men in the best society who practised these acts and many more at Oxford, and that these tastes were perfectly natural in certain people and the law had no right to interfere with them provided they did not harm other people. 'I confess,' he went on, 'I have not many hopes for the present age, but ultimate liberation from conventional slavery and tyranny is as inevitable as death.' And on the subject of *Salome* prosecuting counsel produced a review of it, written by Douglas when he was at Oxford, in which he said that he supposed the play to be 'unhealthy, morbid, unwholesome and un-English, but it had, nevertheless, the beauty of a perfect work of art, a joy forever, ambrosia to feed their souls and honey of sweet-bitter thoughts'.

It was not difficult for counsel to discredit Douglas who also clashed with Judge Darling; it was not their first encounter, as Darling had presided in the Ransome case in which, Douglas felt, he had treated him unfairly and been the main cause of his defeat. On this occasion he showed him no respect, telling him he would not be bullied again and would answer questions in his own way. Later, during Darling's summing up, he again let himself go. 'You lie. You are a damned liar,' he shouted as he was ushered out of the court, only to reappear, rather ridiculously, a few minutes later to ask permission to retrieve his top hat.

It cannot be said that Douglas did much to help Billing's case, but Billing won it all the same. The main issue had been not the alleged lesbianism of Maud Allan but the perniciousness of *Salome* and the cult of decadence which Billing had been at pains to emphasize was essentially Germanic; and at that moment of the war, when anti-German feelings were more frenzied than ever, the verdict was predictable and wildly popular.

The Billing case was the last public instance of what Ross called 'kicking Oscar's corpse'. In the post-war years came a different moral climate; the movement away from Victorian values – religion, respectability, convention – gathered pace; lifestyles became more relaxed, literature and the theatre more explicit and people talked more freely of subjects that had once been taboo. In this atmosphere Wilde and his works became less abhorrent: people could enjoy his plays with a clear conscience, they were even performed in schools and his *bons mots* were quoted from the pulpit. Homosexuality did not immediately come 'out of the closet'; acts between consenting adults remained illegal until the coming of the so-called permissive society in the 1960s. Then, indeed, Wilde came into his own; many groups and cults claimed him as their progenitor and he has been acclaimed as, among others, the first existentialist and the first pop star. To homosexuals he has become the holy and blessed martyr who suffered and died on their behalf and whose sayings and writings amount almost to holy writ. But to Wilde such adulation would surely have been an embarrassment. Certainly he did at times have somewhat grandiose ideas about his art, but at heart he knew that he was an entertainer rather than a gospeller. 'In all art,' he said, 'style is of more importance than sincerity.' This must be the essence of Wilde.

Not everyone, of course, has joined in the worship of Wilde's works. To his friend, Max Beerbohm* he was not a born writer as was shown by the fact that he never concentrated on one form of literature. To W.B. Yeats, Irish poet and playwright, his literary fame was mainly due to his disgrace and martyrdom. Unexpectedly harsh censure comes from Lord David Cecil, author and academic. In uncharacteristically caustic terms he wrote of him (in his life of Max Beerbohm):

> For in fact poor Oscar was far from being a fine flower of civilisation. Though posing to himself and to others as the champion of culture and sensibility and whose life was dedicated to the disinterested contemplation of beauty, he was in fact nothing of the kind, but rather a genial, brilliant, spirited Irish buccaneer, with a thirst for self-advertisement, incurably crude taste and a strong streak of sentimental vulgarity ... Oscar Wilde's art is an accurate reflection of the man who created it. He was an admirable entertainer; his jokes were delightful: *The Importance of Being Earnest* is a masterpiece in its kind. But when he went in for being beautiful or moving or profound he succeeded only in being derivative and meretricious.

In the turmoil of argument about Wilde's works and ways one of his

---

* He has been described as 'the best essayist, parodist and cartoonist of his age'.

traits is often overlooked – one considered by Sir Rupert Hart Davis, who edited some thousand of his letters, as being all-important: that he was 'irresistible in his charm, kindness and generosity'.

Date Chart

1893

July	20	Esterhazy's first contact with Schwartzkoppen.

1894

September	26	*Bordereau* comes to Statistical Section.
October	15	Arrest of Dreyfus.
December	19–22	First court martial of Dreyfus.

1895

January	5	Degradation of Dreyfus.	
February	21	Dreyfus sails for French Guiana.	
March	1		Wilde prosecutes Queensberry for criminal libel.
	9		Case of Wilde versus Queensberry begins.
April	5		Wilde arrested.
	13	Dreyfus reaches Devil's Island.	
	26		Wilde's first trial begins.
May	2		Wilde sentenced to 2 years' hard labour.
July	1	Picquart appointed director of Statistical Section.	
November	12		Wilde declared bankrupt.

| | 21 | | Wilde transferred to Reading gaol. |

1896

| March | 15 | Discovery of *Petit Bleu* incriminating Esterhazy. | |
| November | 10 | Facsimile of *Bordereau* printed in *Le Matin*. | |

1897

January	6	Picquart sent to Algeria.	
May	19		Wilde released from prison.
August	28		Wilde reunited with Douglas at Rouen.
September			Wilde and Douglas in Naples.
November	1	Schwartzkoppen leaves Paris.	

1898

January	10	Court martial of Esterhazy.	
	13	Zola's letter ('J'accuse') appears in *L'Aurore*.	
February	7		
		Trial of Zola begins.	Carlos Blacker arrives in Paris.
	9		*Ballad of Reading Gaol* published.
	13		Wilde arrives in Paris.
	23	Zola sentenced.	
March	13		Blacker meets Wilde; reveals secrets of Dreyfus Affair as told him by Panizzardi.
April	4	'Letter from Diplomat' in *Le Siècle*.	
	7		Death of Constance Wilde.
	8	Letter of Casella in *Le Siècle*.	
	11	Article of Rowland Strong in *New York Times*.	
June	1	Article of Conybeare ('Huguenot') in *National Review*.	
	5	Reprinted in *Le Siècle*.	
	25		

Blacker Writes to Wilde termi-
nating friendship.

July	7	Statement of Cavalgnac in chamber, quoting documents re Dreyfus.
	18	Panizzardi recalled to Rome.
August	13	Forgery of *Faux Henry* discovered.
	31	Suicide of Henry.
September	27	Government sends appeal of Lucie Dreyfus to Court of Criminal Appeal.

1899

February	26	Appeal passed to United Appeal Court.
June	3	Court gives judgement.
	9	Dreyfus leaves Devil's Island.
	30	Dreyfus arrives in France.
August	7	Court martial at Rennes begins.
September	9	Dreyfus found guilty with 'extenuating circumstances'.
	19	Dreyfus pardoned by President.

1900

| November | 30 | | Death of Wilde. |
| December | 24 | Amnesty law passed. | |

1906

June	18	Dreyfus appeal before Court of Appeal.
July	12	Dreyfus finally and irrevocably acquitted.
	13	Dreyfus reinstated in army.

Sources and Bibliography

For the most part in this book sources have been secondary. The main works consulted are listed below. The original sources are the papers of Carlos Blacker – his letters, diary and the memorandum he wrote (undated but probably c. 1899) about his role in the Dreyfus Affair. For his financial quarrel with Wilde there is only Wilde's account in two letters to Robert Ross (27 June and July 1898). These were not printed in full in *Letters of Oscar Wilde* edited by Rupert Hart Davis out of consideration for Blacker's close family. They are quoted here with the consent of Blacker's surviving descendants.

The transmission of Blacker's information from Panizzardi via Wilde to Zola depends on the published works of Christopher Healy as well as some inexplicit comments by F.C. Conybeare. The conversation between Wilde and Esterhazy is described by Lord Alfred Douglas in his autobiography and by Frank Harris in *Oscar Wilde, His Life and Confessions*, although this is denied and scorned by Robert Sherard in his biographical works.

The later life of Carlos Blacker is based on his diaries and the memoranda left by his son, Dr C.P. Blacker.

Chapters II, VIII–XI, XV

Chapman, Guy, *The Dreyfus Case – A Reassessment* (1955).
Burns, Michael, *Dreyfus – A Family Affair*, (1991).
Kayser, Jacques, *The Dreyfus Affair*, (1931).
Drouin, Michel (ed.), *L'Affaire Dreyfus A à Z*, (1994).
Johnson, Douglas, *France and the Dreyfus Affair*, (1966).

For dealings between Esterhazy and Schwartzkoppen

Blacker, Carlos, Memorandum (c. 1899).

Schwartzkoppen (ed. Schwertfeger), *The Truth About Dreyfus*, (1930).

Chapter III–VI, XII

Ellman, Richard, *Oscar Wilde*, (1987).
Montgomery Hyde, *Oscar Wilde*, (1976); *Trials of Oscar Wilde*, (1948); and *Lord Alfred Douglas*, (1985).
Pearson, Hesketh, *Oscar Wilde*, (1946).
Hart Davis, Rupert, *Letters of Oscar Wilde*, (1962).
Douglas, Lord Alfred, *Autobiography*, (1929); *Without Apology*, (1938); and *Oscar Wilde – A Summing Up*, (1940).
Aronson, Theo, *Prince Eddy and the Homosexual Underworld*, (1994).

Chapter XIII

Blacker, Carlos, Memorandum and diary.
Maguire, Robert, Entry on Blacker in *L'Affaire Dreyfus A à Z*, (Drouin ed.).
'Oscar Wilde and the Dreyfus Affair' in *Victorian Studies* Autumn 1997.
Masters, Brian, *The Dukes*, (1975).
Conybeare, F. C., *The Dreyfus Case*, (1898) and article in National Review (1 June 1898).
Healy, Christopher, *Confessions of a Journalist*, (1906) and article in *Today* (8 October 1902).
Ellman, Richard, Op. cit.
Reinach, Joseph, *Histoire de l'Affaire Dreyfus*, (1901–8).

Chapter XIV

Hart Davis, Rupert, *Letters of Oscar Wilde*, (1962).
Blacker, C., Letters and diary.
Ross, Robert, Letters.

Chapter XVI

Burns, Michael, Op. cit.
Blacker, Carlos, Diaries and papers.
Blacker, Dr C. P., Memoranda.
Montgomery Hyde, Op. cit.
Douglas, Lord Alfred, Op. cit.
Hoare, Philip, *Wilde's Last Stand*, (1997).

Index